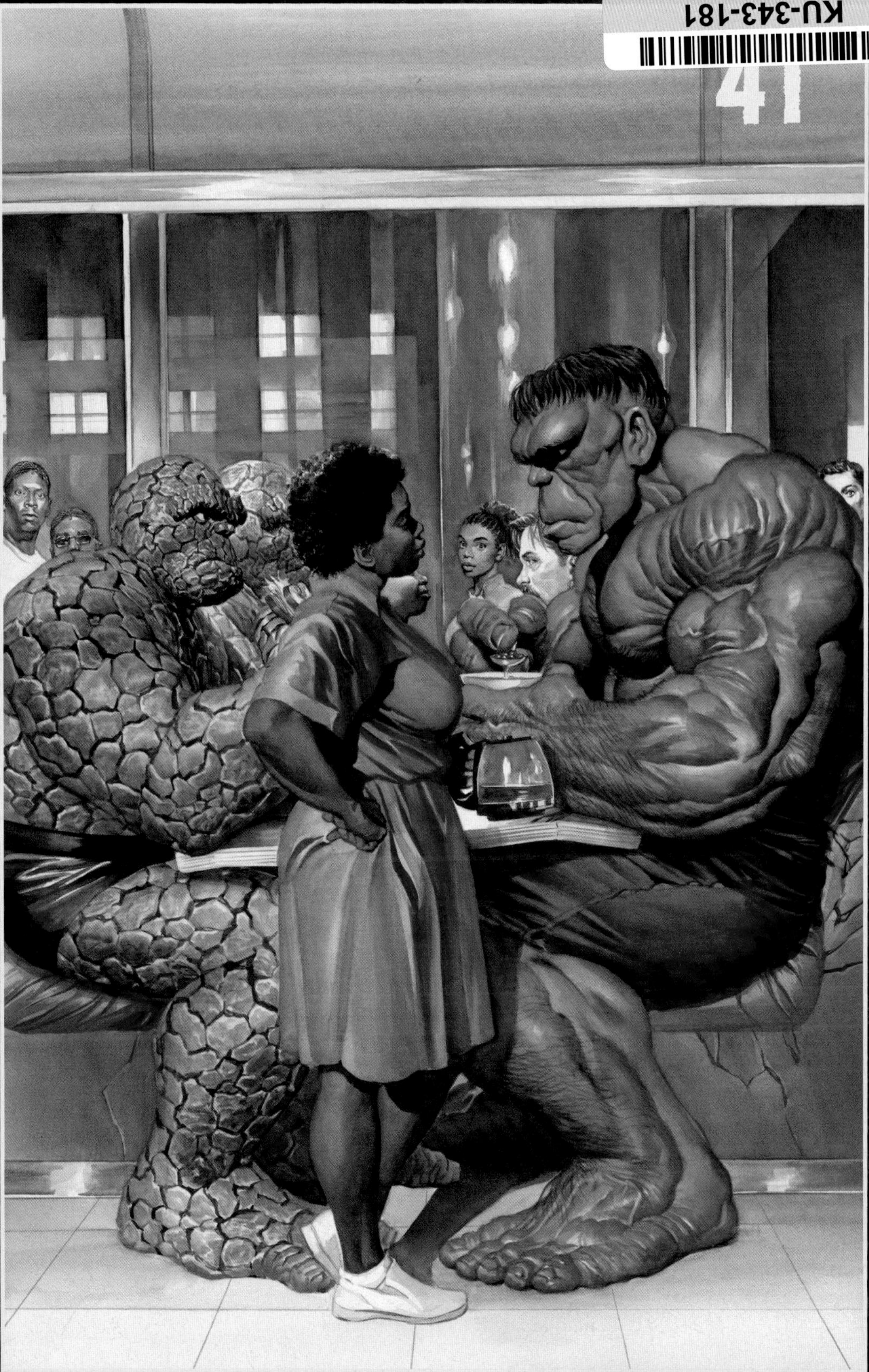

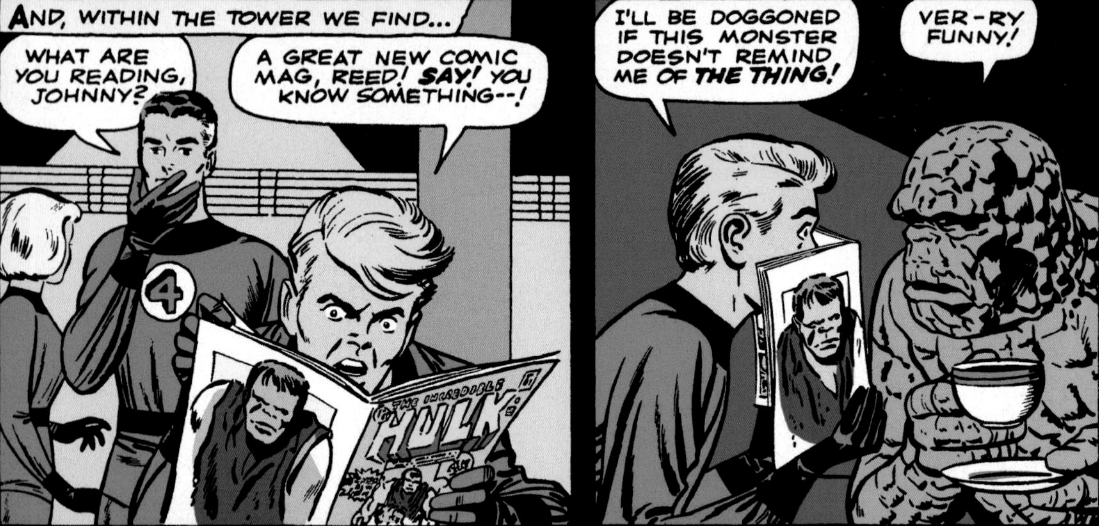
AND, WITHIN THE TOWER WE FIND...
WHAT ARE YOU READING, JOHNNY?
A GREAT NEW COMIC MAG, REED! SAY! YOU KNOW SOMETHING--!
THE INCREDIBLE HULK
I'LL BE DOGGONED IF THIS MONSTER DOESN'T REMIND ME OF THE THING!
VER-RY FUNNY!

—STAN LEE & JACK KIRBY
FANTASTIC FOUR #5,
"PRISONERS OF DOCTOR DOOM!"

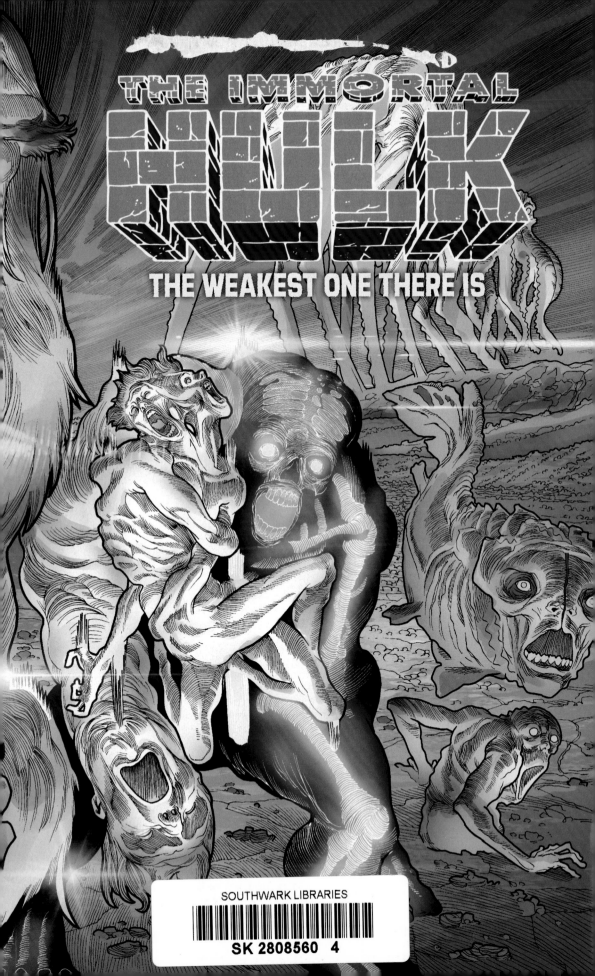

THE IMMORTAL HULK

THE WEAKEST ONE THERE IS

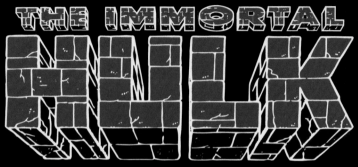

THE IMMORTAL HULK

THE WEAKEST ONE THERE IS

AL EWING
WRITER

ISSUES #41, #43-45

JOE BENNETT
PENCILER

RUY JOSÉ & BELARDINO BRABO
INKERS

PAUL MOUNTS
COLOR ARTIST

ISSUE #42

LEADER SEQUENCE

ALEX LINS
ARTIST

CHRIS O'HALLORAN
COLOR ARTIST

GAMMA FLIGHT SEQUENCE

ADAM GORHAM
ARTIST

CHRIS O'HALLORAN
COLOR ARTIST

JACKIE McGEE SEQUENCE

RACHAEL STOTT
ARTIST

CHRIS O'HALLORAN
COLOR ARTIST

U-FOES SEQUENCE

JOE BENNETT
PENCILER

RUY JOSÉ
INKER

PAUL MOUNTS
COLOR ARTIST

VC's CORY PETIT
LETTERER

ALEX ROSS
COVER ARTIST

SARAH BRUNSTAD
ASSOCIATE EDITOR

WIL MOSS
EDITOR

TOM BREVOORT
EXECUTIVE EDITOR

COLLECTION EDITOR: JENNIFER GRÜNWALD
ASSISTANT EDITOR: DANIEL KIRCHHOFFER
ASSISTANT MANAGING EDITOR: MAIA LOY
ASSISTANT MANAGING EDITOR: LISA MONTALBANO

VP, PRODUCTION & SPECIAL PROJECTS: JEFF YOUNGQUIST
BOOK DESIGNERS: STACIE ZUCKER & ADAM DEL RE
SVP PRINT, SALES & MARKETING: DAVID GABRIEL
EDITOR IN CHIEF: C.B. CEBULSKI

HULK
CREATED BY
STAN LEE &
JACK KIRBY

IMMORTAL HULK VOL. 9: THE WEAKEST ONE THERE IS. Contains material originally published in magazine form as IMMORTAL HULK (2018) #41-45. First printing 2021. ISBN 978-1-302-92597-0. Published by MARVEL WORLDWIDE, INC., a subsidiary of MARVEL ENTERTAINMENT, LLC. OFFICE OF PUBLICATION: 1290 Avenue of the Americas, New York, NY 10104. © 2021 MARVEL No similarity between any of the names, characters, persons, and/or institutions in this magazine with those of any living or dead person or institution is intended, and any such similarity which may exist is purely coincidental. Printed in Canada. KEVIN FEIGE, Chief Creative Officer; DAN BUCKLEY, President, Marvel Entertainment; JOE QUESADA, EVP & Creative Director; DAVID BOGART, Associate Publisher & SVP of Talent Affairs; TOM BREVOORT, VP, Executive Editor; NICK LOWE, Executive Editor, VP of Content, Digital Publishing; DAVID GABRIEL, VP of Print & Digital Publishing; JEFF YOUNGQUIST, VP of Production & Special Projects; ALEX MORALES, Director of Publishing Operations; DAN EDINGTON, Managing Editor; RICKEY PURDIN, Director of Talent Relations; JENNIFER GRÜNWALD, Senior Editor, Special Projects; SUSAN CRESPI, Production Manager; STAN LEE, Chairman Emeritus. For information regarding advertising in Marvel Comics or on Marvel.com, please contact Vit DeBellis, Custom Solutions & Integrated Advertising Manager, at vdebellis@marvel.com. For Marvel subscription inquiries, please call 888-511-5480. Manufactured between 4/16/2021 and 5/18/2021 by SOLISCO PRINTERS, SCOTT, QC, CANADA.

10 9 8 7 6 5 4 3 2 1

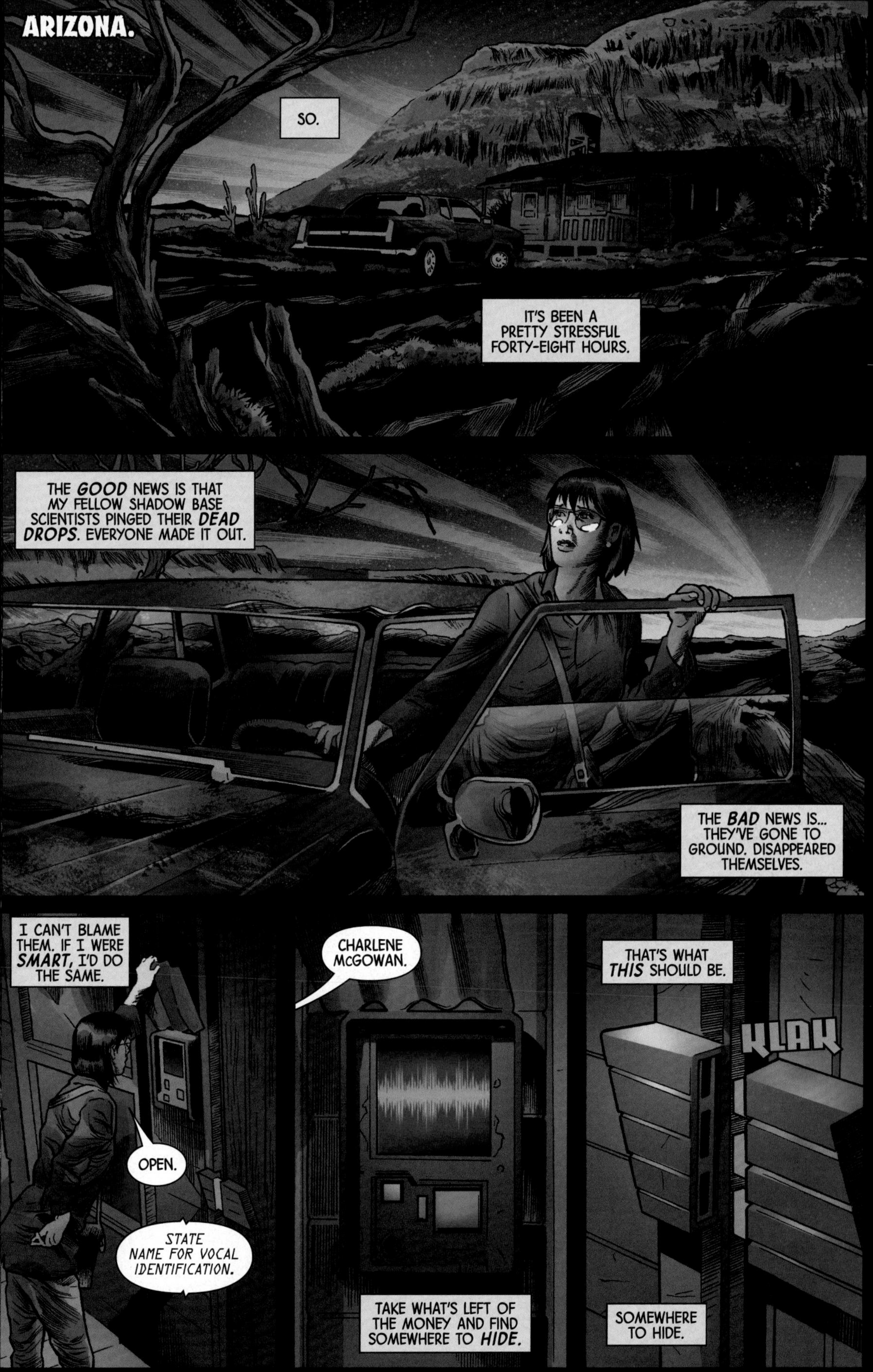
ARIZONA.
SO.
IT'S BEEN A PRETTY STRESSFUL FORTY-EIGHT HOURS.
THE GOOD NEWS IS THAT MY FELLOW SHADOW BASE SCIENTISTS PINGED THEIR DEAD DROPS. EVERYONE MADE IT OUT.
THE BAD NEWS IS... THEY'VE GONE TO GROUND. DISAPPEARED THEMSELVES.
I CAN'T BLAME THEM. IF I WERE SMART, I'D DO THE SAME.
OPEN.
STATE NAME FOR VOCAL IDENTIFICATION.
CHARLENE McGOWAN.
TAKE WHAT'S LEFT OF THE MONEY AND FIND SOMEWHERE TO HIDE.
THAT'S WHAT THIS SHOULD BE.
KLAK
SOMEWHERE TO HIDE.

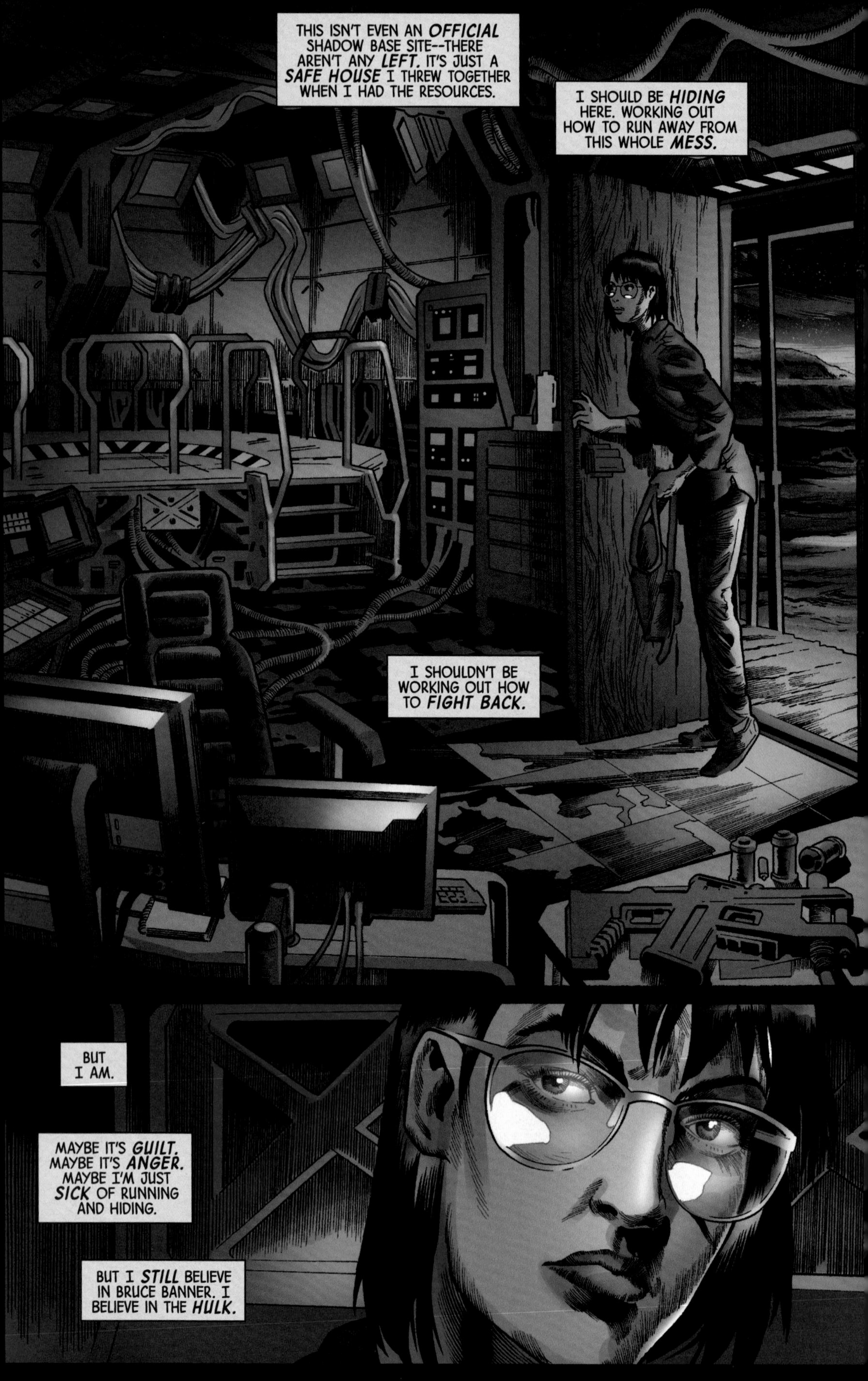
THIS ISN'T EVEN AN OFFICIAL SHADOW BASE SITE--THERE AREN'T ANY LEFT. IT'S JUST A SAFE HOUSE I THREW TOGETHER WHEN I HAD THE RESOURCES.
I SHOULD BE HIDING HERE. WORKING OUT HOW TO RUN AWAY FROM THIS WHOLE MESS.
I SHOULDN'T BE WORKING OUT HOW TO FIGHT BACK.
BUT I AM.
MAYBE IT'S GUILT. MAYBE IT'S ANGER. MAYBE I'M JUST SICK OF RUNNING AND HIDING.
BUT I STILL BELIEVE IN BRUCE BANNER. I BELIEVE IN THE HULK.

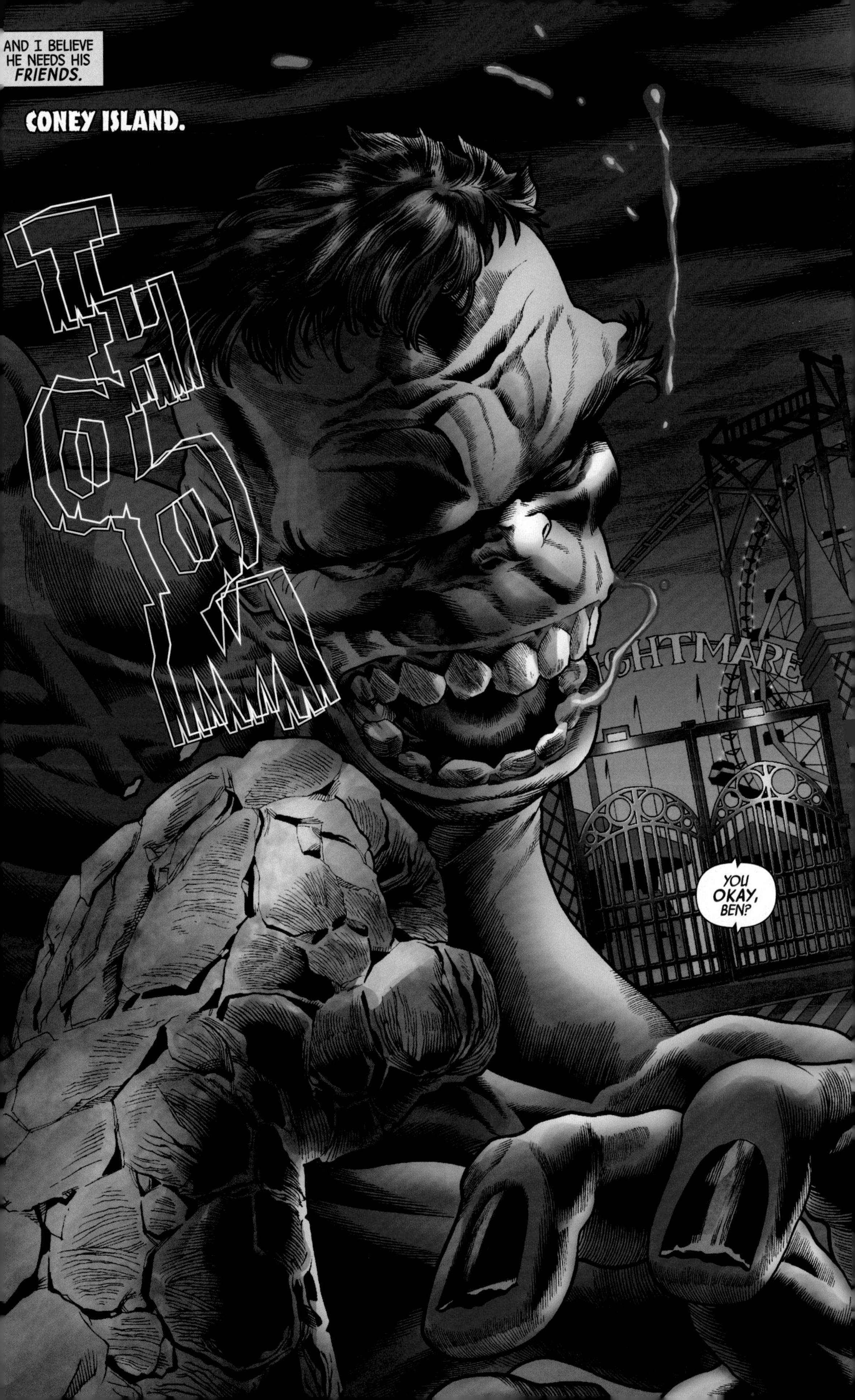
AND I BELIEVE HE NEEDS HIS *FRIENDS.*
CONEY ISLAND.
THOOM
YOU OKAY, BEN?

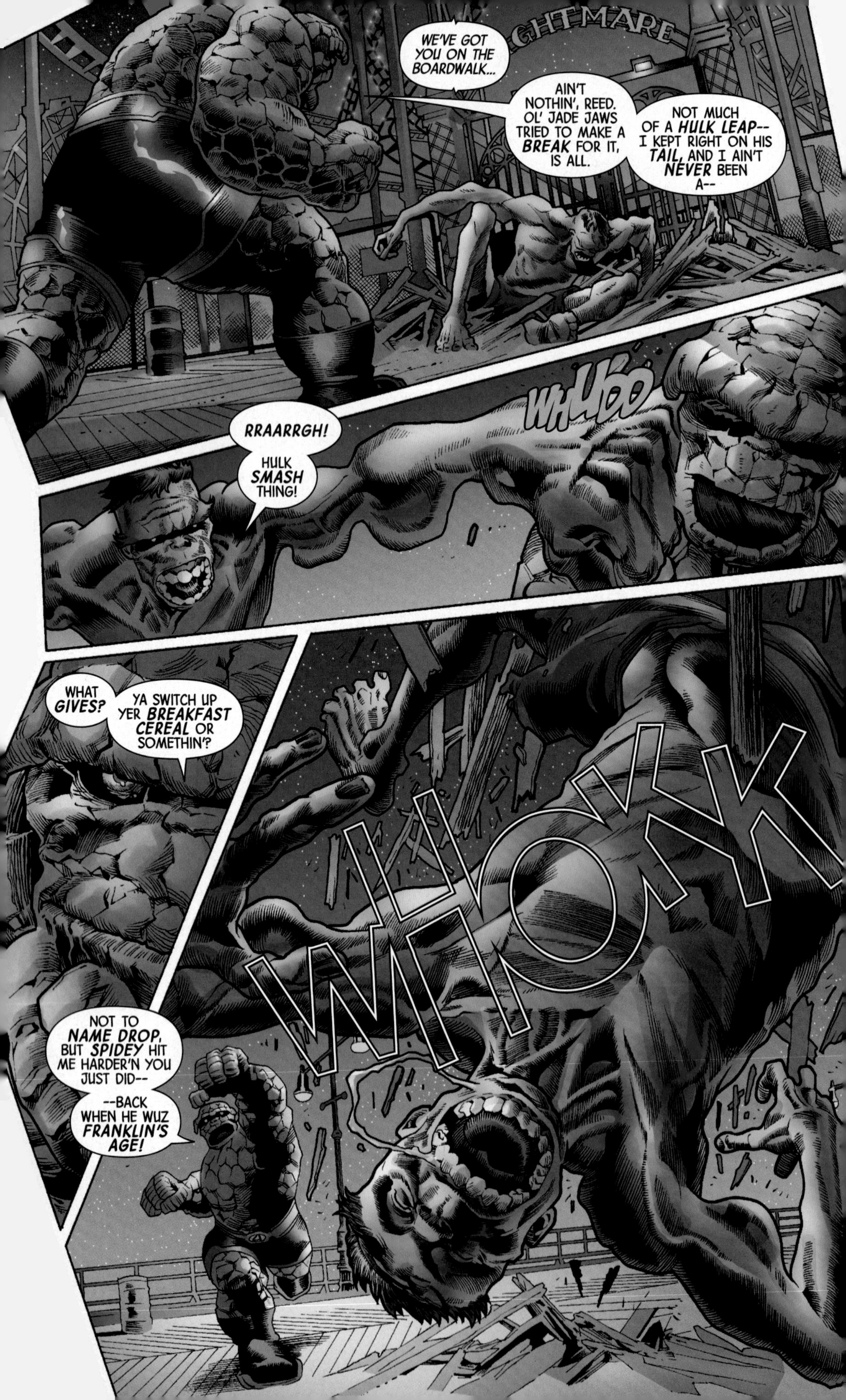

...GHTMARE
WE'VE GOT YOU ON THE BOARDWALK...
AIN'T NOTHIN', REED. OL' JADE JAWS TRIED TO MAKE A BREAK FOR IT, IS ALL.
NOT MUCH OF A HULK LEAP-- I KEPT RIGHT ON HIS TAIL, AND I AIN'T NEVER BEEN A--
WHUDD
RRAARRGH!
HULK SMASH THING!
WHAT GIVES?
YA SWITCH UP YER BREAKFAST CEREAL OR SOMETHIN'?
WHOK
NOT TO NAME DROP, BUT SPIDEY HIT ME HARDER'N YOU JUST DID--
--BACK WHEN HE WUZ FRANKLIN'S AGE!

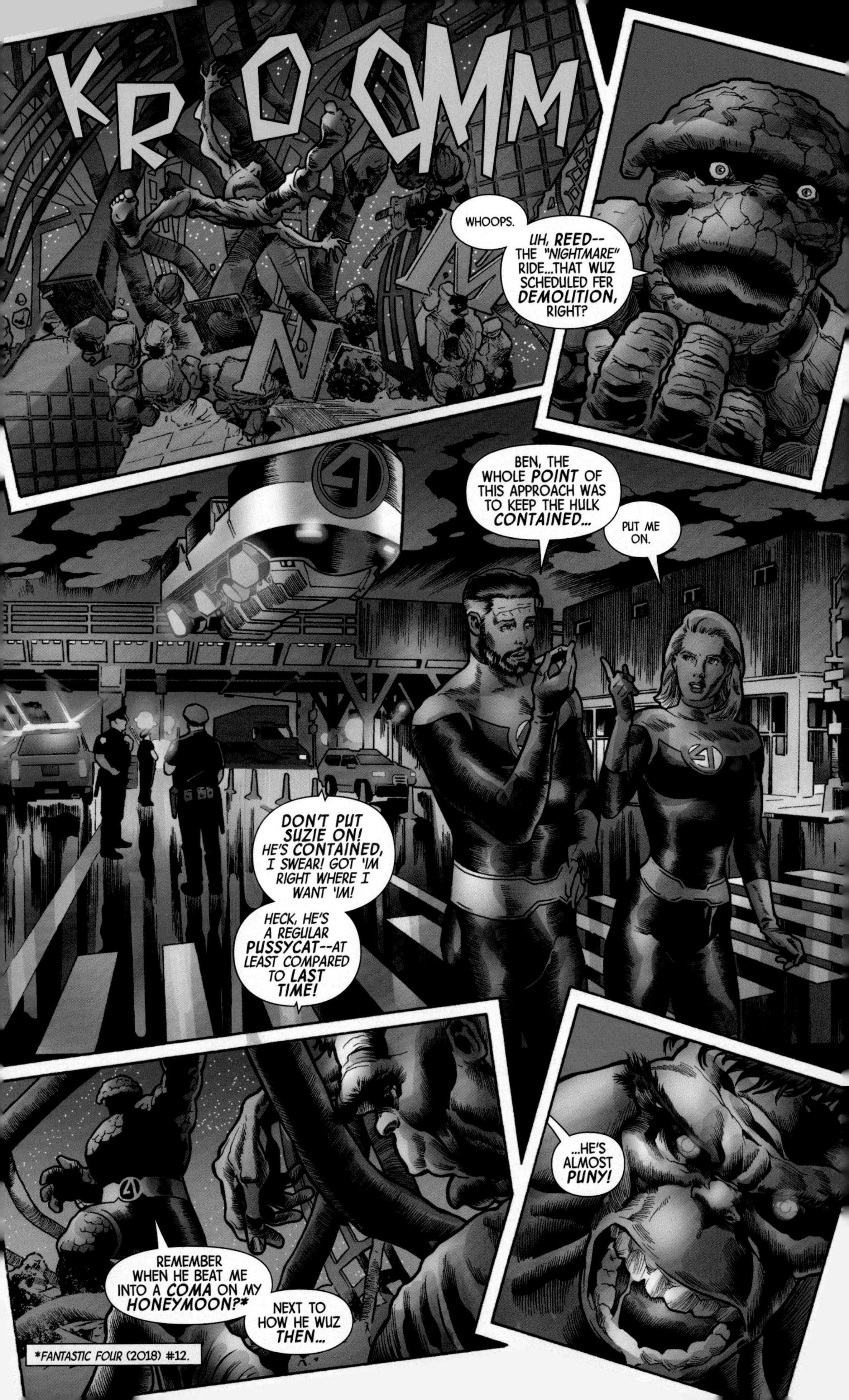
KROOMM
WHOOPS.
UH, REED-- THE "NIGHTMARE" RIDE...THAT WUZ SCHEDULED FER DEMOLITION, RIGHT?
BEN, THE WHOLE POINT OF THIS APPROACH WAS TO KEEP THE HULK CONTAINED...
PUT ME ON.
DON'T PUT SUZIE ON! HE'S CONTAINED, I SWEAR! GOT 'IM RIGHT WHERE I WANT 'IM!
HECK, HE'S A REGULAR PUSSYCAT--AT LEAST COMPARED TO LAST TIME!
REMEMBER WHEN HE BEAT ME INTO A COMA ON MY HONEYMOON?*
NEXT TO HOW HE WUZ THEN...
...HE'S ALMOST PUNY!
*FANTASTIC FOUR (2018) #12.

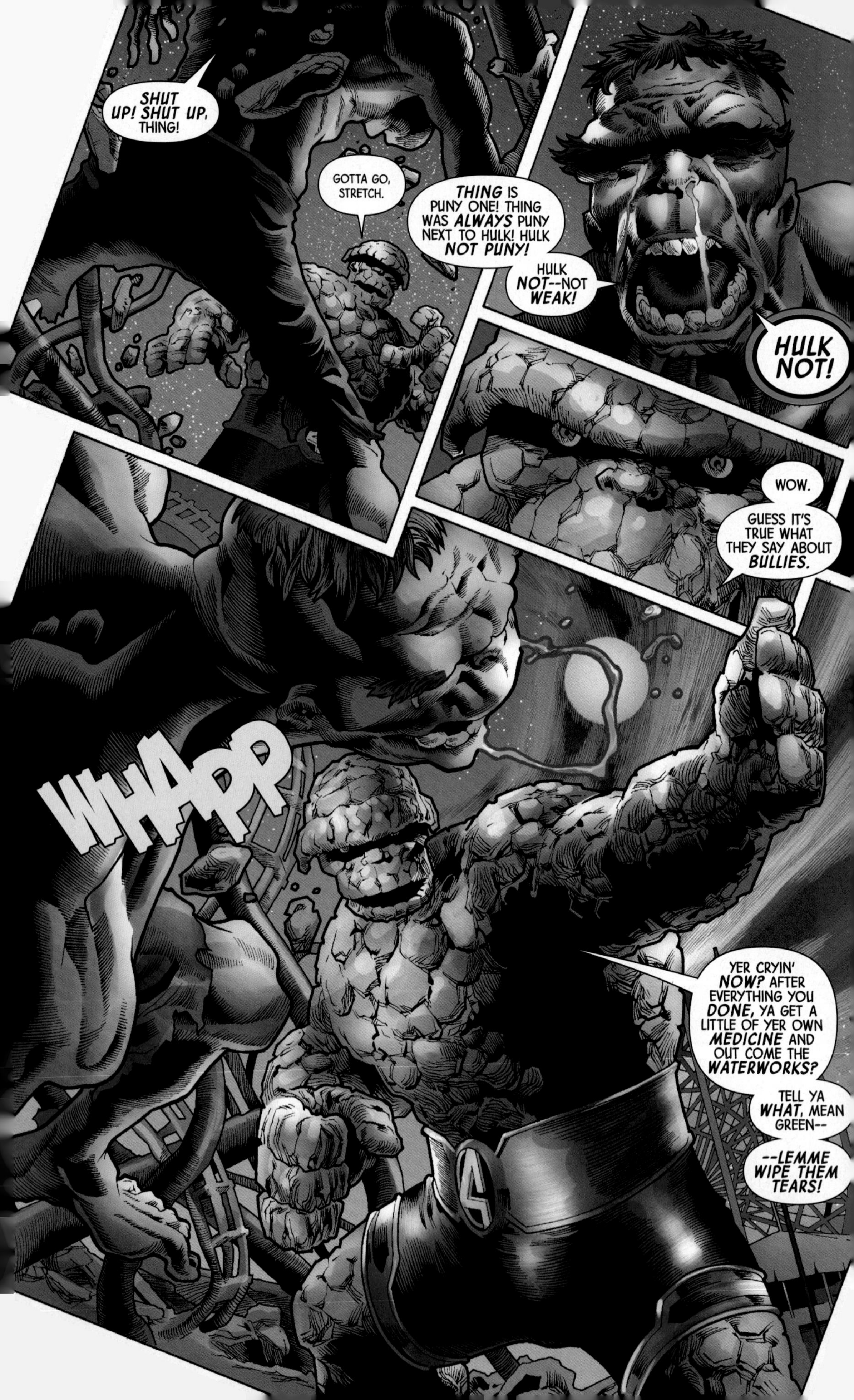
SHUT UP! SHUT UP, THING!
GOTTA GO, STRETCH.
THING IS PUNY ONE! THING WAS ALWAYS PUNY NEXT TO HULK! HULK NOT PUNY!
HULK NOT--NOT WEAK!
HULK NOT!
WOW.
GUESS IT'S TRUE WHAT THEY SAY ABOUT BULLIES.
WHAPP
YER CRYIN' NOW? AFTER EVERYTHING YOU DONE, YA GET A LITTLE OF YER OWN MEDICINE AND OUT COME THE WATERWORKS?
TELL YA WHAT, MEAN GREEN--
--LEMME WIPE THEM TEARS!

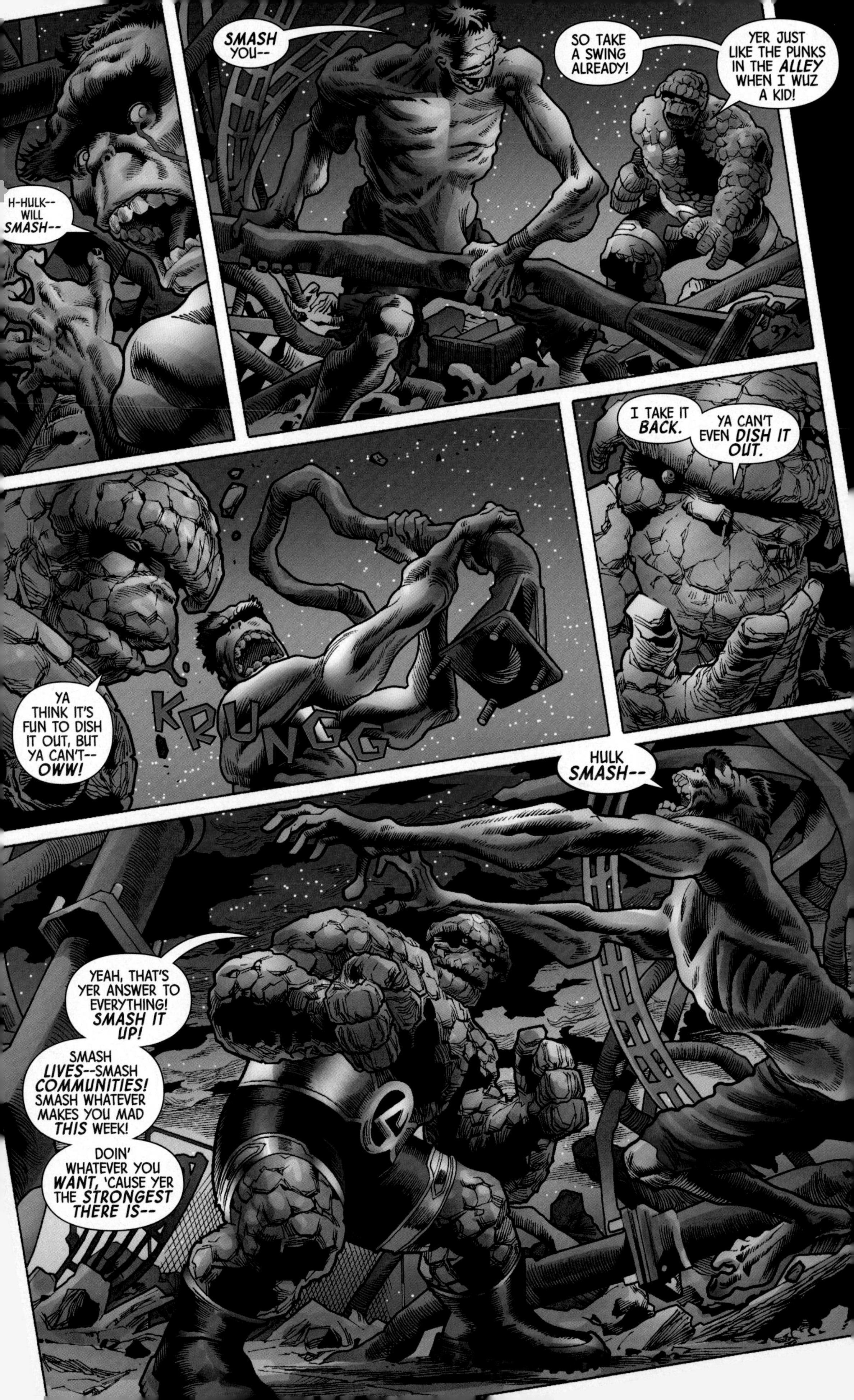
H-HULK--
WILL
SMASH--
SMASH
YOU--
SO TAKE
A SWING
ALREADY!
YER JUST
LIKE THE PUNKS
IN THE ALLEY
WHEN I WUZ
A KID!
YA
THINK IT'S
FUN TO DISH
IT OUT, BUT
YA CAN'T--
OWW!
KRUNGG
I TAKE IT
BACK.
YA CAN'T
EVEN DISH IT
OUT.
HULK
SMASH--
YEAH, THAT'S
YER ANSWER TO
EVERYTHING!
SMASH IT
UP!
SMASH
LIVES--SMASH
COMMUNITIES!
SMASH WHATEVER
MAKES YOU MAD
THIS WEEK!
DOIN'
WHATEVER YOU
WANT, 'CAUSE YER
THE STRONGEST
THERE IS--

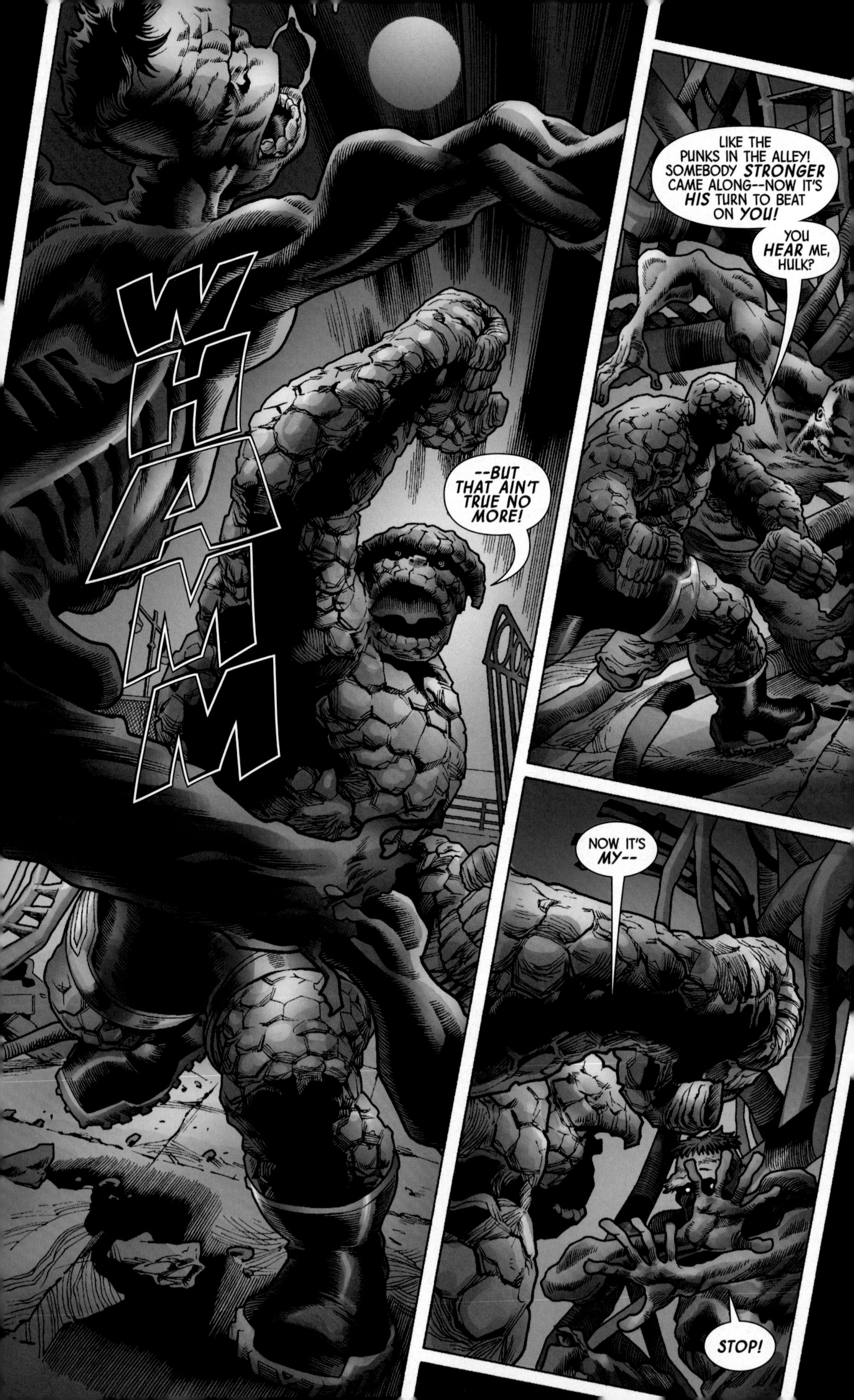
WHAMM
--BUT THAT AIN'T TRUE NO MORE!
LIKE THE PUNKS IN THE ALLEY! SOMEBODY STRONGER CAME ALONG--NOW IT'S HIS TURN TO BEAT ON YOU!
YOU HEAR ME, HULK?
NOW IT'S MY--
STOP!

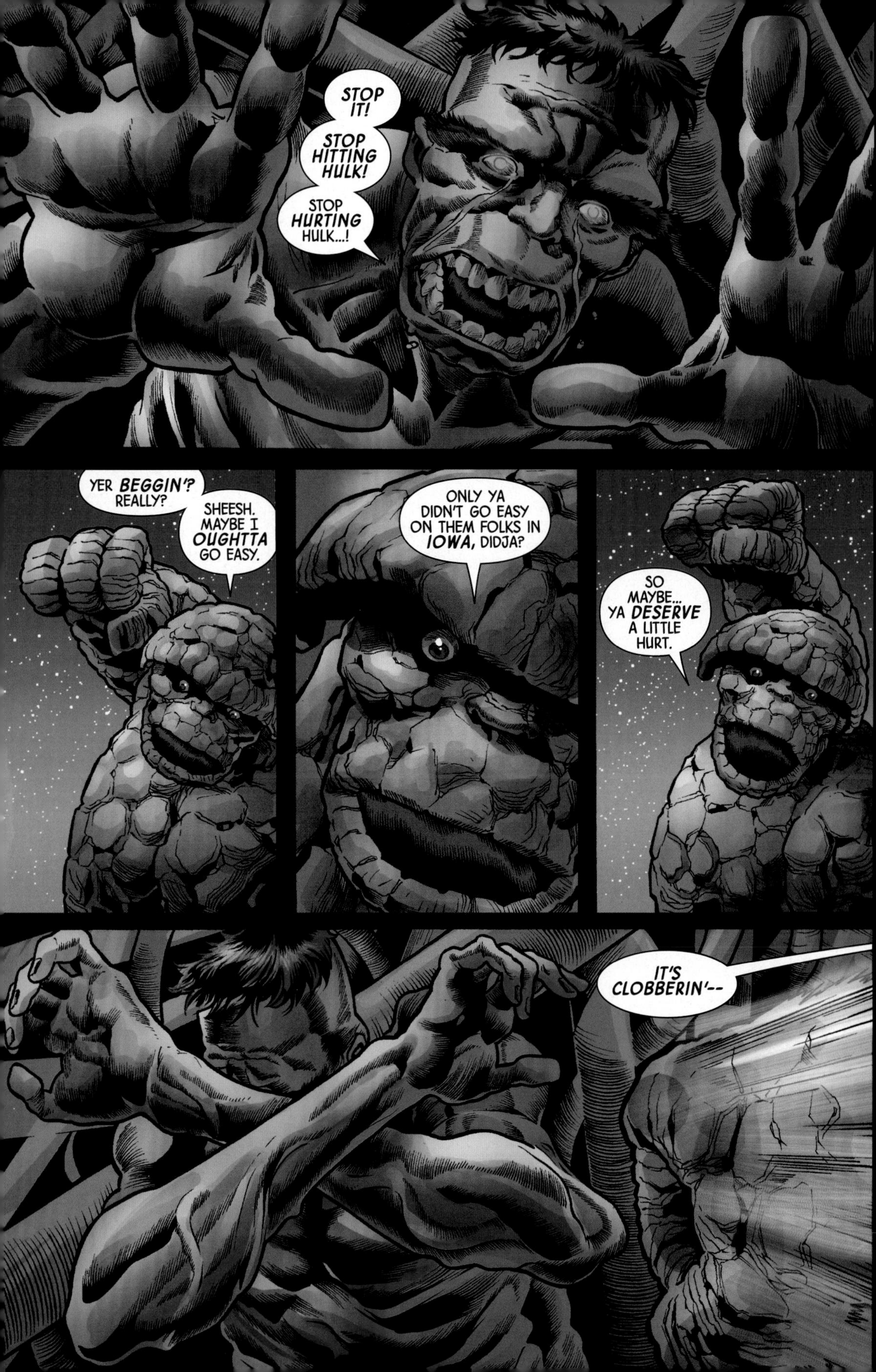
STOP IT!
STOP HITTING HULK!
STOP HURTING HULK...!
YER BEGGIN'? REALLY?
SHEESH. MAYBE I OUGHTTA GO EASY.
ONLY YA DIDN'T GO EASY ON THEM FOLKS IN IOWA, DIDJA?
SO MAYBE... YA DESERVE A LITTLE HURT.
IT'S CLOBBERIN'--

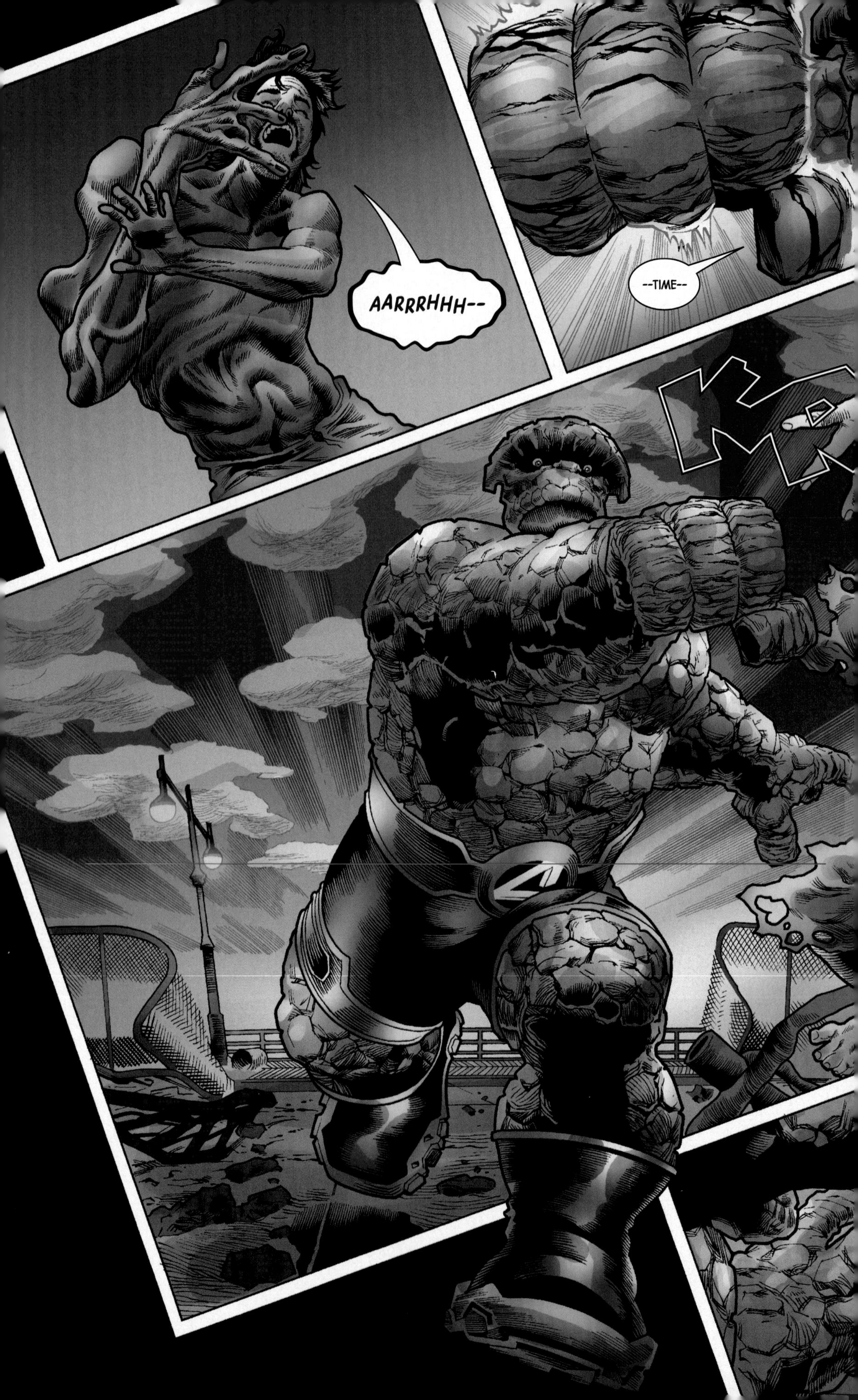
AARRRHHH--
--TIME--

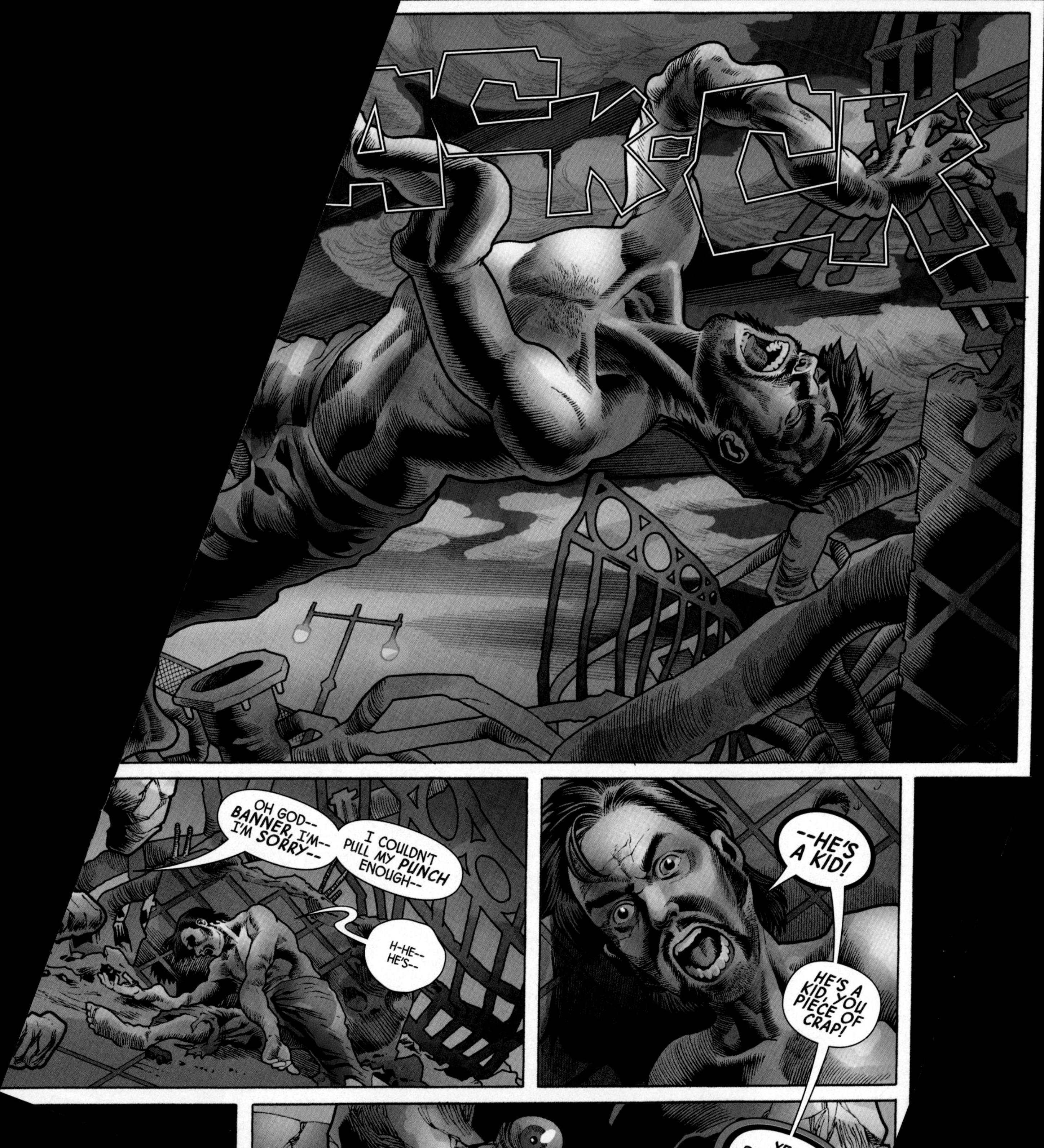
ACK-CK
OH GOD-- BANNER, I'M-- I'M SORRY--
I COULDN'T PULL MY PUNCH ENOUGH--
H-HE-- HE'S--
--HE'S A KID!
HE'S A KID, YOU PIECE OF CRAP!

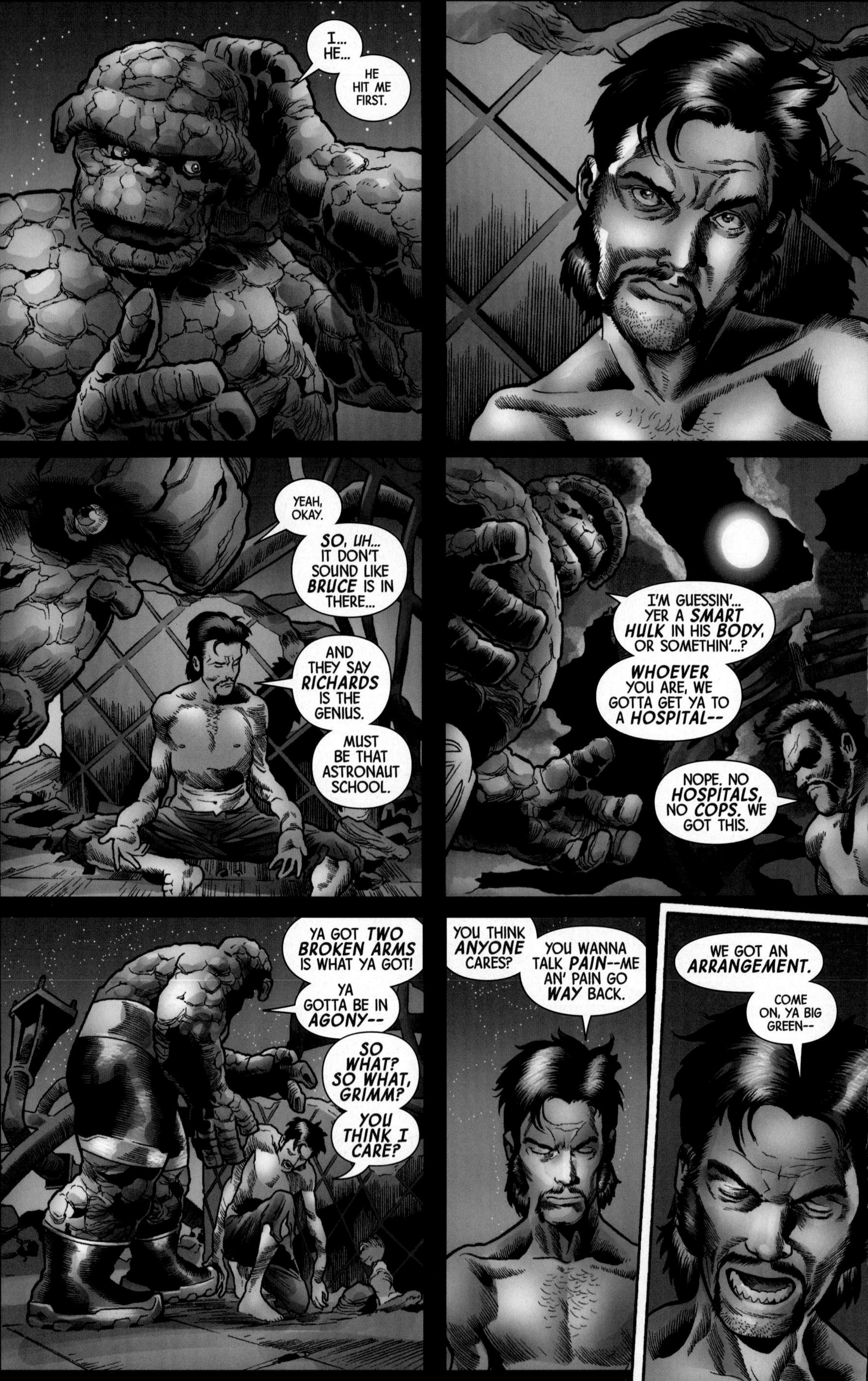
I... HE...
HE HIT ME FIRST.
YEAH, OKAY.
SO, UH... IT DON'T SOUND LIKE BRUCE IS IN THERE...
AND THEY SAY RICHARDS IS THE GENIUS.
MUST BE THAT ASTRONAUT SCHOOL.
I'M GUESSIN'... YER A SMART HULK IN HIS BODY, OR SOMETHIN'...?
WHOEVER YOU ARE, WE GOTTA GET YA TO A HOSPITAL--
NOPE. NO HOSPITALS, NO COPS. WE GOT THIS.
YA GOT TWO BROKEN ARMS IS WHAT YA GOT!
YA GOTTA BE IN AGONY--
SO WHAT? SO WHAT, GRIMM?
YOU THINK I CARE?
YOU THINK ANYONE CARES?
YOU WANNA TALK PAIN--ME AN' PAIN GO WAY BACK.
WE GOT AN ARRANGEMENT.
COME ON, YA BIG GREEN--

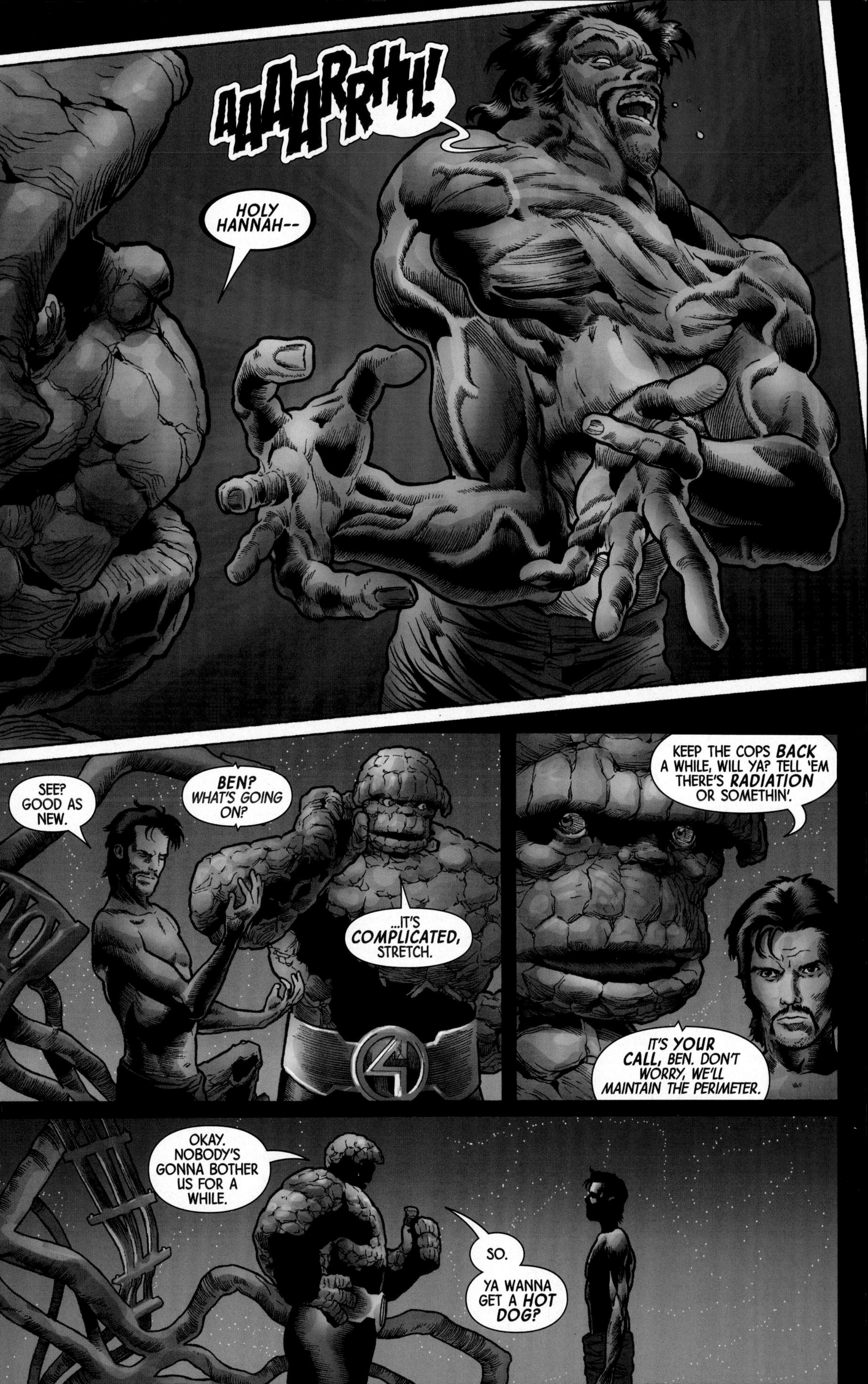
AAAARRHH!
HOLY HANNAH--
SEE? GOOD AS NEW.
BEN? WHAT'S GOING ON?
...IT'S COMPLICATED, STRETCH.
KEEP THE COPS BACK A WHILE, WILL YA? TELL 'EM THERE'S RADIATION OR SOMETHIN'.
IT'S YOUR CALL, BEN. DON'T WORRY, WE'LL MAINTAIN THE PERIMETER.
OKAY. NOBODY'S GONNA BOTHER US FOR A WHILE.
SO.
YA WANNA GET A HOT DOG?

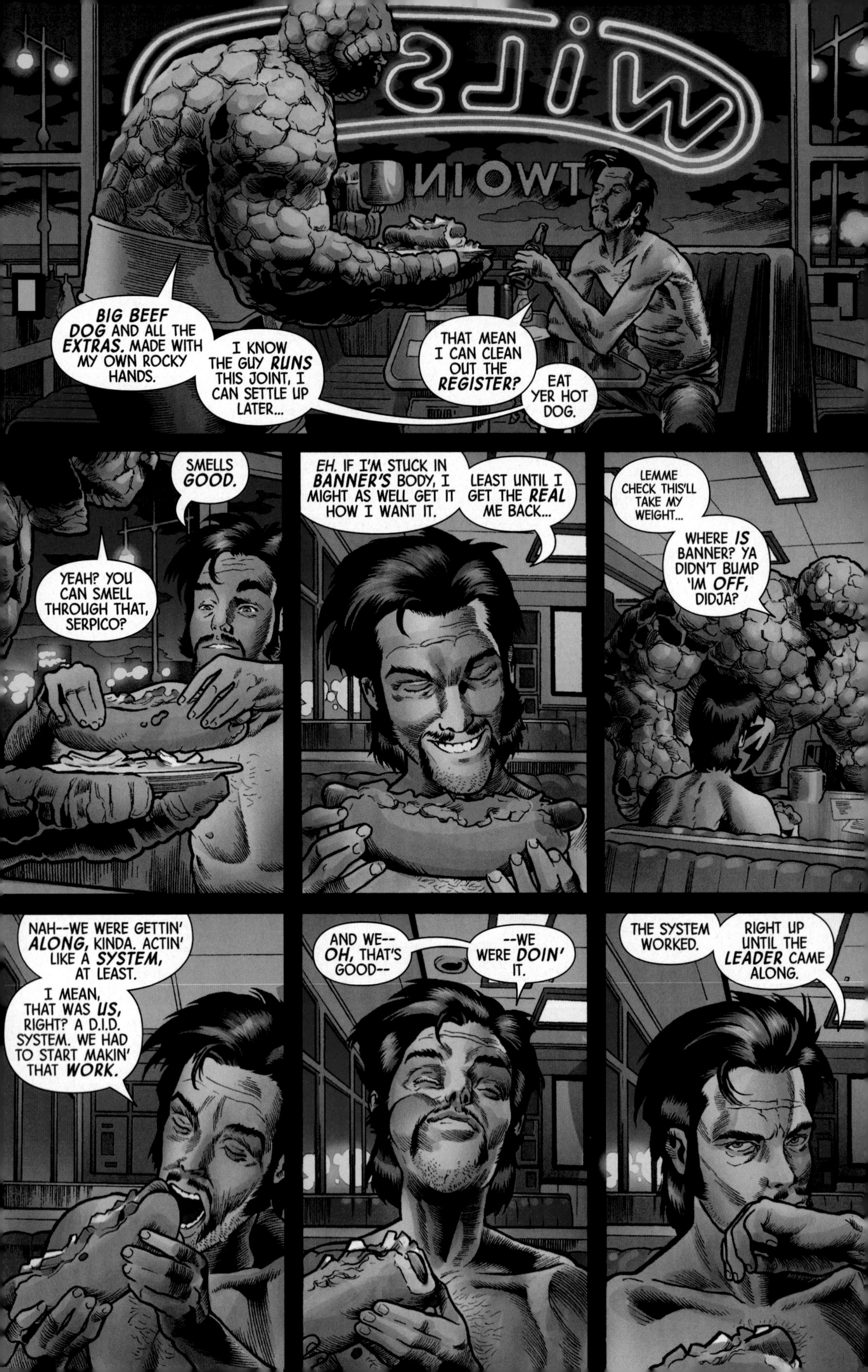

TWO IN
BIG BEEF DOG AND ALL THE EXTRAS. MADE WITH MY OWN ROCKY HANDS.
I KNOW THE GUY RUNS THIS JOINT, I CAN SETTLE UP LATER...
THAT MEAN I CAN CLEAN OUT THE REGISTER?
EAT YER HOT DOG.
SMELLS GOOD.
YEAH? YOU CAN SMELL THROUGH THAT, SERPICO?
EH. IF I'M STUCK IN BANNER'S BODY, I MIGHT AS WELL GET IT HOW I WANT IT.
LEAST UNTIL I GET THE REAL ME BACK...
LEMME CHECK THIS'LL TAKE MY WEIGHT...
WHERE IS BANNER? YA DIDN'T BUMP 'IM OFF, DIDJA?
NAH--WE WERE GETTIN' ALONG, KINDA. ACTIN' LIKE A SYSTEM, AT LEAST.
I MEAN, THAT WAS US, RIGHT? A D.I.D. SYSTEM. WE HAD TO START MAKIN' THAT WORK.
AND WE-- OH, THAT'S GOOD--
--WE WERE DOIN' IT.
THE SYSTEM WORKED.
RIGHT UP UNTIL THE LEADER CAME ALONG.

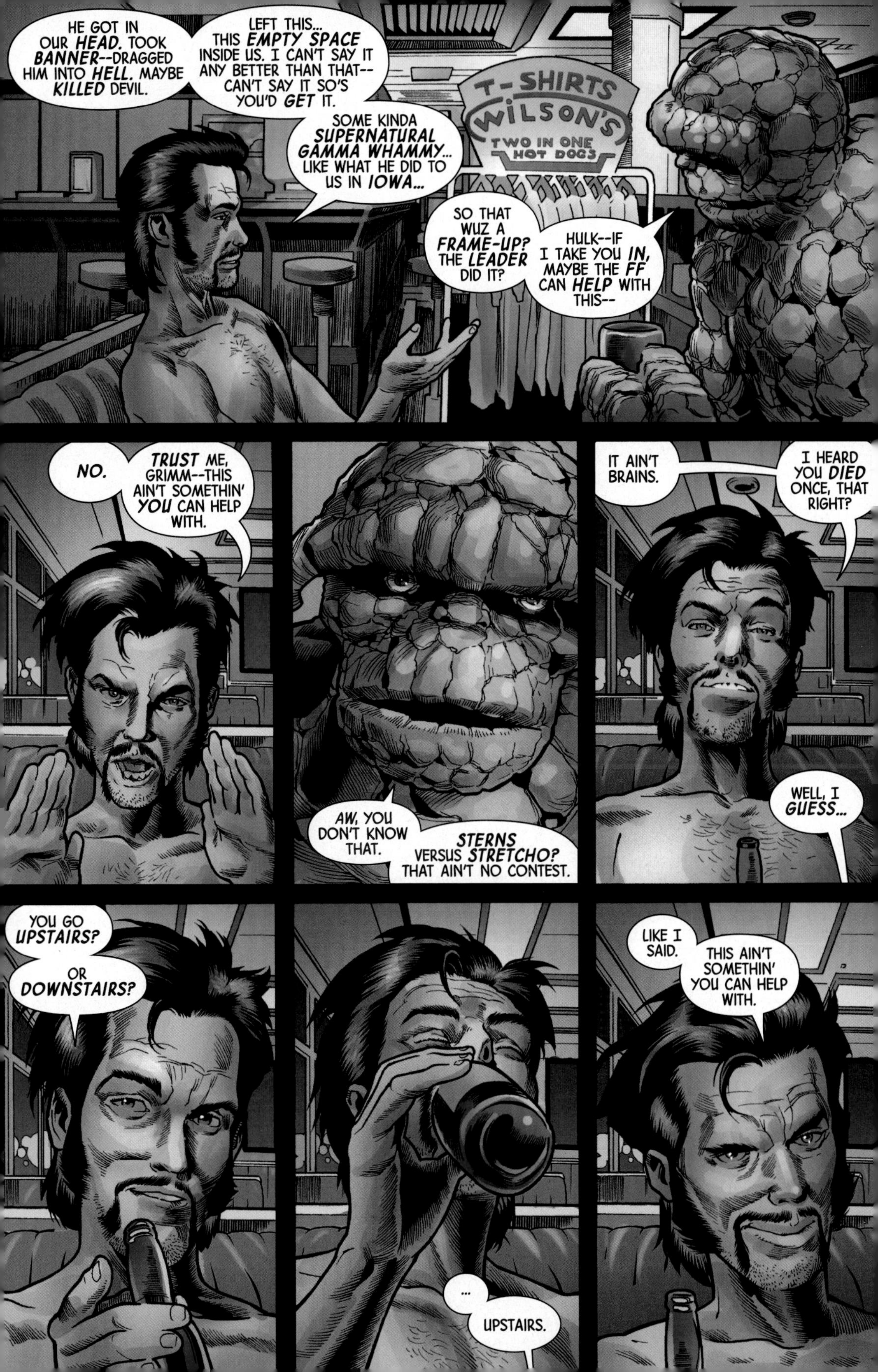
HE GOT IN OUR HEAD. TOOK BANNER--DRAGGED HIM INTO HELL. MAYBE KILLED DEVIL.
LEFT THIS... THIS EMPTY SPACE INSIDE US. I CAN'T SAY IT ANY BETTER THAN THAT-- CAN'T SAY IT SO'S YOU'D GET IT.
SOME KINDA SUPERNATURAL GAMMA WHAMMY... LIKE WHAT HE DID TO US IN IOWA...
T-SHIRTS
WILSON'S
TWO IN ONE HOT DOGS
SO THAT WUZ A FRAME-UP? THE LEADER DID IT?
HULK--IF I TAKE YOU IN, MAYBE THE FF CAN HELP WITH THIS--
NO.
TRUST ME, GRIMM--THIS AIN'T SOMETHIN' YOU CAN HELP WITH.
AW, YOU DON'T KNOW THAT.
STERNS VERSUS STRETCHO? THAT AIN'T NO CONTEST.
IT AIN'T BRAINS.
I HEARD YOU DIED ONCE, THAT RIGHT?
WELL, I GUESS...
YOU GO UPSTAIRS?
OR DOWNSTAIRS?
...
UPSTAIRS.
LIKE I SAID.
THIS AIN'T SOMETHIN' YOU CAN HELP WITH.

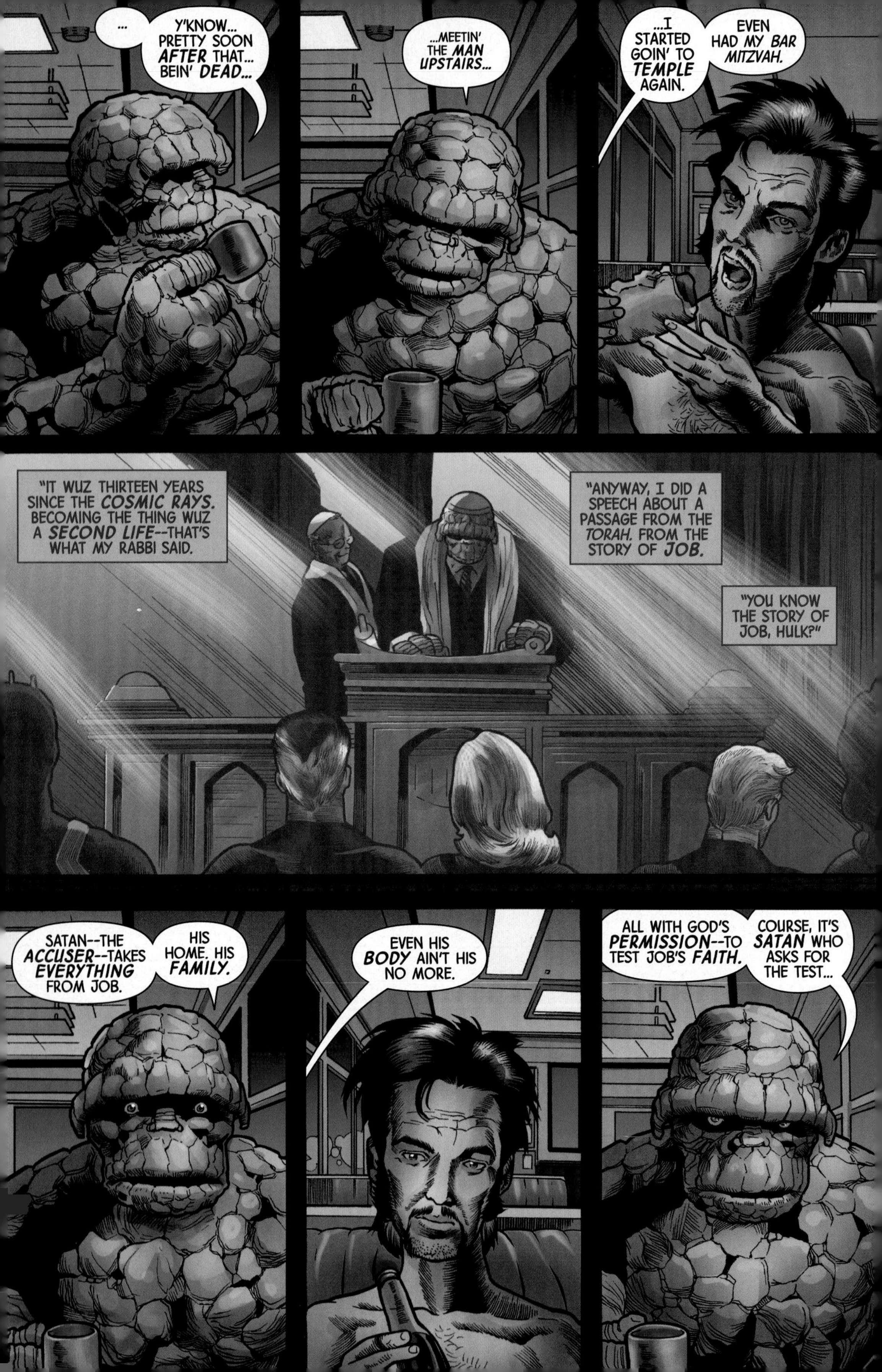
...
Y'KNOW... PRETTY SOON AFTER THAT... BEIN' DEAD...
...MEETIN' THE MAN UPSTAIRS...
...I STARTED GOIN' TO TEMPLE AGAIN.
EVEN HAD MY BAR MITZVAH.
"IT WUZ THIRTEEN YEARS SINCE THE COSMIC RAYS. BECOMING THE THING WUZ A SECOND LIFE--THAT'S WHAT MY RABBI SAID.
"ANYWAY, I DID A SPEECH ABOUT A PASSAGE FROM THE TORAH. FROM THE STORY OF JOB.
"YOU KNOW THE STORY OF JOB, HULK?"
SATAN--THE ACCUSER--TAKES EVERYTHING FROM JOB.
HIS HOME. HIS FAMILY.
EVEN HIS BODY AIN'T HIS NO MORE.
ALL WITH GOD'S PERMISSION--TO TEST JOB'S FAITH.
COURSE, IT'S SATAN WHO ASKS FOR THE TEST...

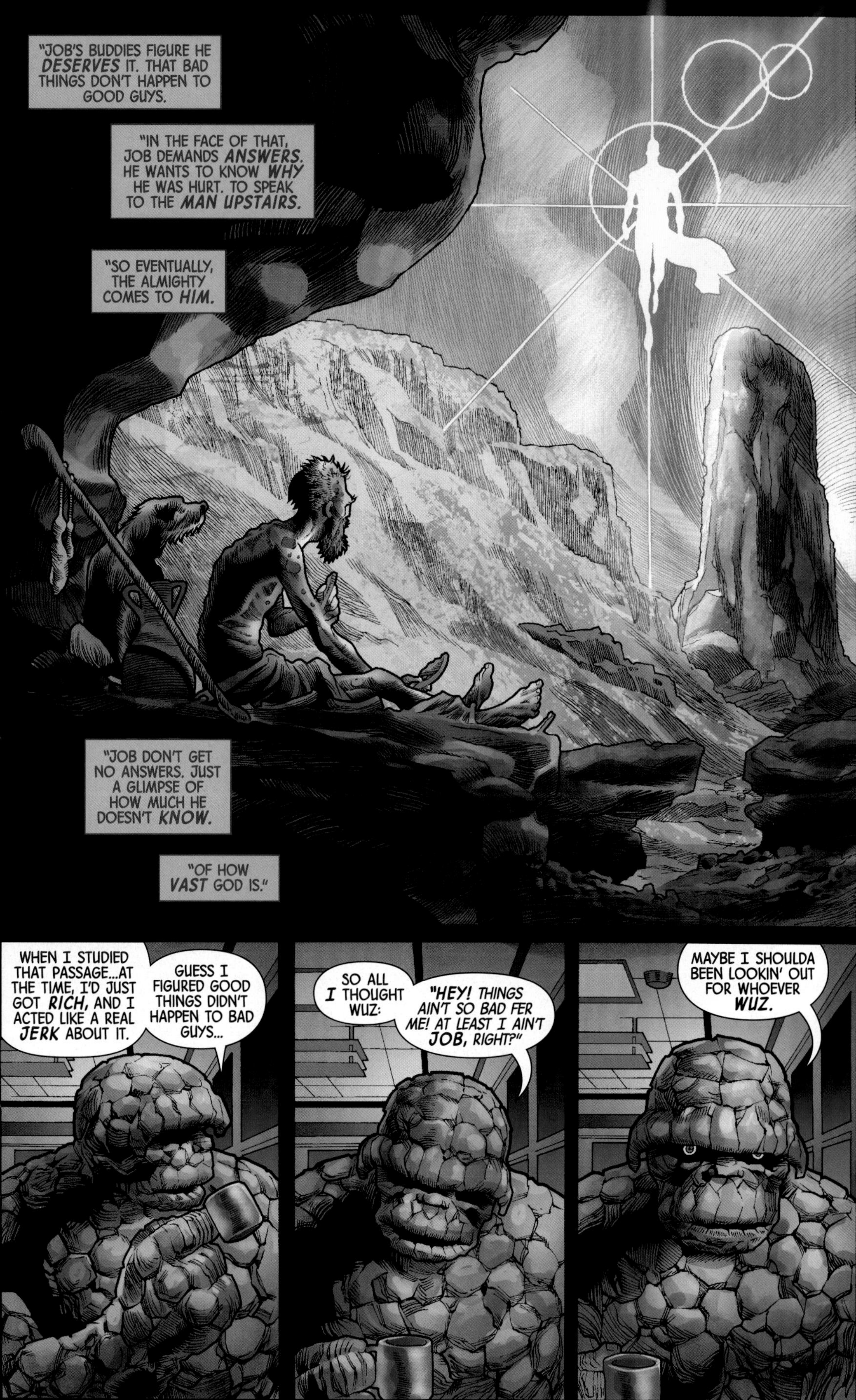
"JOB'S BUDDIES FIGURE HE DESERVES IT. THAT BAD THINGS DON'T HAPPEN TO GOOD GUYS.
"IN THE FACE OF THAT, JOB DEMANDS ANSWERS. HE WANTS TO KNOW WHY HE WAS HURT. TO SPEAK TO THE MAN UPSTAIRS.
"SO EVENTUALLY, THE ALMIGHTY COMES TO HIM.
"JOB DON'T GET NO ANSWERS. JUST A GLIMPSE OF HOW MUCH HE DOESN'T KNOW.
"OF HOW VAST GOD IS."
WHEN I STUDIED THAT PASSAGE...AT THE TIME, I'D JUST GOT RICH, AND I ACTED LIKE A REAL JERK ABOUT IT.
GUESS I FIGURED GOOD THINGS DIDN'T HAPPEN TO BAD GUYS...
SO ALL I THOUGHT WUZ:
"HEY! THINGS AIN'T SO BAD FER ME! AT LEAST I AIN'T JOB, RIGHT?"
MAYBE I SHOULDA BEEN LOOKIN' OUT FOR WHOEVER WUZ.

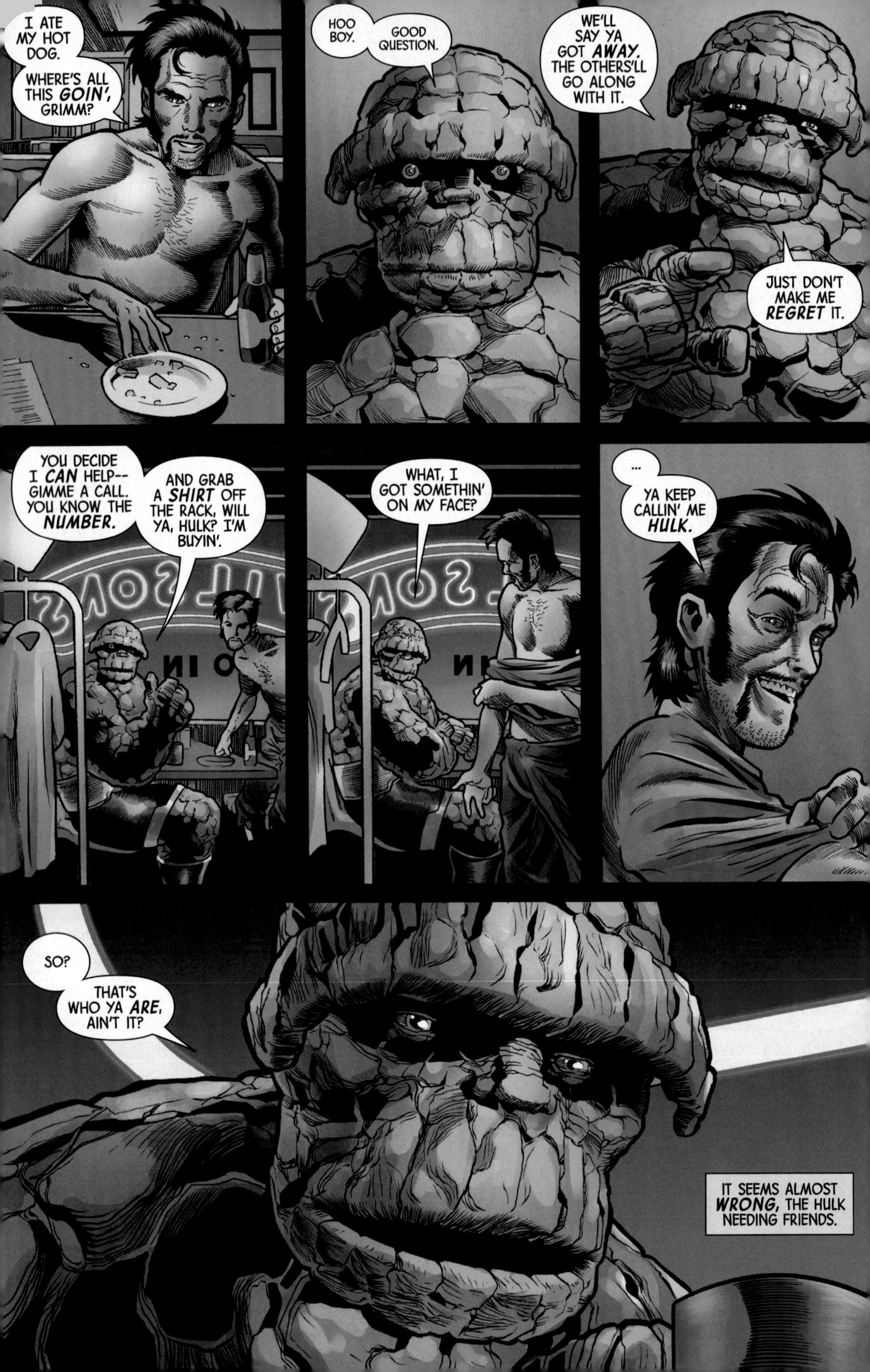
I ATE MY HOT DOG.
WHERE'S ALL THIS GOIN', GRIMM?
HOO BOY.
GOOD QUESTION.
WE'LL SAY YA GOT AWAY. THE OTHERS'LL GO ALONG WITH IT.
JUST DON'T MAKE ME REGRET IT.
YOU DECIDE I CAN HELP-- GIMME A CALL. YOU KNOW THE NUMBER.
AND GRAB A SHIRT OFF THE RACK, WILL YA, HULK? I'M BUYIN'.
WHAT, I GOT SOMETHIN' ON MY FACE?
...
YA KEEP CALLIN' ME HULK.
SO?
THAT'S WHO YA ARE, AIN'T IT?
IT SEEMS ALMOST WRONG, THE HULK NEEDING FRIENDS.

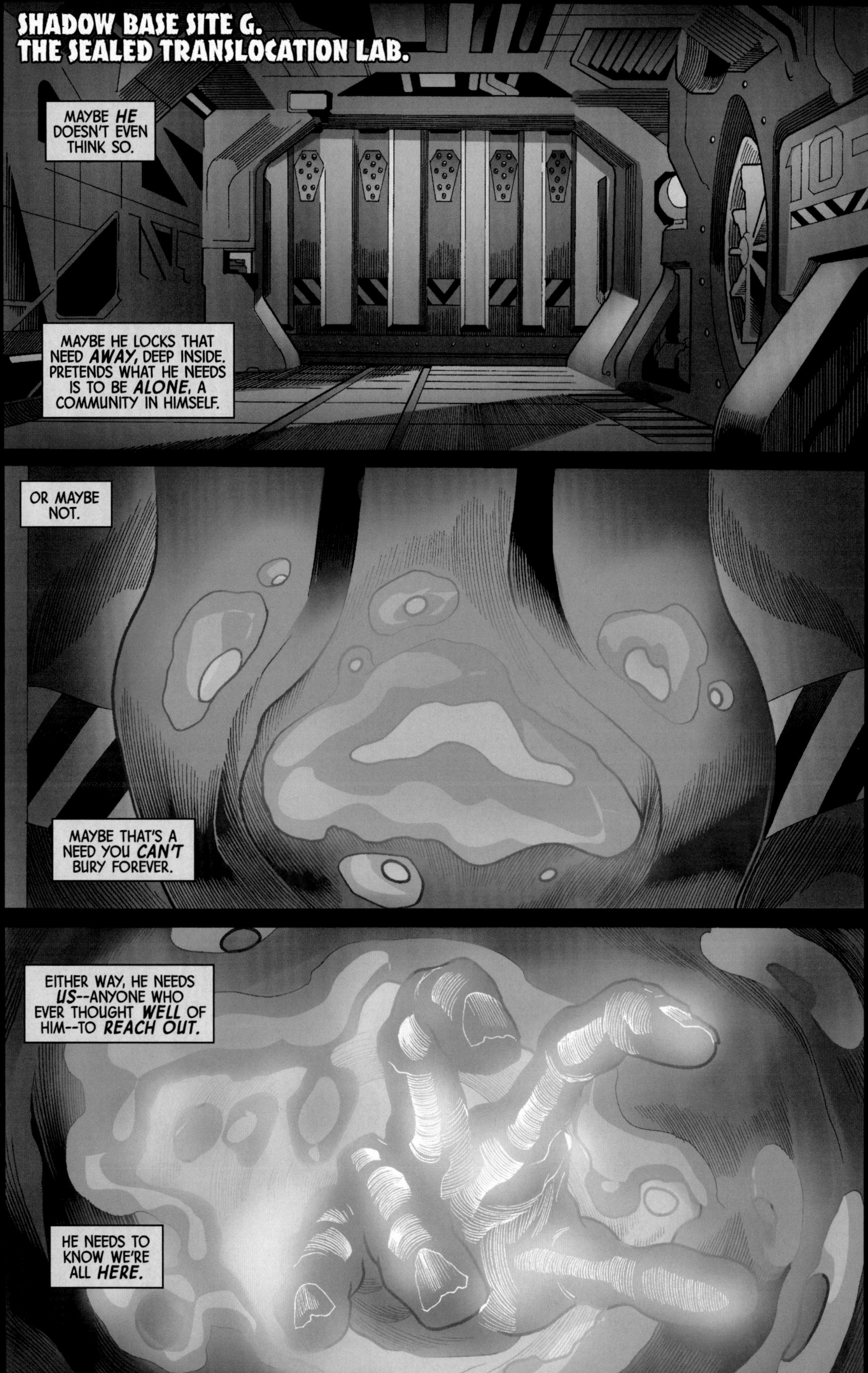
SHADOW BASE SITE G.
THE SEALED TRANSLOCATION LAB.
MAYBE HE DOESN'T EVEN THINK SO.
MAYBE HE LOCKS THAT NEED AWAY, DEEP INSIDE. PRETENDS WHAT HE NEEDS IS TO BE ALONE, A COMMUNITY IN HIMSELF.
OR MAYBE NOT.
MAYBE THAT'S A NEED YOU CAN'T BURY FOREVER.
EITHER WAY, HE NEEDS US--ANYONE WHO EVER THOUGHT WELL OF HIM--TO REACH OUT.
HE NEEDS TO KNOW WE'RE ALL HERE.

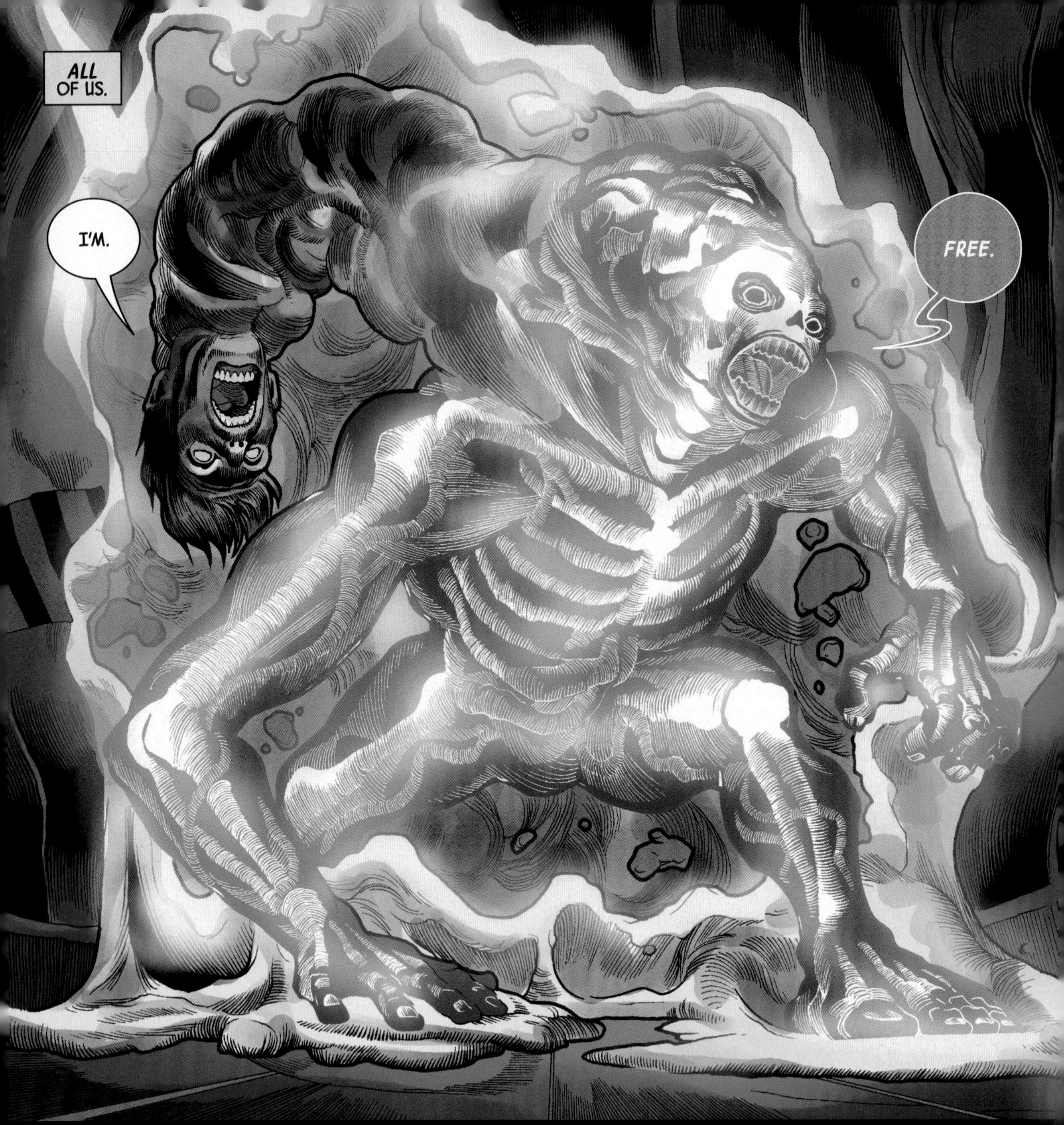
ALL OF US.
I'M.
FREE.

THE MAN DOWNSTAIRS

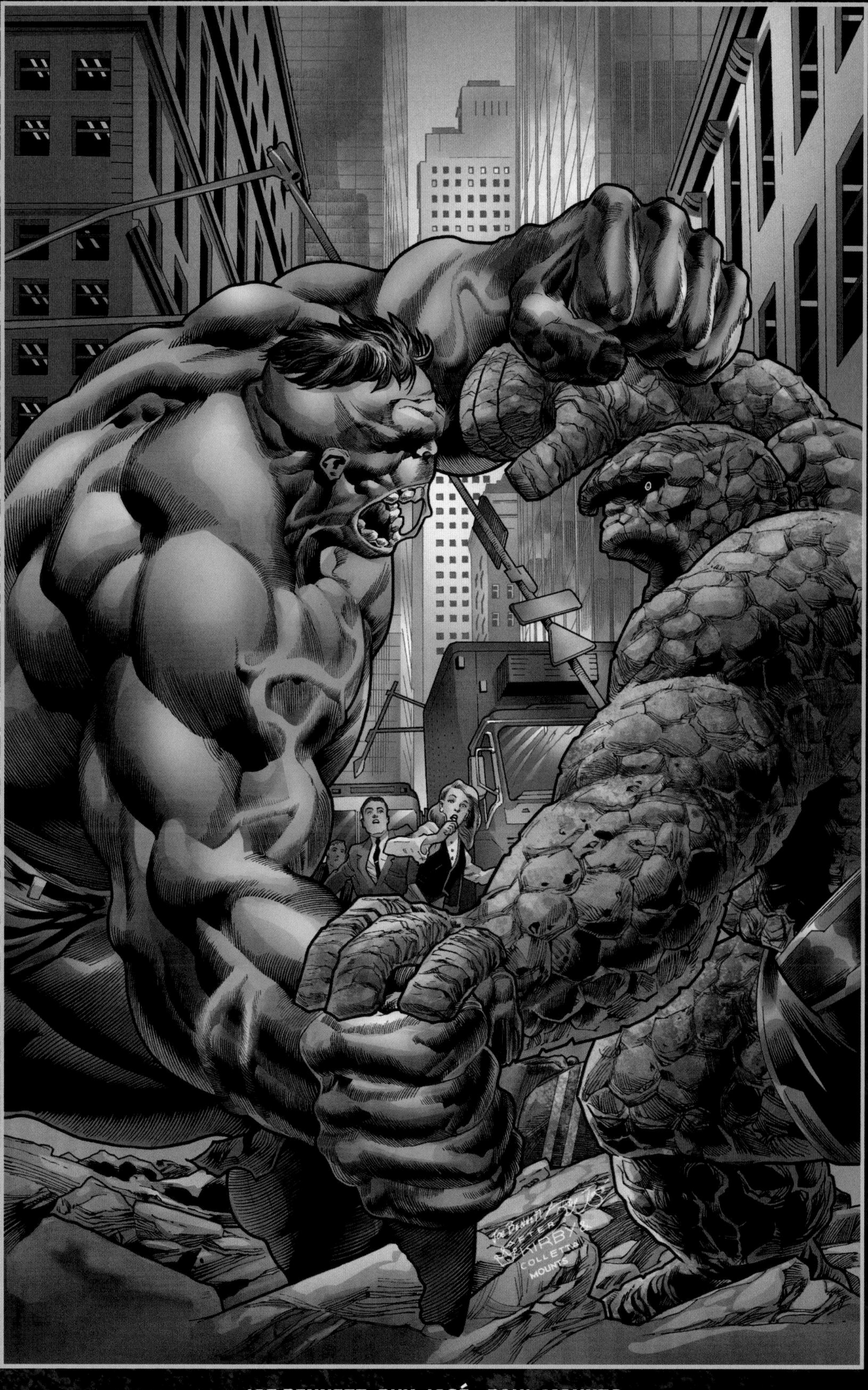
AFTER
KIRBY
COLLETTA
MOUNTS

JOE BENNETT, RUY JOSÉ & PAUL MOUNTS
#41 VARIANT

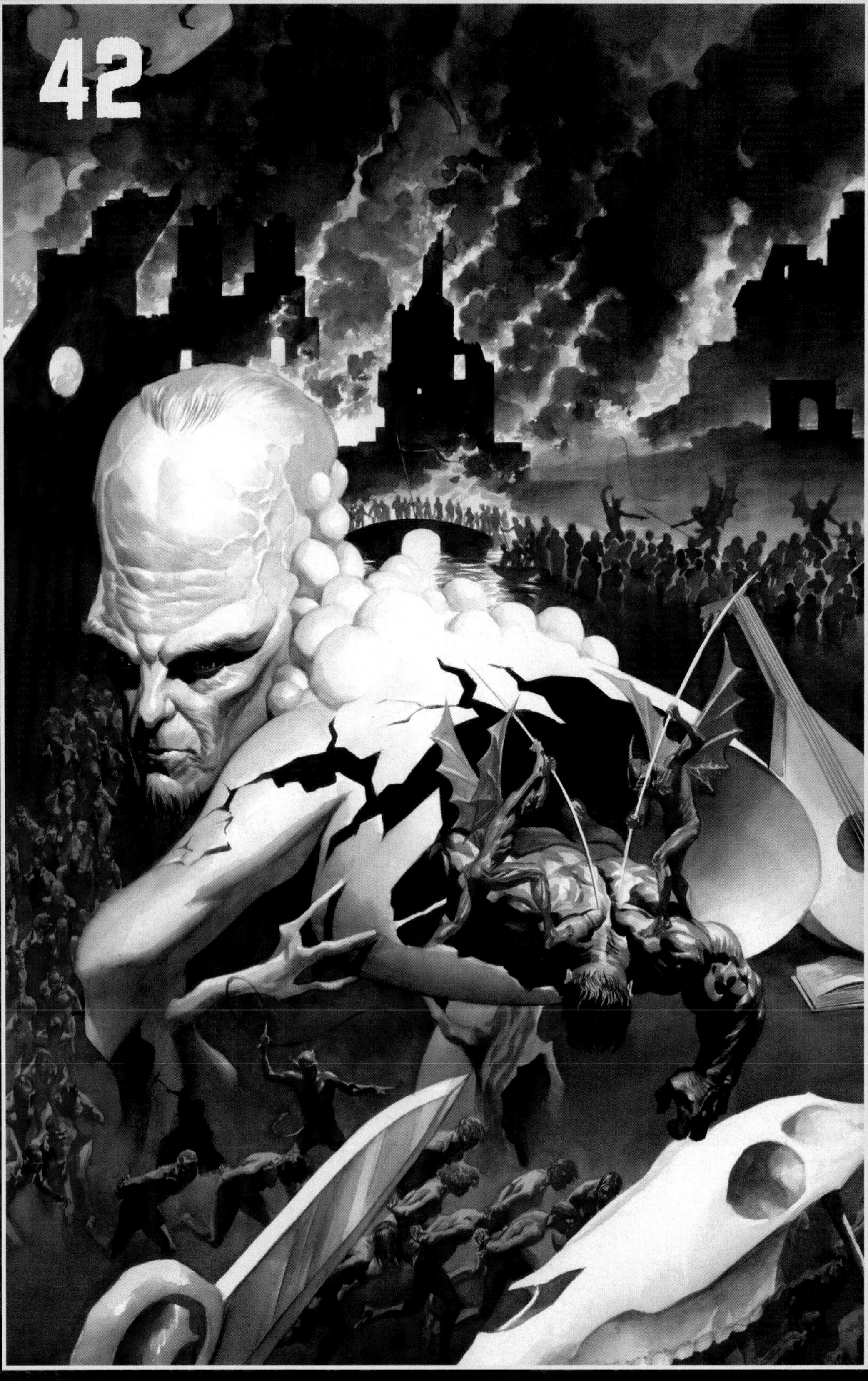
42

"CONSEQUENCES ARE UNPITYING. OUR DEEDS CARRY THEIR TERRIBLE CONSEQUENCES, QUITE APART FROM ANY FLUCTUATIONS THAT WENT BEFORE— CONSEQUENCES THAT ARE HARDLY EVER CONFINED TO OURSELVES."

— GEORGE ELIOT, *ADAM BEDE*

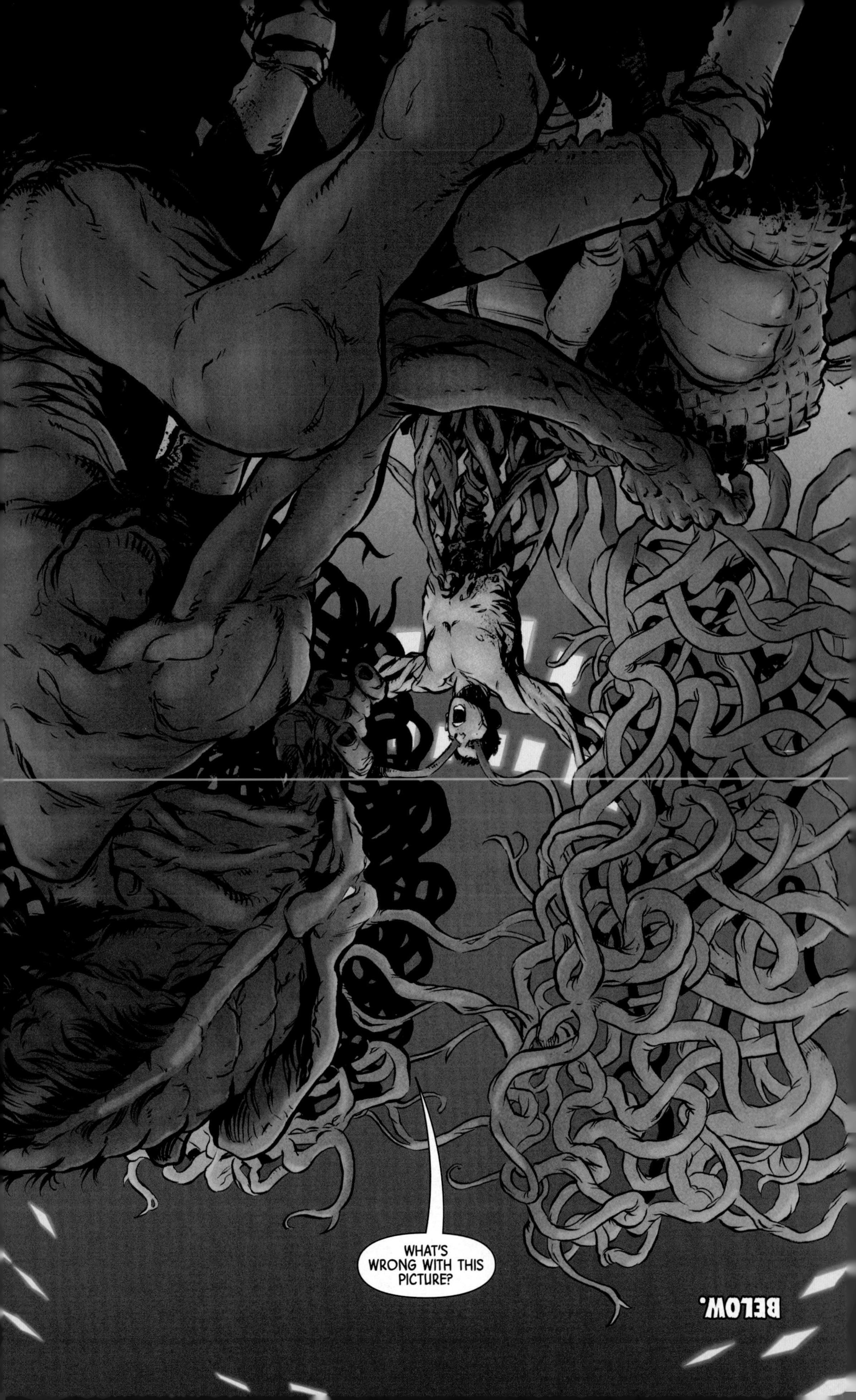

WHAT'S WRONG WITH THIS PICTURE?
BELOW.

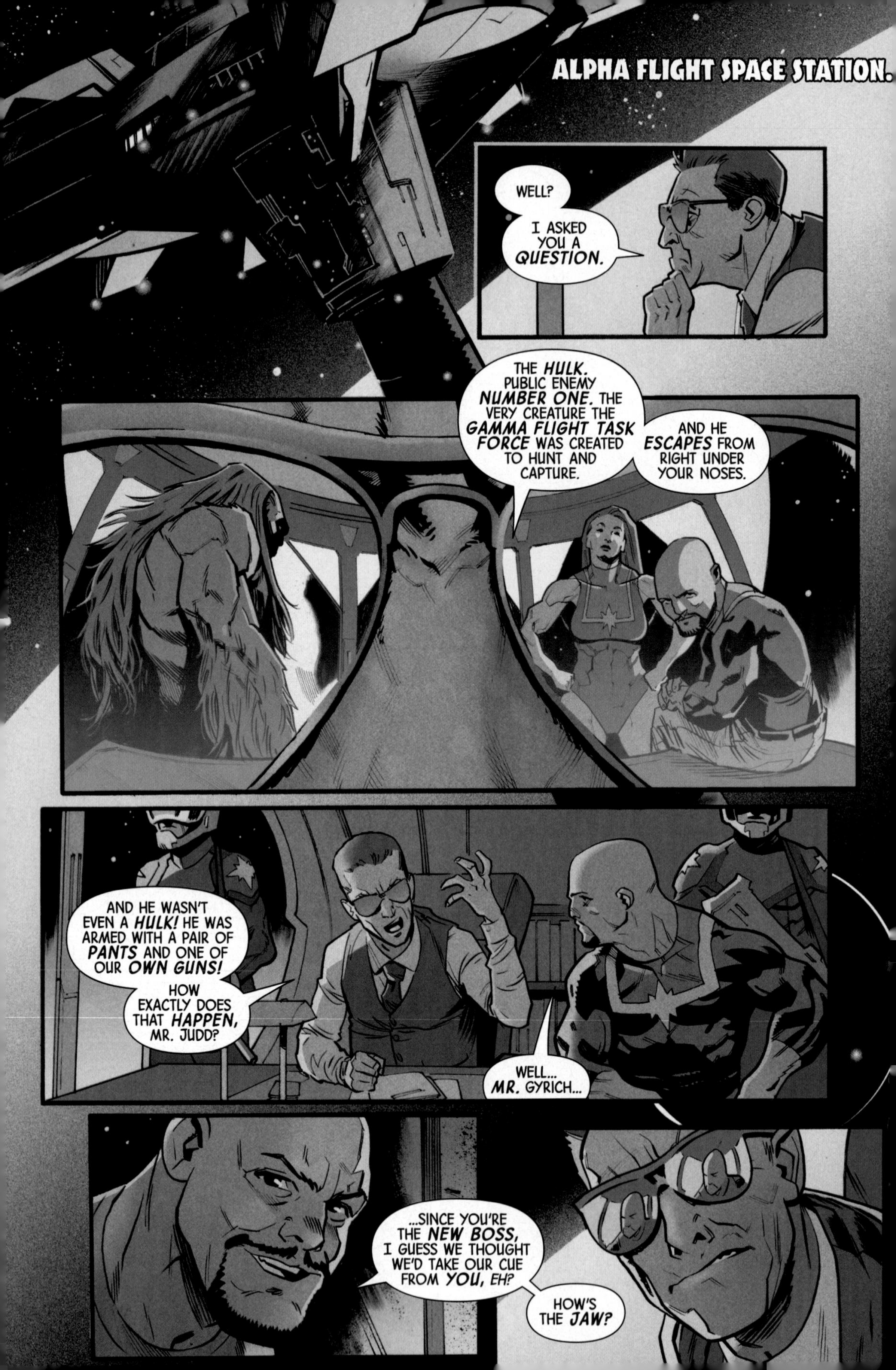
ALPHA FLIGHT SPACE STATION.
WELL?
I ASKED YOU A QUESTION.
THE HULK. PUBLIC ENEMY NUMBER ONE. THE VERY CREATURE THE GAMMA FLIGHT TASK FORCE WAS CREATED TO HUNT AND CAPTURE.
AND HE ESCAPES FROM RIGHT UNDER YOUR NOSES.
AND HE WASN'T EVEN A HULK! HE WAS ARMED WITH A PAIR OF PANTS AND ONE OF OUR OWN GUNS!
HOW EXACTLY DOES THAT HAPPEN, MR. JUDD?
WELL... MR. GYRICH...
...SINCE YOU'RE THE NEW BOSS, I GUESS WE THOUGHT WE'D TAKE OUR CUE FROM YOU, EH?
HOW'S THE JAW?

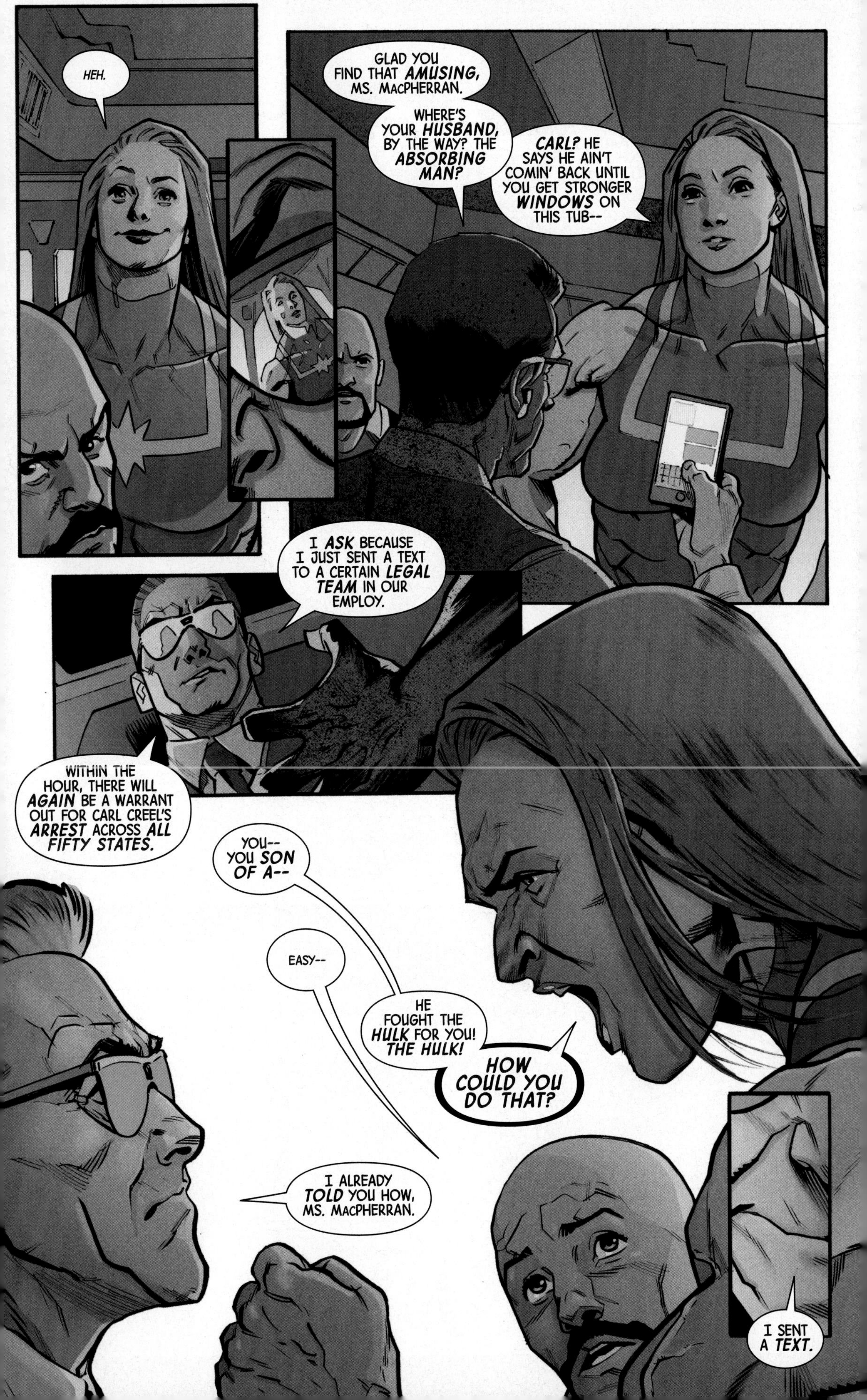
HEH.
GLAD YOU FIND THAT AMUSING, MS. MacPHERRAN.
WHERE'S YOUR HUSBAND, BY THE WAY? THE ABSORBING MAN?
CARL? HE SAYS HE AIN'T COMIN' BACK UNTIL YOU GET STRONGER WINDOWS ON THIS TUB--
I ASK BECAUSE I JUST SENT A TEXT TO A CERTAIN LEGAL TEAM IN OUR EMPLOY.
WITHIN THE HOUR, THERE WILL AGAIN BE A WARRANT OUT FOR CARL CREEL'S ARREST ACROSS ALL FIFTY STATES.
YOU-- YOU SON OF A--
EASY--
HE FOUGHT THE HULK FOR YOU! THE HULK!
HOW COULD YOU DO THAT?
I ALREADY TOLD YOU HOW, MS. MacPHERRAN.
I SENT A TEXT.

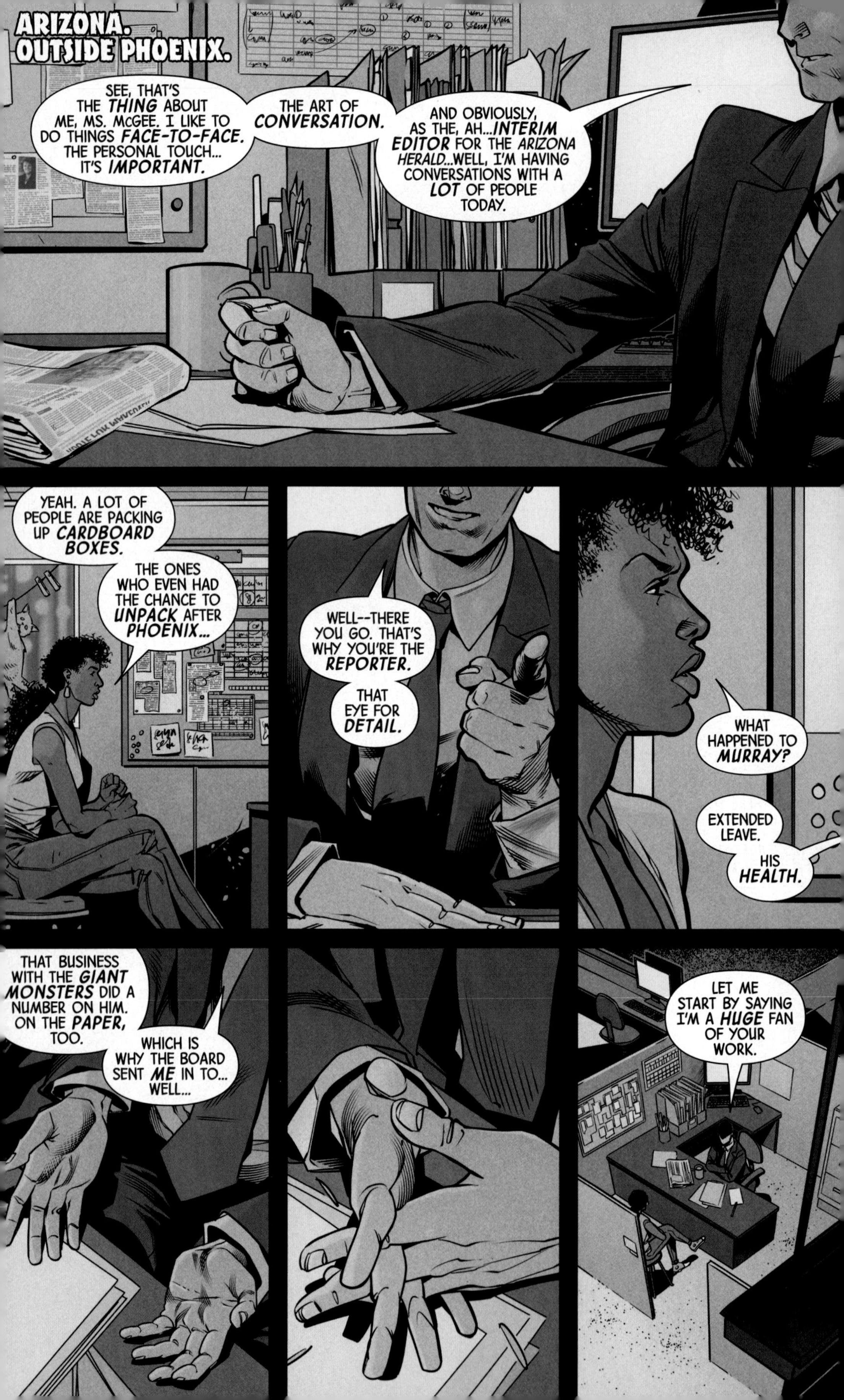
ARIZONA. OUTSIDE PHOENIX.
SEE, THAT'S THE THING ABOUT ME, MS. McGEE. I LIKE TO DO THINGS FACE-TO-FACE. THE PERSONAL TOUCH... IT'S IMPORTANT.
THE ART OF CONVERSATION.
AND OBVIOUSLY, AS THE, AH...INTERIM EDITOR FOR THE ARIZONA HERALD...WELL, I'M HAVING CONVERSATIONS WITH A LOT OF PEOPLE TODAY.
YEAH. A LOT OF PEOPLE ARE PACKING UP CARDBOARD BOXES.
THE ONES WHO EVEN HAD THE CHANCE TO UNPACK AFTER PHOENIX...
WELL--THERE YOU GO. THAT'S WHY YOU'RE THE REPORTER.
THAT EYE FOR DETAIL.
WHAT HAPPENED TO MURRAY?
EXTENDED LEAVE.
HIS HEALTH.
THAT BUSINESS WITH THE GIANT MONSTERS DID A NUMBER ON HIM. ON THE PAPER, TOO.
WHICH IS WHY THE BOARD SENT ME IN TO... WELL...
LET ME START BY SAYING I'M A HUGE FAN OF YOUR WORK.

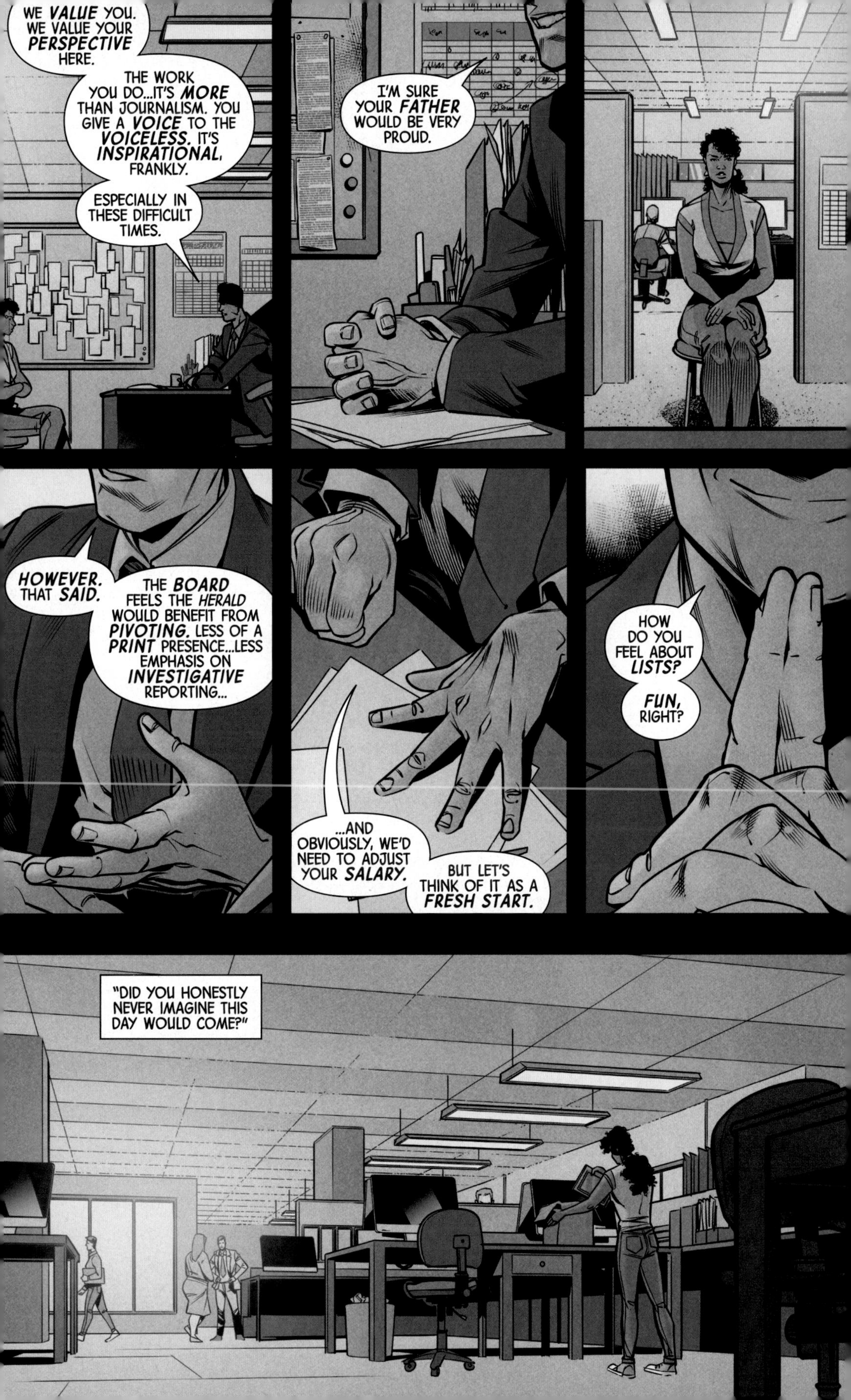
WE VALUE YOU. WE VALUE YOUR PERSPECTIVE HERE.
THE WORK YOU DO...IT'S MORE THAN JOURNALISM. YOU GIVE A VOICE TO THE VOICELESS. IT'S INSPIRATIONAL, FRANKLY.
ESPECIALLY IN THESE DIFFICULT TIMES.
I'M SURE YOUR FATHER WOULD BE VERY PROUD.
HOWEVER. THAT SAID.
THE BOARD FEELS THE HERALD WOULD BENEFIT FROM PIVOTING. LESS OF A PRINT PRESENCE...LESS EMPHASIS ON INVESTIGATIVE REPORTING...
...AND OBVIOUSLY, WE'D NEED TO ADJUST YOUR SALARY.
BUT LET'S THINK OF IT AS A FRESH START.
HOW DO YOU FEEL ABOUT LISTS?
FUN, RIGHT?
"DID YOU HONESTLY NEVER IMAGINE THIS DAY WOULD COME?"

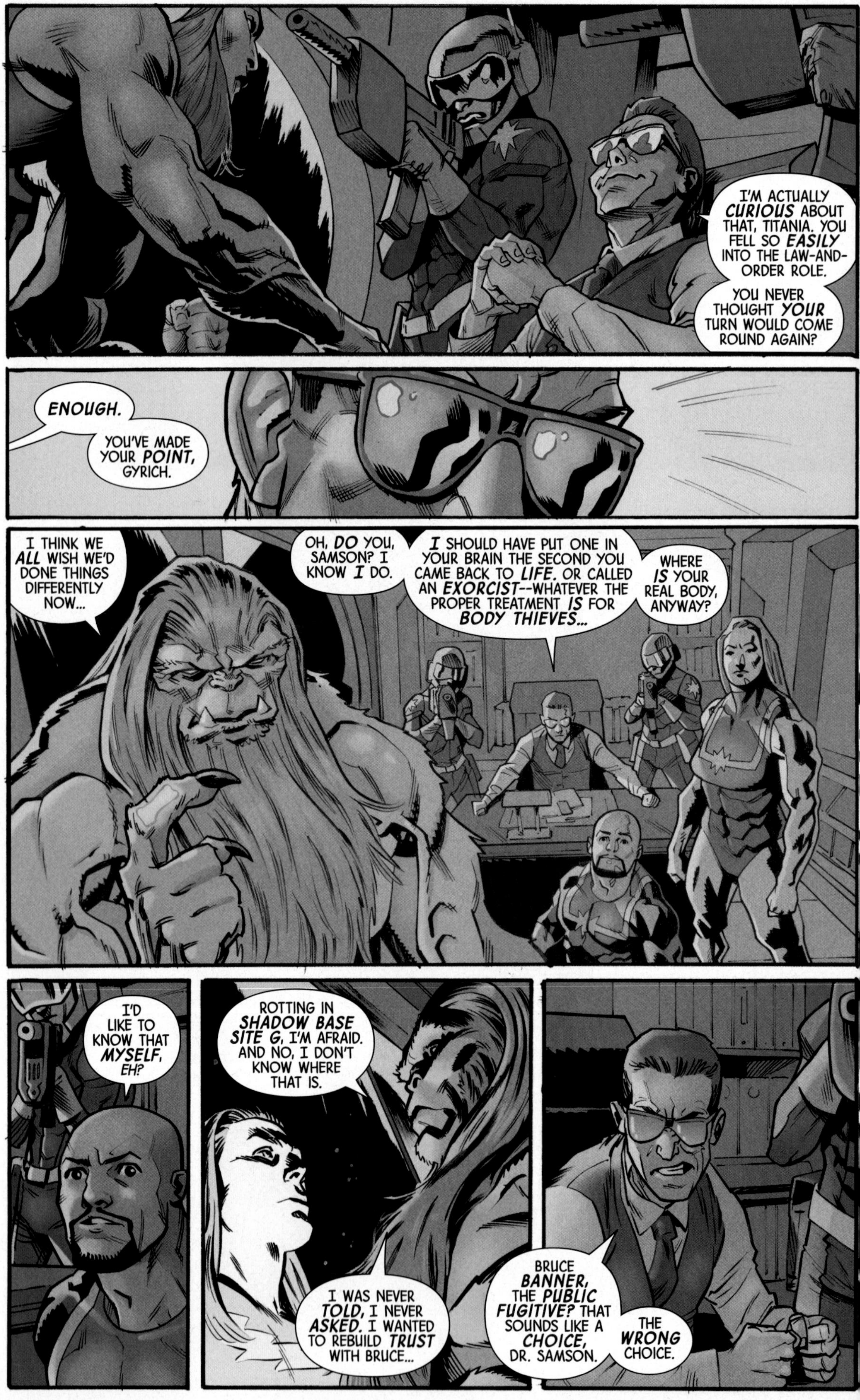
I'M ACTUALLY CURIOUS ABOUT THAT, TITANIA. YOU FELL SO EASILY INTO THE LAW-AND-ORDER ROLE.
YOU NEVER THOUGHT YOUR TURN WOULD COME ROUND AGAIN?
ENOUGH.
YOU'VE MADE YOUR POINT, GYRICH.
I THINK WE ALL WISH WE'D DONE THINGS DIFFERENTLY NOW...
OH, DO YOU, SAMSON? I KNOW I DO.
I SHOULD HAVE PUT ONE IN YOUR BRAIN THE SECOND YOU CAME BACK TO LIFE. OR CALLED AN EXORCIST--WHATEVER THE PROPER TREATMENT IS FOR BODY THIEVES...
WHERE IS YOUR REAL BODY, ANYWAY?
I'D LIKE TO KNOW THAT MYSELF, EH?
ROTTING IN SHADOW BASE SITE G, I'M AFRAID. AND NO, I DON'T KNOW WHERE THAT IS.
I WAS NEVER TOLD, I NEVER ASKED. I WANTED TO REBUILD TRUST WITH BRUCE...
BRUCE BANNER, THE PUBLIC FUGITIVE? THAT SOUNDS LIKE A CHOICE, DR. SAMSON.
THE WRONG CHOICE.

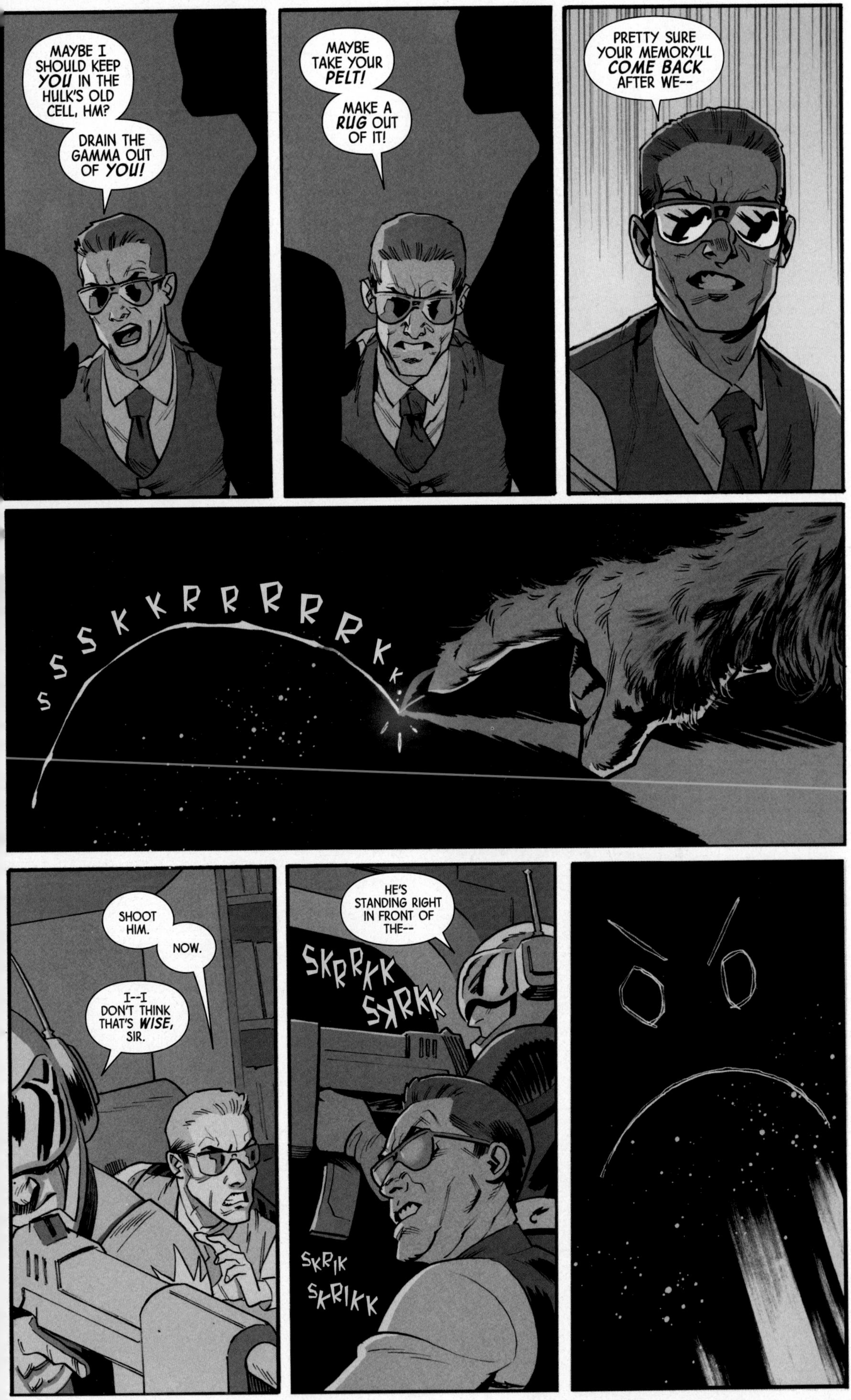
MAYBE I SHOULD KEEP YOU IN THE HULK'S OLD CELL, HM?
DRAIN THE GAMMA OUT OF YOU!
MAYBE TAKE YOUR PELT!
MAKE A RUG OUT OF IT!
PRETTY SURE YOUR MEMORY'LL COME BACK AFTER WE--
SSSKKRRRRRRKK
SHOOT HIM.
NOW.
I--I DON'T THINK THAT'S WISE, SIR.
HE'S STANDING RIGHT IN FRONT OF THE--
SKRRKK
SKRKK
SKRIK
SKRIKK

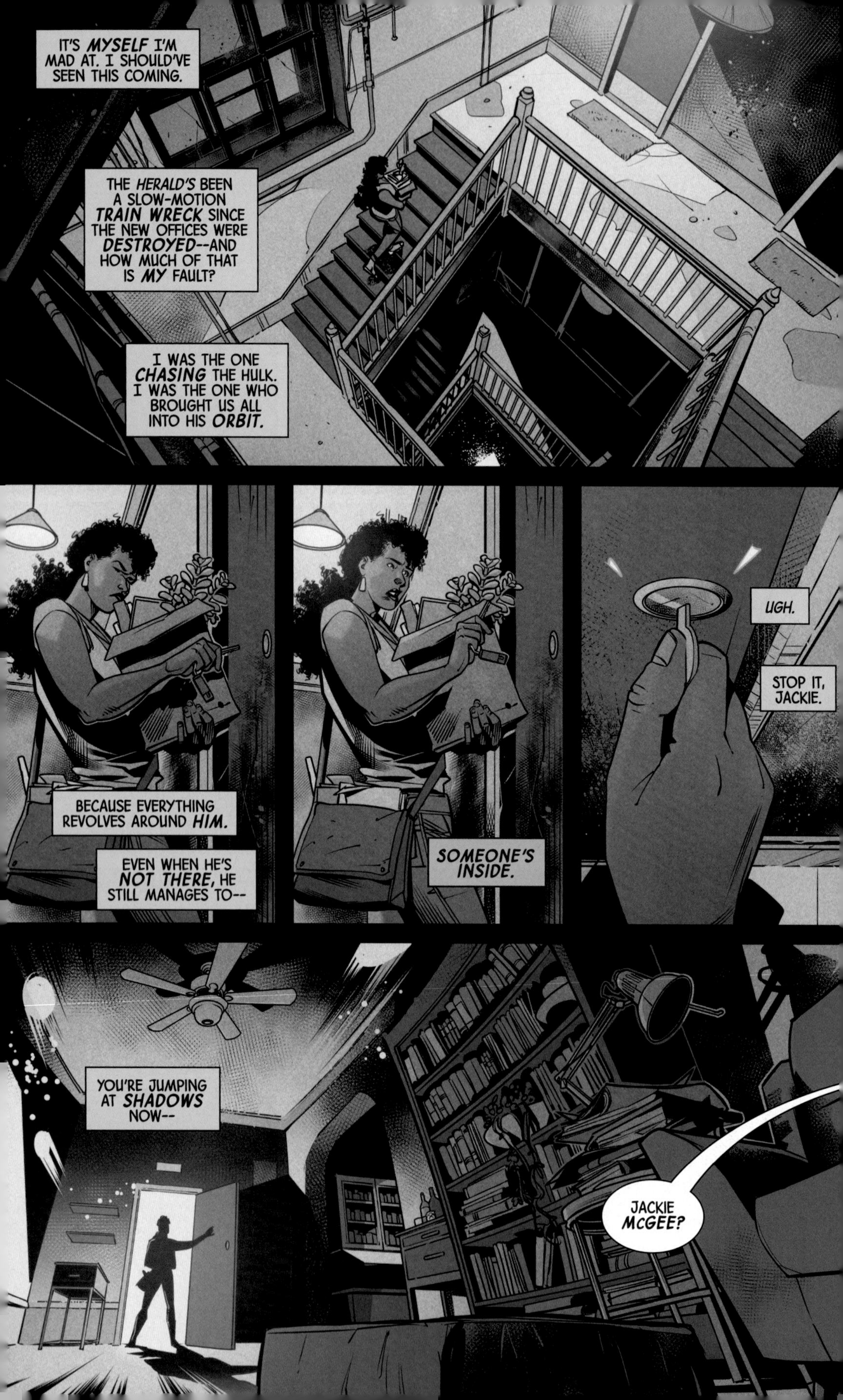
IT'S MYSELF I'M MAD AT. I SHOULD'VE SEEN THIS COMING.
THE HERALD'S BEEN A SLOW-MOTION TRAIN WRECK SINCE THE NEW OFFICES WERE DESTROYED--AND HOW MUCH OF THAT IS MY FAULT?
I WAS THE ONE CHASING THE HULK. I WAS THE ONE WHO BROUGHT US ALL INTO HIS ORBIT.
BECAUSE EVERYTHING REVOLVES AROUND HIM.
EVEN WHEN HE'S NOT THERE, HE STILL MANAGES TO--
SOMEONE'S INSIDE.
UGH.
STOP IT, JACKIE.
YOU'RE JUMPING AT SHADOWS NOW--
JACKIE McGEE?

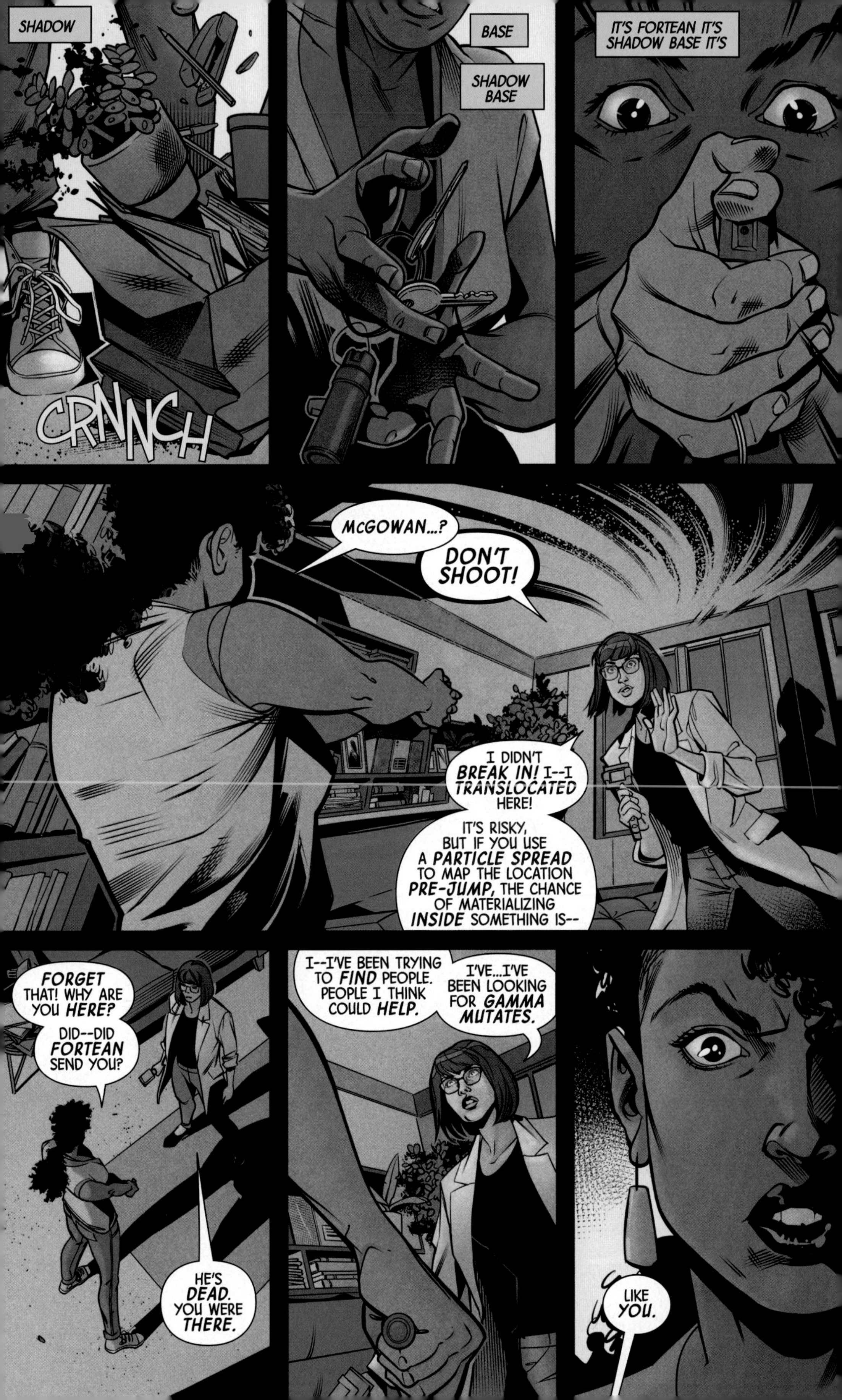

SHADOW
CRNNCH
BASE
SHADOW BASE
IT'S FORTEAN IT'S SHADOW BASE IT'S
McGOWAN...?
DON'T SHOOT!
I DIDN'T BREAK IN! I--I TRANSLOCATED HERE!
IT'S RISKY, BUT IF YOU USE A PARTICLE SPREAD TO MAP THE LOCATION PRE-JUMP, THE CHANCE OF MATERIALIZING INSIDE SOMETHING IS--
FORGET THAT! WHY ARE YOU HERE?
DID--DID FORTEAN SEND YOU?
HE'S DEAD. YOU WERE THERE.
I--I'VE BEEN TRYING TO FIND PEOPLE. PEOPLE I THINK COULD HELP.
I'VE...I'VE BEEN LOOKING FOR GAMMA MUTATES.
LIKE YOU.

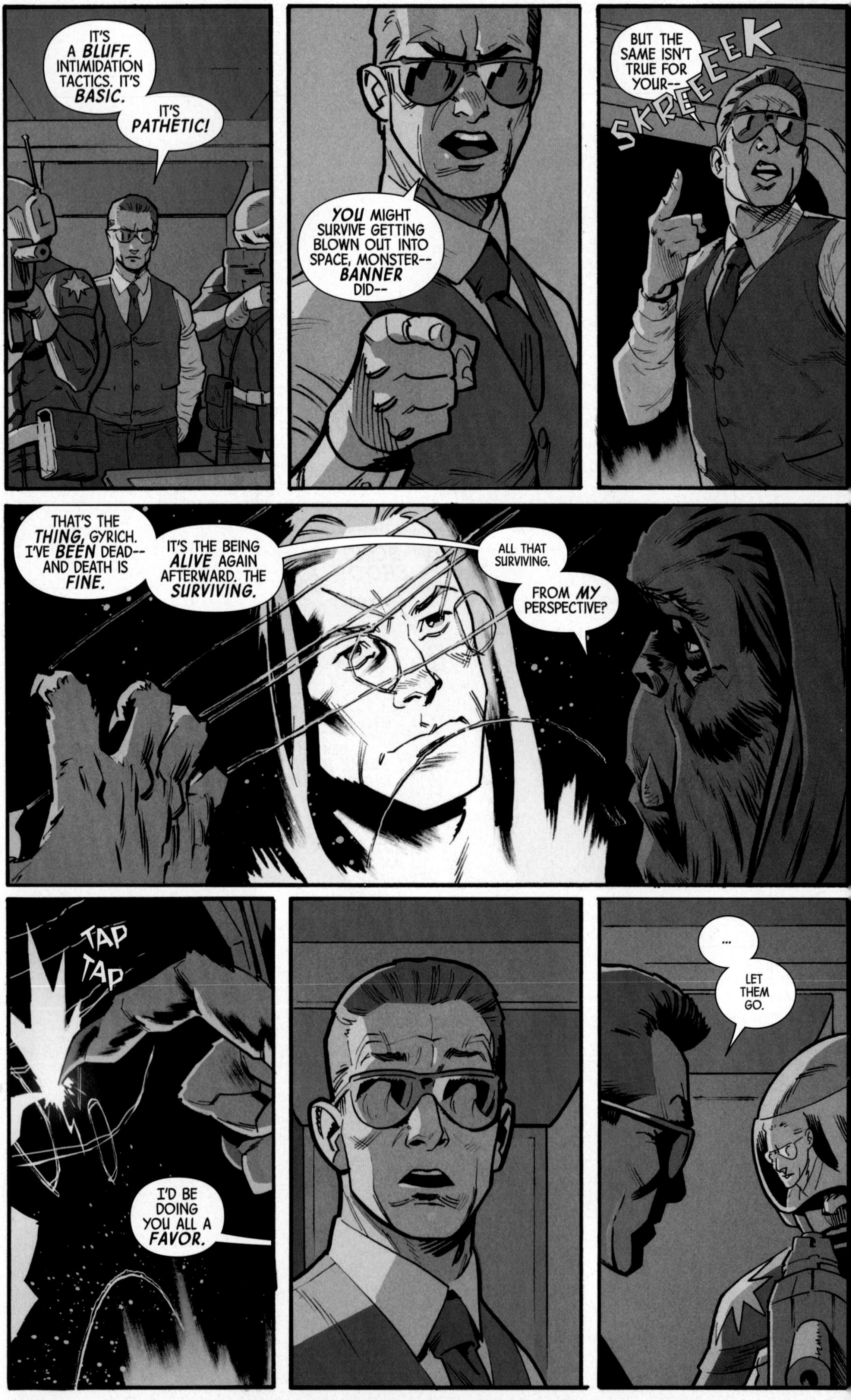

IT'S A BLUFF. INTIMIDATION TACTICS. IT'S BASIC.
IT'S PATHETIC!
YOU MIGHT SURVIVE GETTING BLOWN OUT INTO SPACE, MONSTER-- BANNER DID--
BUT THE SAME ISN'T TRUE FOR YOUR--
SKREEEEK
THAT'S THE THING, GYRICH. I'VE BEEN DEAD-- AND DEATH IS FINE.
IT'S THE BEING ALIVE AGAIN AFTERWARD. THE SURVIVING.
ALL THAT SURVIVING.
FROM MY PERSPECTIVE?
TAP TAP
I'D BE DOING YOU ALL A FAVOR.
...
LET THEM GO.

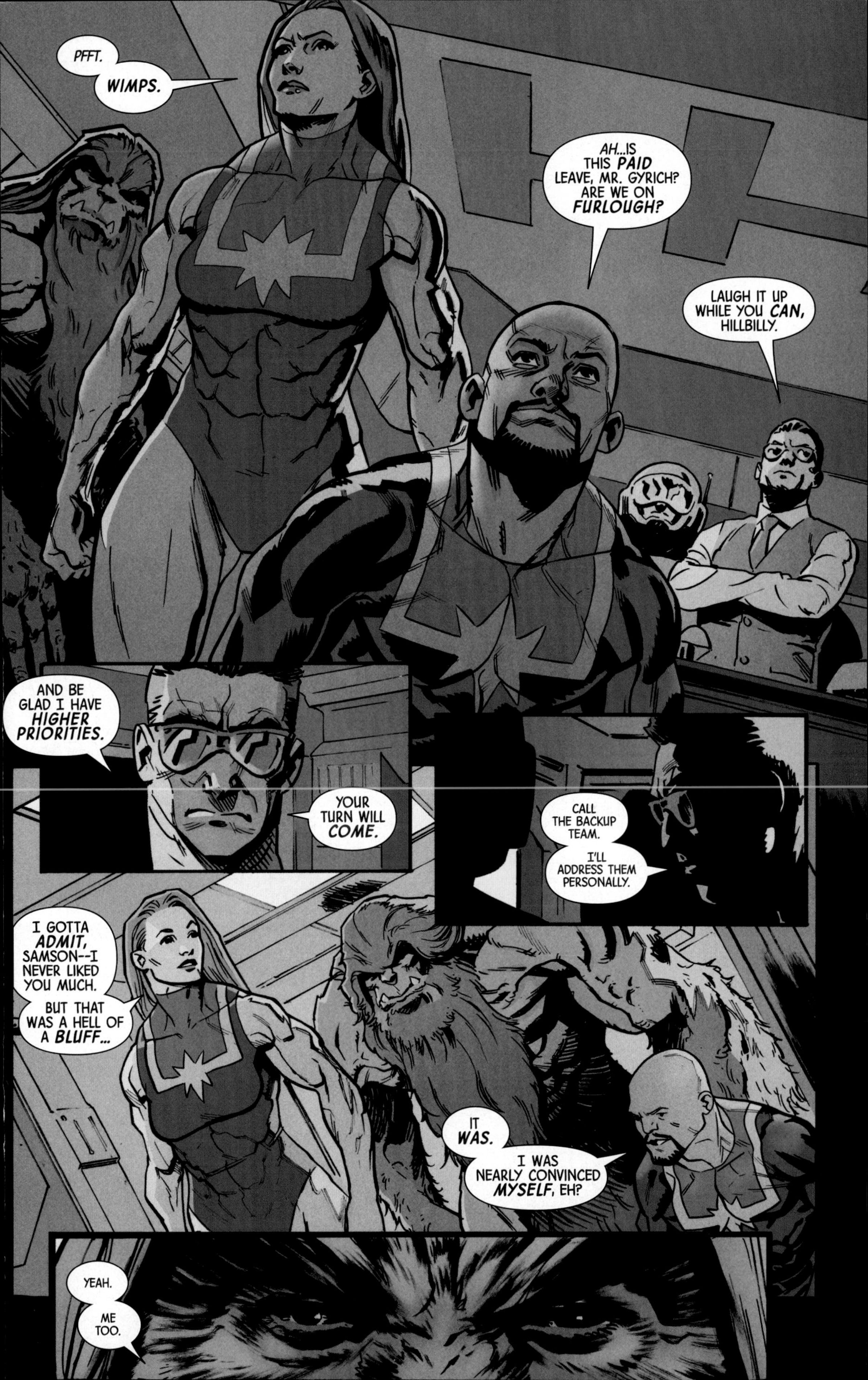
PFFT.
WIMPS.
AH...IS THIS PAID LEAVE, MR. GYRICH? ARE WE ON FURLOUGH?
LAUGH IT UP WHILE YOU CAN, HILLBILLY.
AND BE GLAD I HAVE HIGHER PRIORITIES.
YOUR TURN WILL COME.
CALL THE BACKUP TEAM.
I'LL ADDRESS THEM PERSONALLY.
I GOTTA ADMIT, SAMSON--I NEVER LIKED YOU MUCH.
BUT THAT WAS A HELL OF A BLUFF...
IT WAS.
I WAS NEARLY CONVINCED MYSELF, EH?
YEAH.
ME TOO.

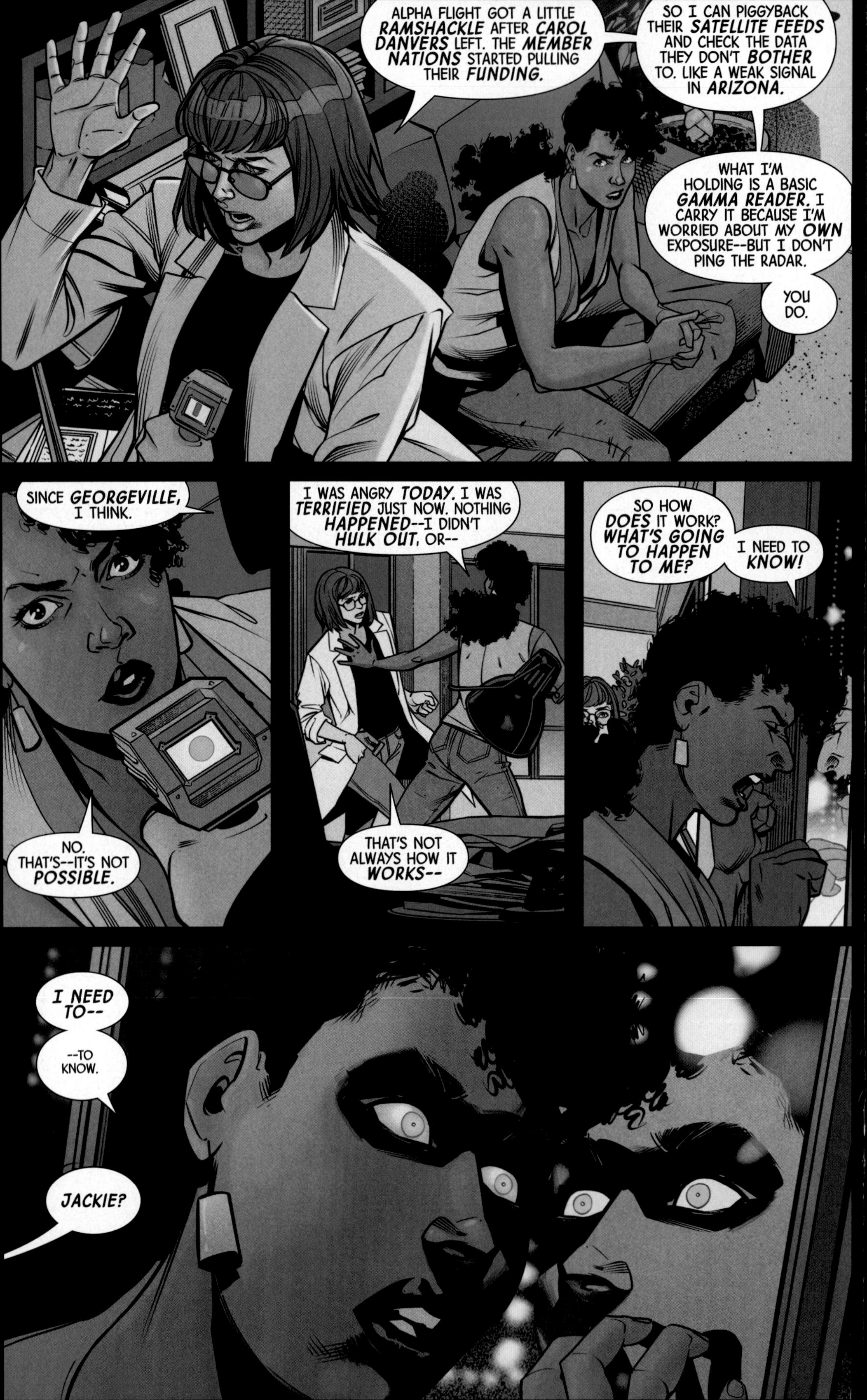
ALPHA FLIGHT GOT A LITTLE RAMSHACKLE AFTER CAROL DANVERS LEFT. THE MEMBER NATIONS STARTED PULLING THEIR FUNDING.
SO I CAN PIGGYBACK THEIR SATELLITE FEEDS AND CHECK THE DATA THEY DON'T BOTHER TO. LIKE A WEAK SIGNAL IN ARIZONA.
WHAT I'M HOLDING IS A BASIC GAMMA READER. I CARRY IT BECAUSE I'M WORRIED ABOUT MY OWN EXPOSURE--BUT I DON'T PING THE RADAR.
YOU DO.
SINCE GEORGEVILLE, I THINK.
NO. THAT'S--IT'S NOT POSSIBLE.
I WAS ANGRY TODAY. I WAS TERRIFIED JUST NOW. NOTHING HAPPENED--I DIDN'T HULK OUT, OR--
THAT'S NOT ALWAYS HOW IT WORKS--
SO HOW DOES IT WORK? WHAT'S GOING TO HAPPEN TO ME?
I NEED TO KNOW!
I NEED TO--
--TO KNOW.
JACKIE?

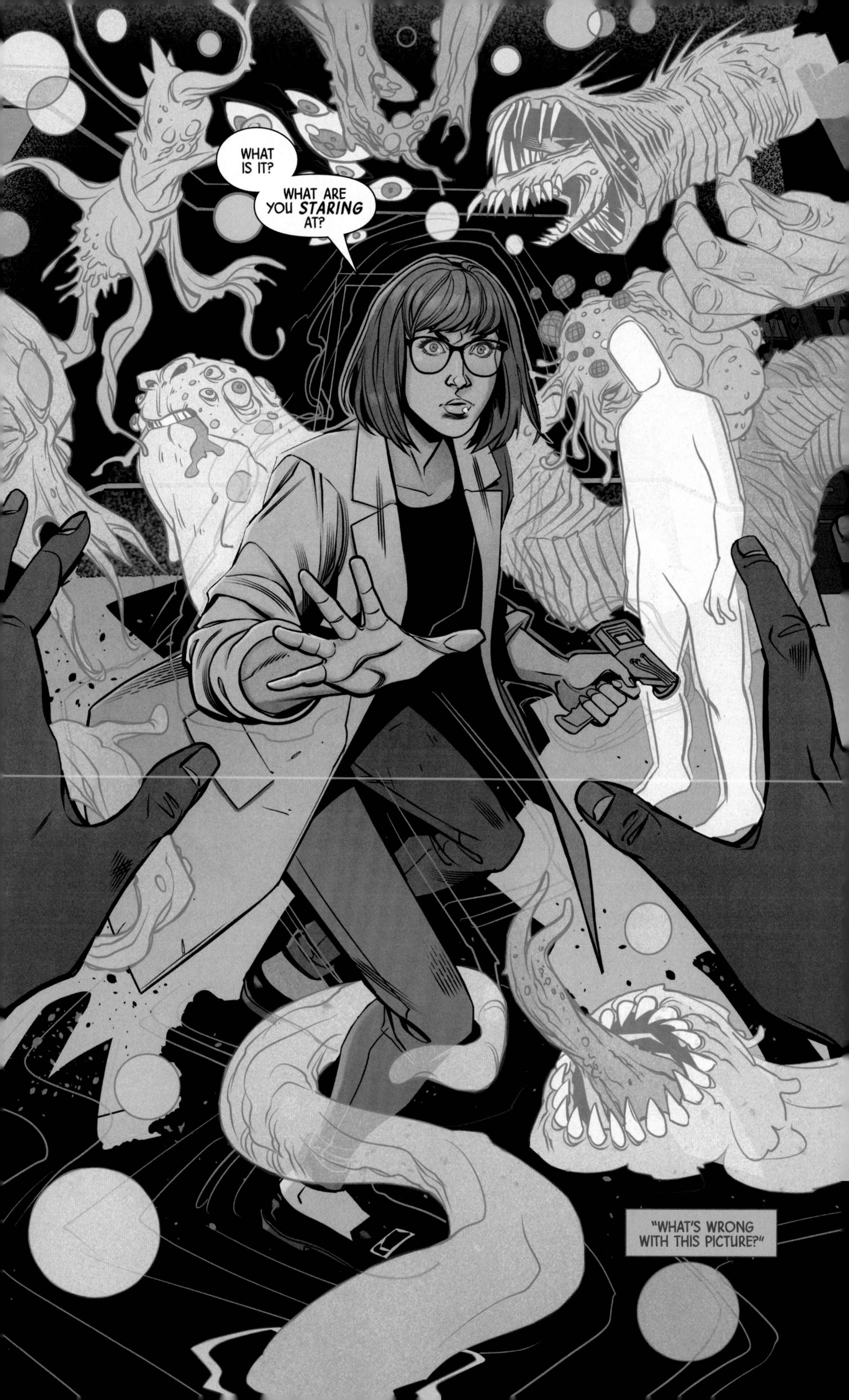
WHAT IS IT?
WHAT ARE YOU STARING AT?
"WHAT'S WRONG WITH THIS PICTURE?"

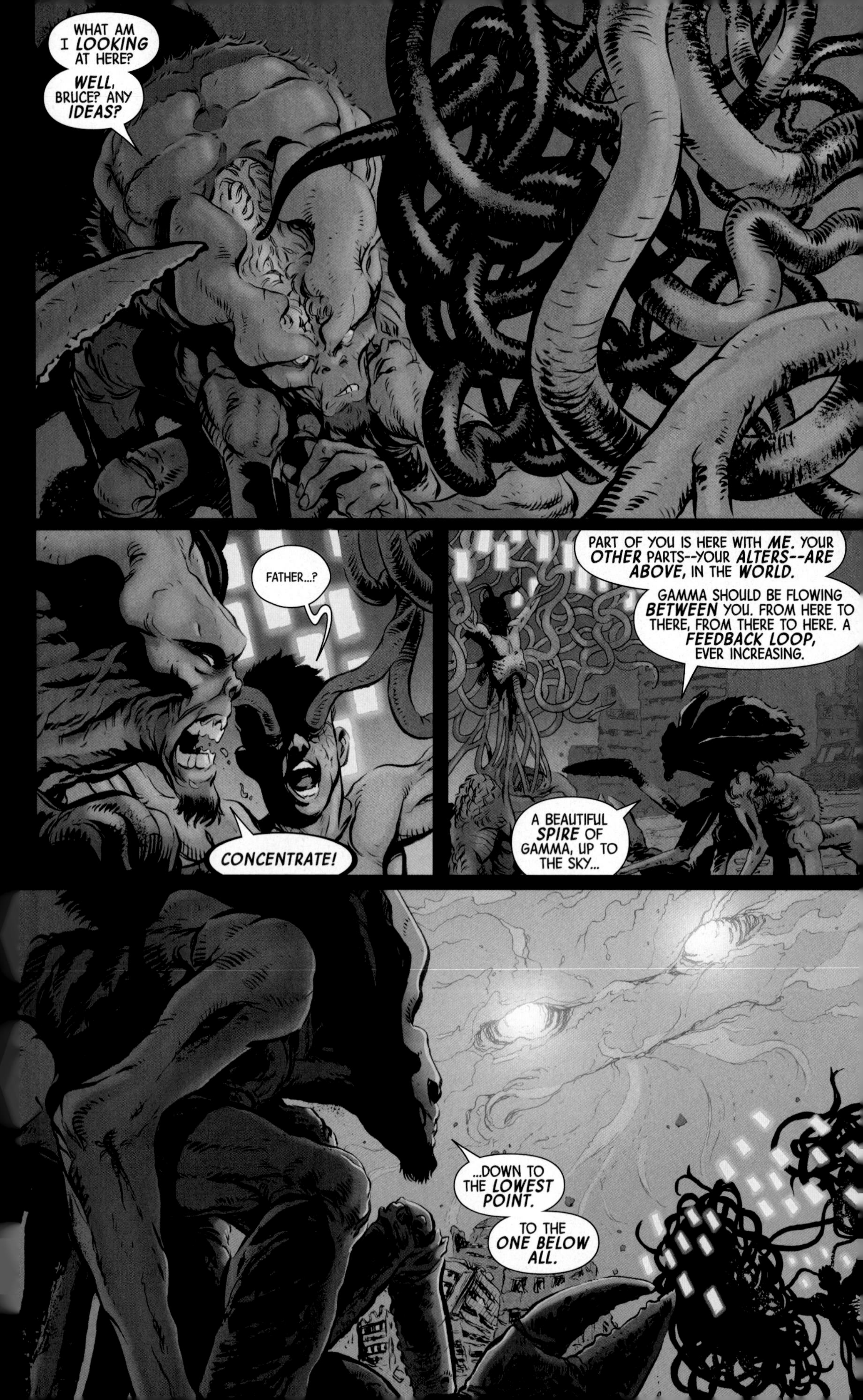
WHAT AM I LOOKING AT HERE?
WELL, BRUCE? ANY IDEAS?
FATHER...?
CONCENTRATE!
PART OF YOU IS HERE WITH ME. YOUR OTHER PARTS--YOUR ALTERS--ARE ABOVE, IN THE WORLD.
GAMMA SHOULD BE FLOWING BETWEEN YOU. FROM HERE TO THERE, FROM THERE TO HERE. A FEEDBACK LOOP, EVER INCREASING.
A BEAUTIFUL SPIRE OF GAMMA, UP TO THE SKY...
...DOWN TO THE LOWEST POINT.
TO THE ONE BELOW ALL.

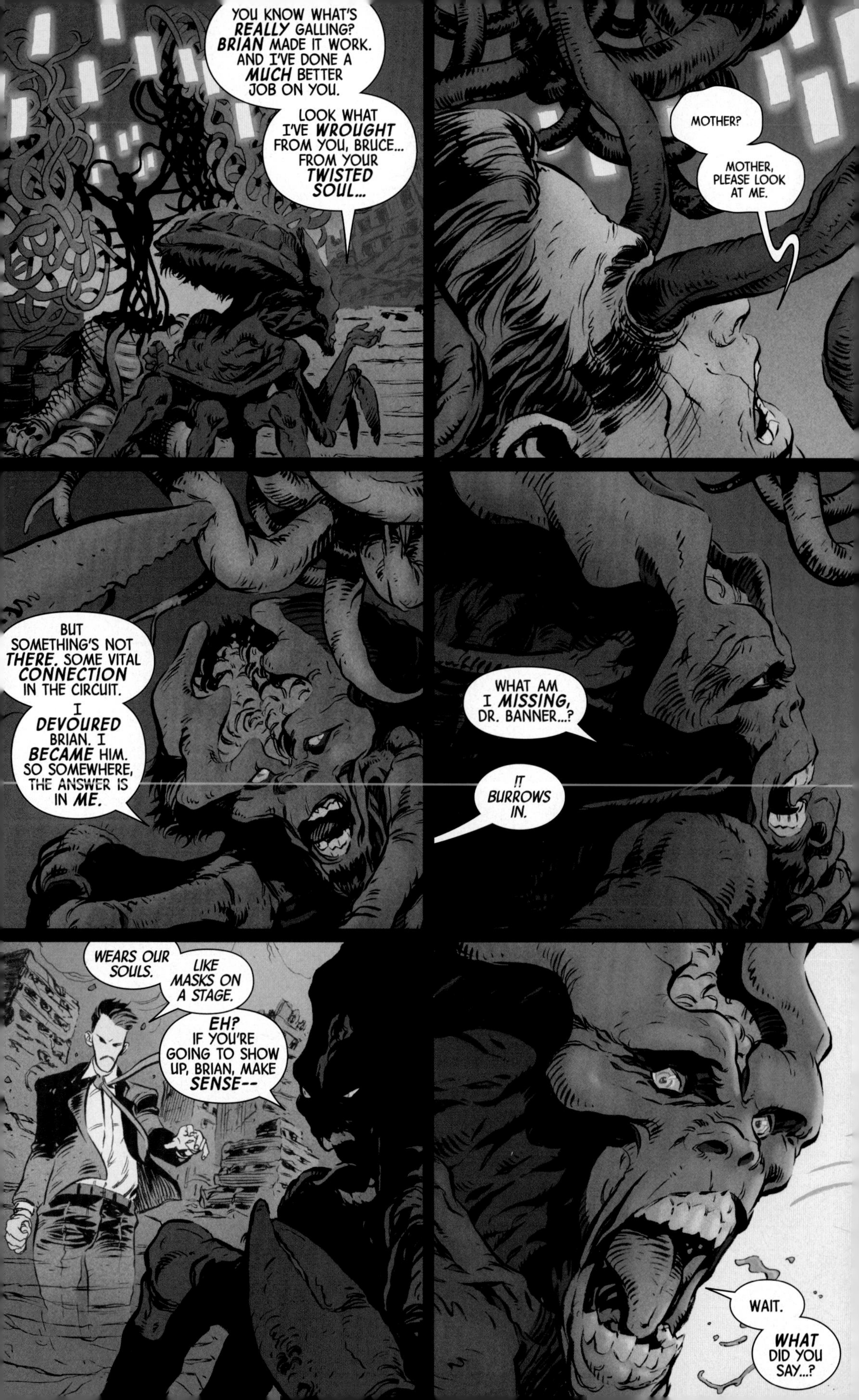
YOU KNOW WHAT'S REALLY GALLING? BRIAN MADE IT WORK. AND I'VE DONE A MUCH BETTER JOB ON YOU.
LOOK WHAT I'VE WROUGHT FROM YOU, BRUCE... FROM YOUR TWISTED SOUL...
MOTHER?
MOTHER, PLEASE LOOK AT ME.
BUT SOMETHING'S NOT THERE. SOME VITAL CONNECTION IN THE CIRCUIT.
I DEVOURED BRIAN. I BECAME HIM. SO SOMEWHERE, THE ANSWER IS IN ME.
WHAT AM I MISSING, DR. BANNER...?
IT BURROWS IN.
WEARS OUR SOULS.
LIKE MASKS ON A STAGE.
EH? IF YOU'RE GOING TO SHOW UP, BRIAN, MAKE SENSE--
WAIT.
WHAT DID YOU SAY...?

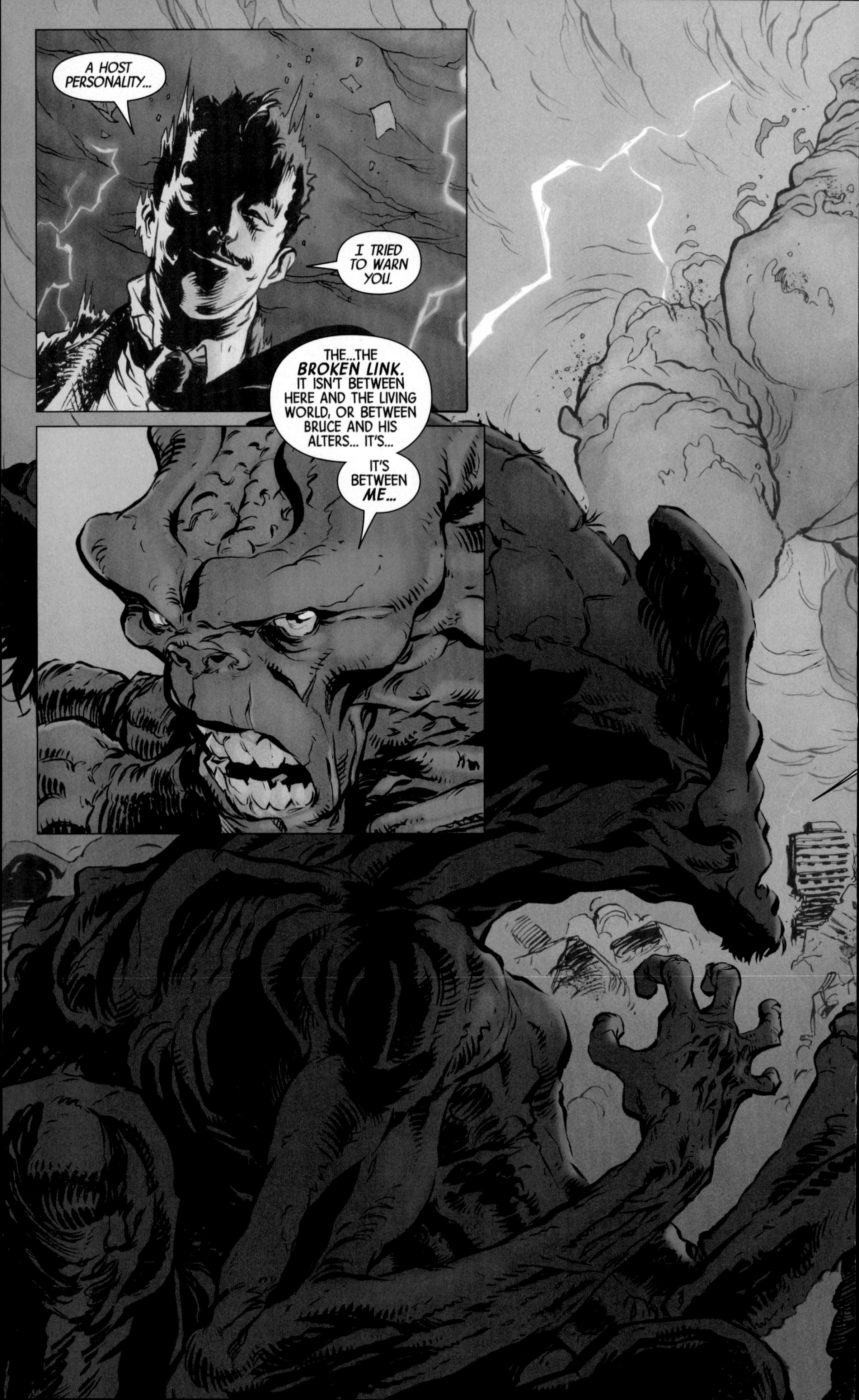
A HOST PERSONALITY...
I TRIED TO WARN YOU.
THE...THE BROKEN LINK. IT ISN'T BETWEEN HERE AND THE LIVING WORLD, OR BETWEEN BRUCE AND HIS ALTERS... IT'S...
IT'S BETWEEN ME...

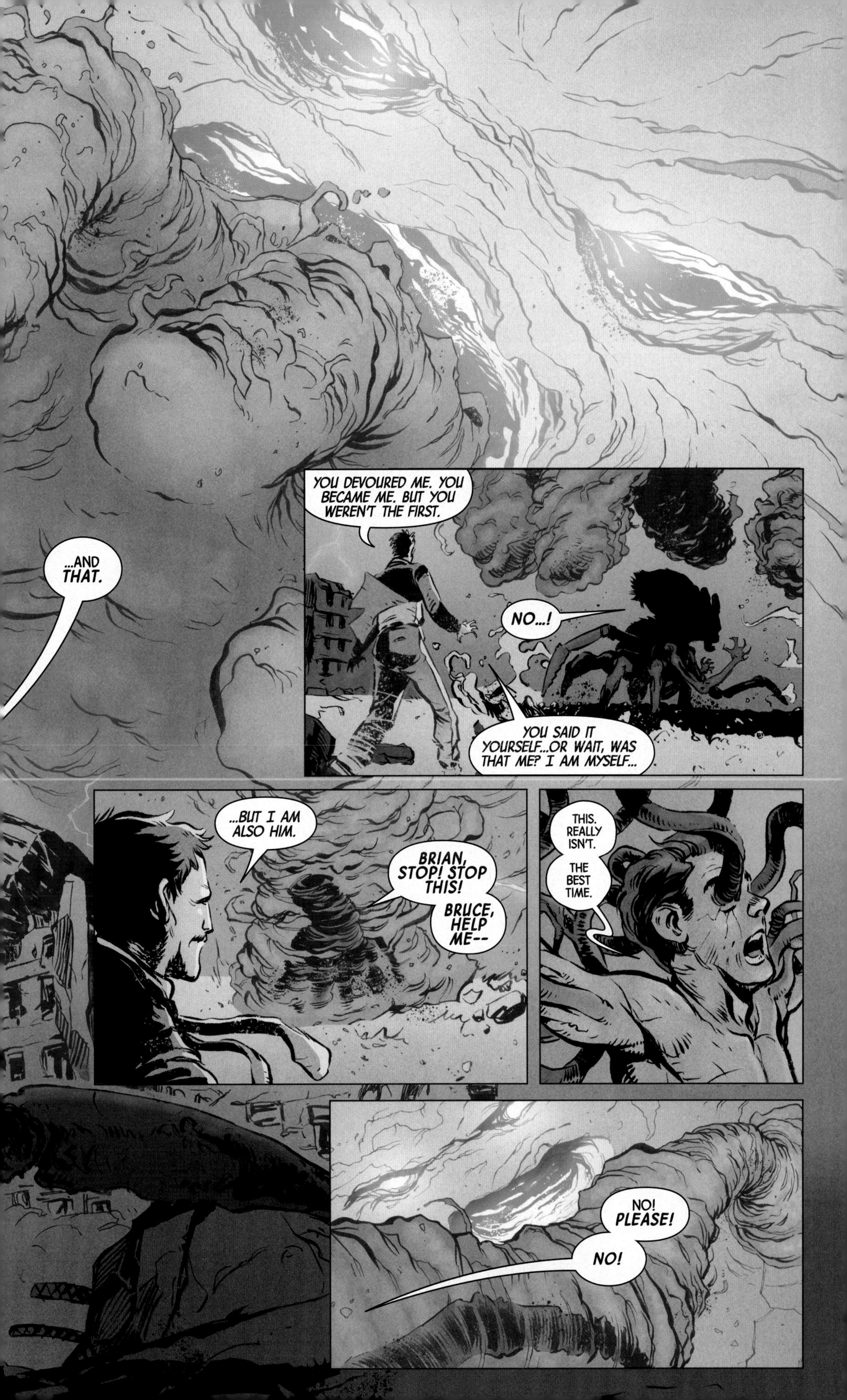

...AND THAT.
YOU DEVOURED ME. YOU BECAME ME. BUT YOU WEREN'T THE FIRST.
NO...!
YOU SAID IT YOURSELF...OR WAIT, WAS THAT ME? I AM MYSELF...
...BUT I AM ALSO HIM.
BRIAN, STOP! STOP THIS!
BRUCE, HELP ME--
THIS. REALLY ISN'T.
THE BEST TIME.
NO! PLEASE!
NO!

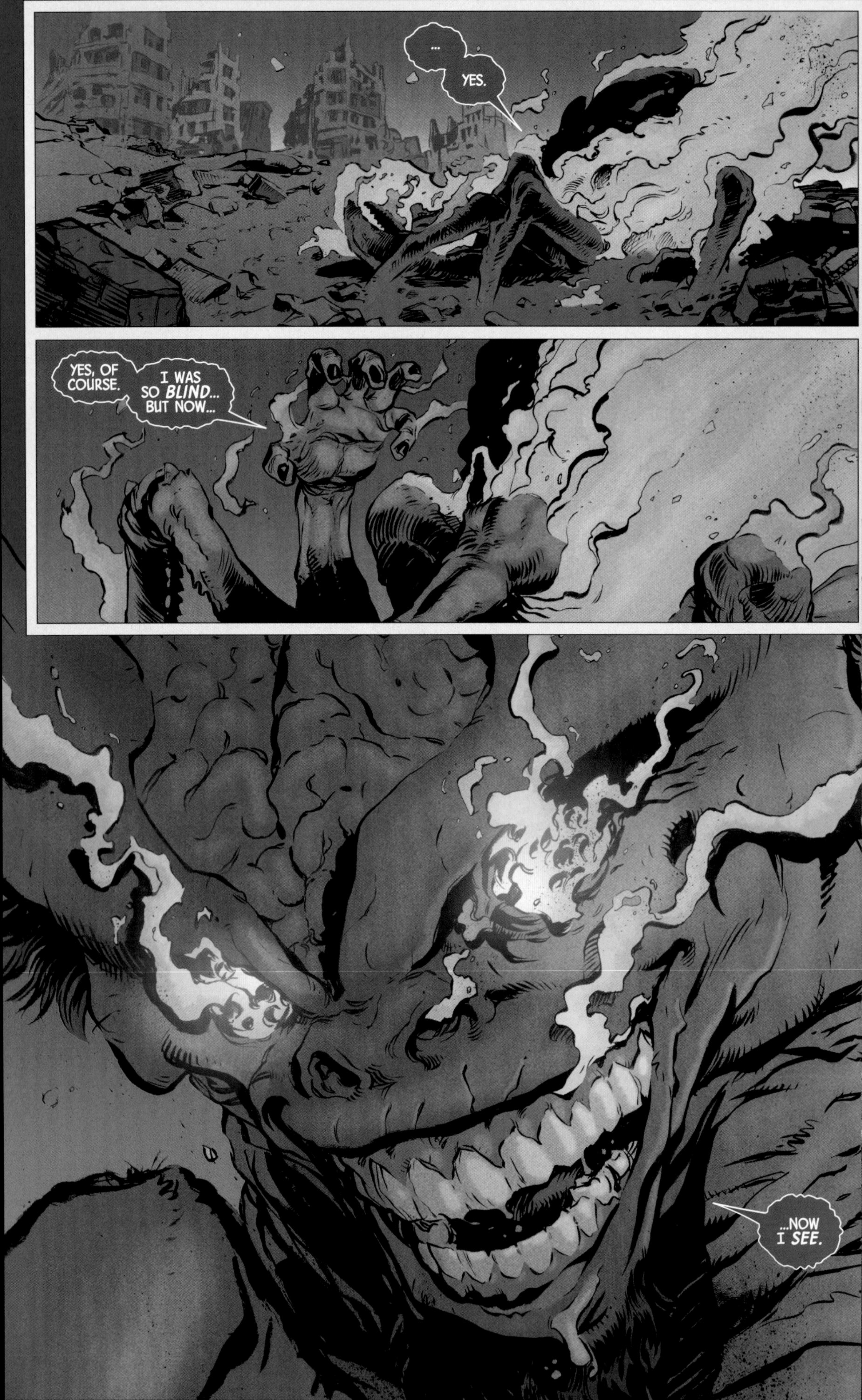
...
YES.
YES, OF COURSE.
I WAS SO BLIND... BUT NOW...
...NOW I SEE.

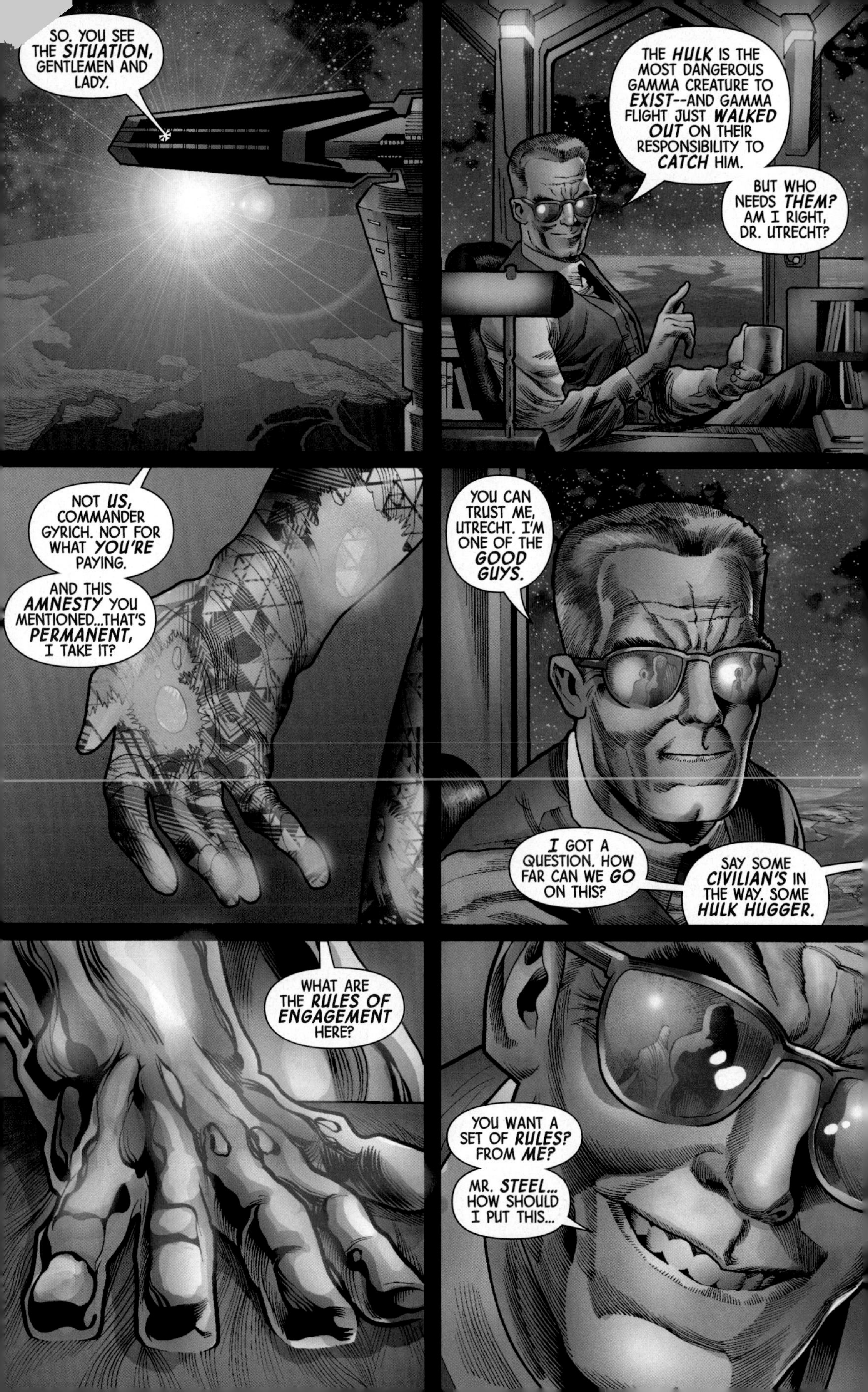
SO, YOU SEE THE SITUATION, GENTLEMEN AND LADY.
THE HULK IS THE MOST DANGEROUS GAMMA CREATURE TO EXIST--AND GAMMA FLIGHT JUST WALKED OUT ON THEIR RESPONSIBILITY TO CATCH HIM.
BUT WHO NEEDS THEM? AM I RIGHT, DR. UTRECHT?
NOT US, COMMANDER GYRICH. NOT FOR WHAT YOU'RE PAYING.
AND THIS AMNESTY YOU MENTIONED...THAT'S PERMANENT, I TAKE IT?
YOU CAN TRUST ME, UTRECHT. I'M ONE OF THE GOOD GUYS.
I GOT A QUESTION. HOW FAR CAN WE GO ON THIS?
SAY SOME CIVILIAN'S IN THE WAY. SOME HULK HUGGER.
WHAT ARE THE RULES OF ENGAGEMENT HERE?
YOU WANT A SET OF RULES? FROM ME?
MR. STEEL... HOW SHOULD I PUT THIS...

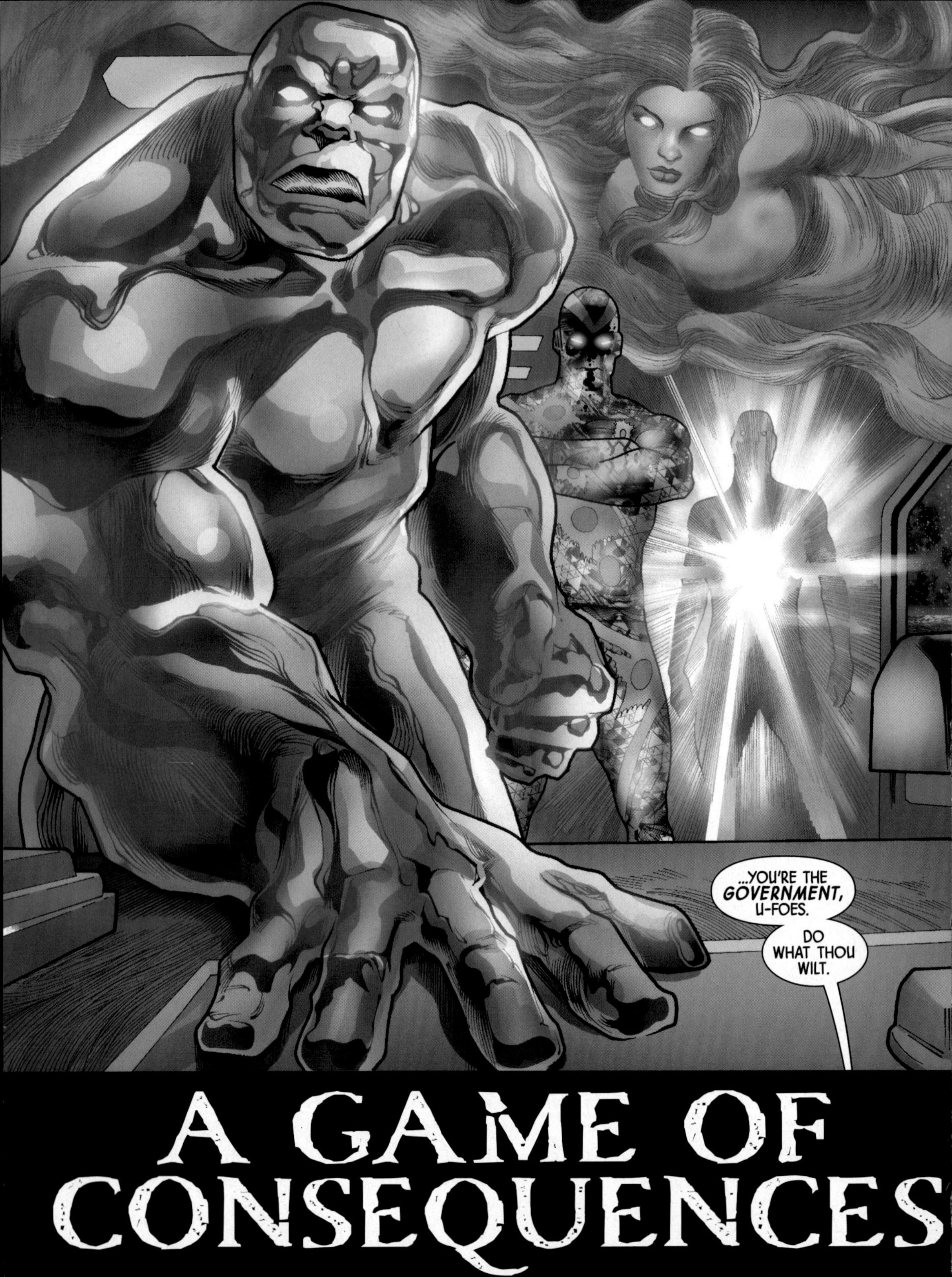
...YOU'RE THE *GOVERNMENT*, U-FOES.
DO WHAT THOU WILT.

A GAME OF CONSEQUENCES

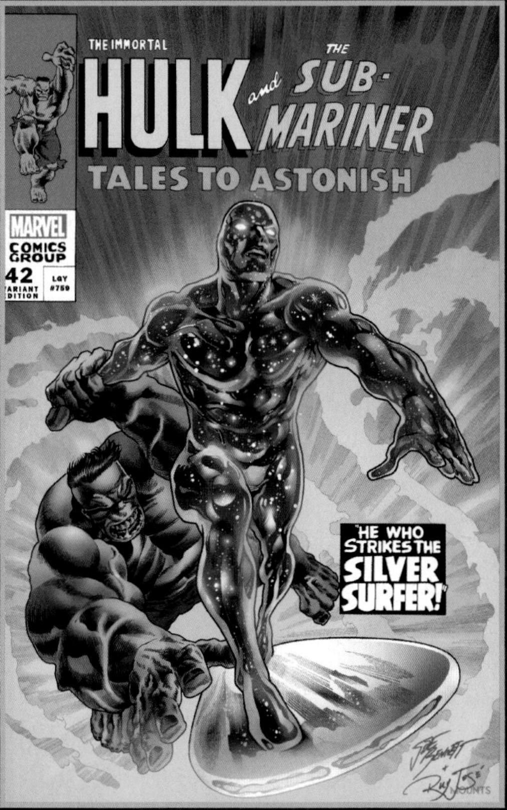
THE IMMORTAL
HULK and THE SUB-MARINER
TALES TO ASTONISH
MARVEL COMICS GROUP
42 VARIANT EDITION
LGY #759
"HE WHO STRIKES THE SILVER SURFER!"

JOE BENNETT, RUY JOSÉ & PAUL MOUNTS
#42 HOMAGE VARIANT

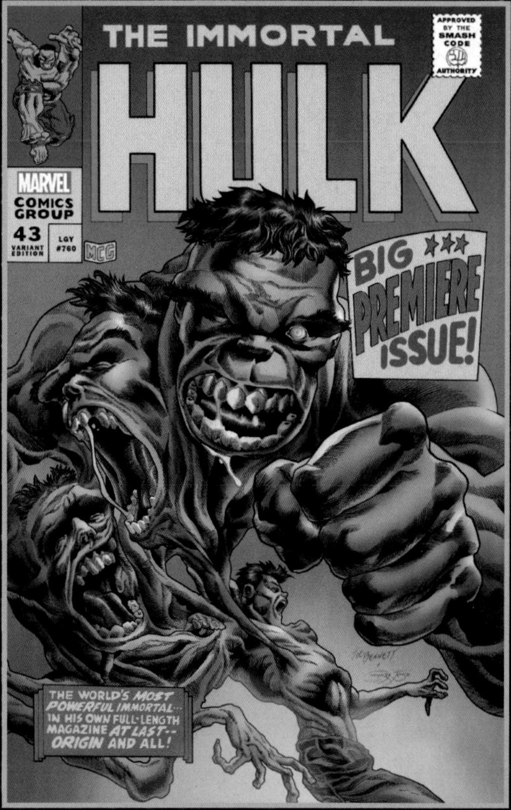
THE IMMORTAL
HULK
APPROVED BY THE SMASH CODE AUTHORITY
MARVEL COMICS GROUP
43 VARIANT EDITION
LGY #760
MCG
BIG PREMIERE ISSUE!
THE WORLD'S MOST POWERFUL IMMORTAL... IN HIS OWN FULL-LENGTH MAGAZINE AT LAST-- ORIGIN AND ALL!

JOE BENNETT, RUY JOSÉ & PAUL MOUNTS
#43 HOMAGE VARIANT

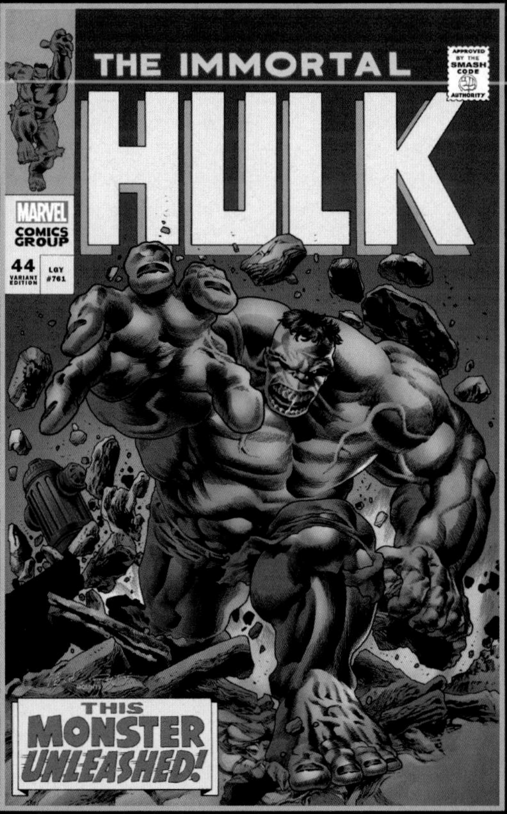
THE IMMORTAL
HULK
APPROVED BY THE SMASH CODE AUTHORITY
MARVEL COMICS GROUP
44 VARIANT EDITION
LGY #761
THIS MONSTER UNLEASHED!

JOE BENNETT, RUY JOSÉ & PAUL MOUNTS

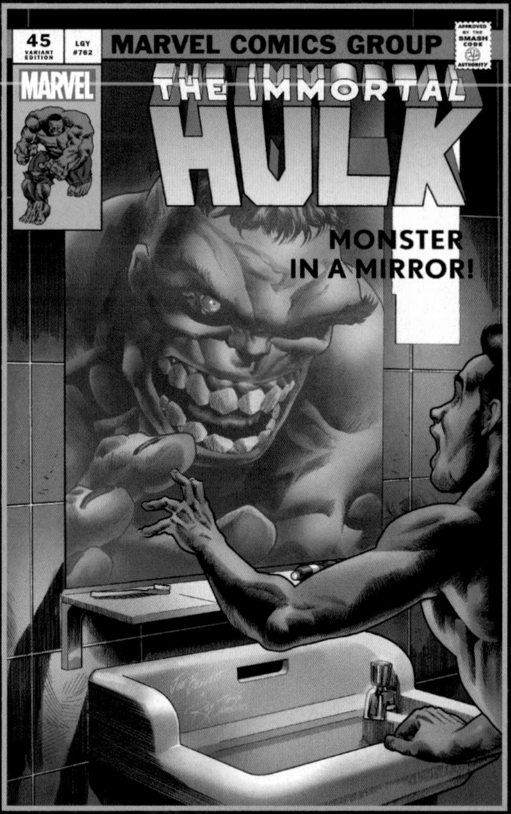
45 VARIANT EDITION
LGY #762
MARVEL COMICS GROUP
APPROVED BY THE SMASH CODE AUTHORITY
MARVEL
THE IMMORTAL
HULK
MONSTER IN A MIRROR!

JOE BENNETT, RUY JOSÉ & PAUL MOUNTS

43

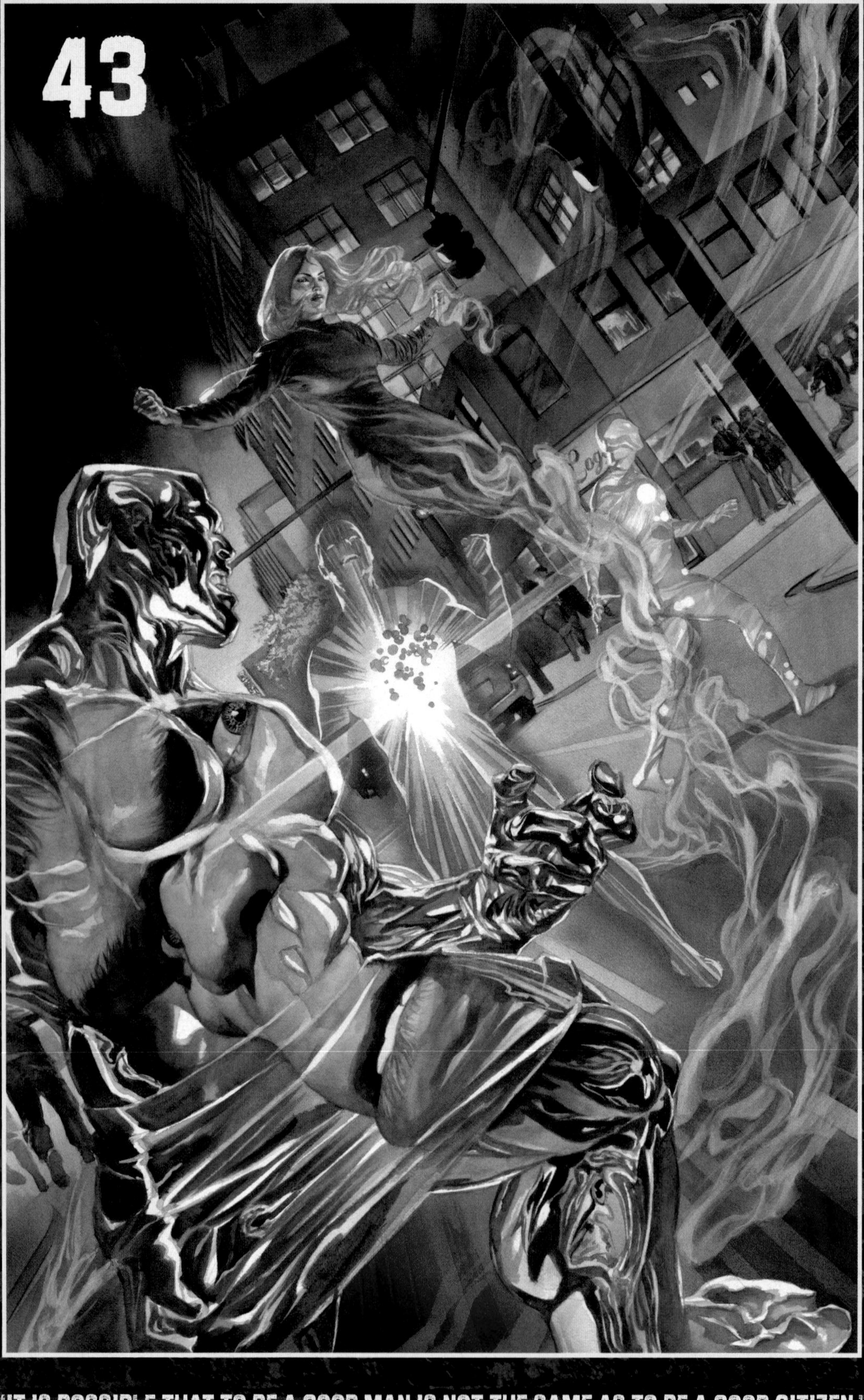

"IT IS POSSIBLE THAT TO BE A GOOD MAN IS NOT THE SAME AS TO BE A GOOD CITIZEN."

– ARISTOTLE, *THE NICOMACHEAN ETHICS*

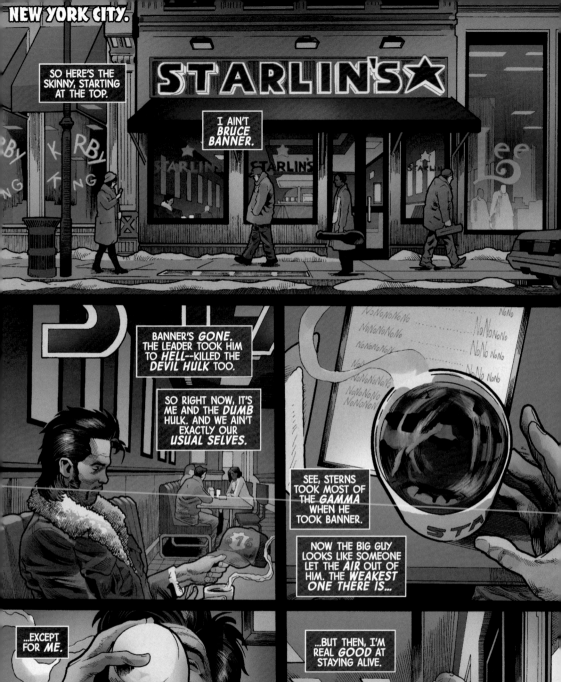

NEW YORK CITY.

SO HERE'S THE SKINNY, STARTING AT THE TOP.

STARLIN'S★

I AIN'T *BRUCE BANNER.*

BANNER'S *GONE.* THE LEADER TOOK HIM TO *HELL*--KILLED THE *DEVIL HULK* TOO.

SO RIGHT NOW, IT'S ME AND THE *DUMB HULK.* AND WE AIN'T EXACTLY OUR *USUAL SELVES.*

SEE, STERNS TOOK MOST OF THE *GAMMA* WHEN HE TOOK BANNER.

NOW THE BIG GUY LOOKS LIKE SOMEONE LET THE *AIR* OUT OF HIM. THE *WEAKEST ONE* THERE IS...

...EXCEPT FOR *ME.*

I USED TO BE THE *GREY HULK.* NOW-- DON'T ASK ME *WHY*--I'M STUCK IN *BANNER'S* BODY.

ONE MORE *PUNY HUMAN,* JUST TRYING TO STAY *ALIVE...*

...BUT THEN, I'M REAL *GOOD* AT STAYING ALIVE.

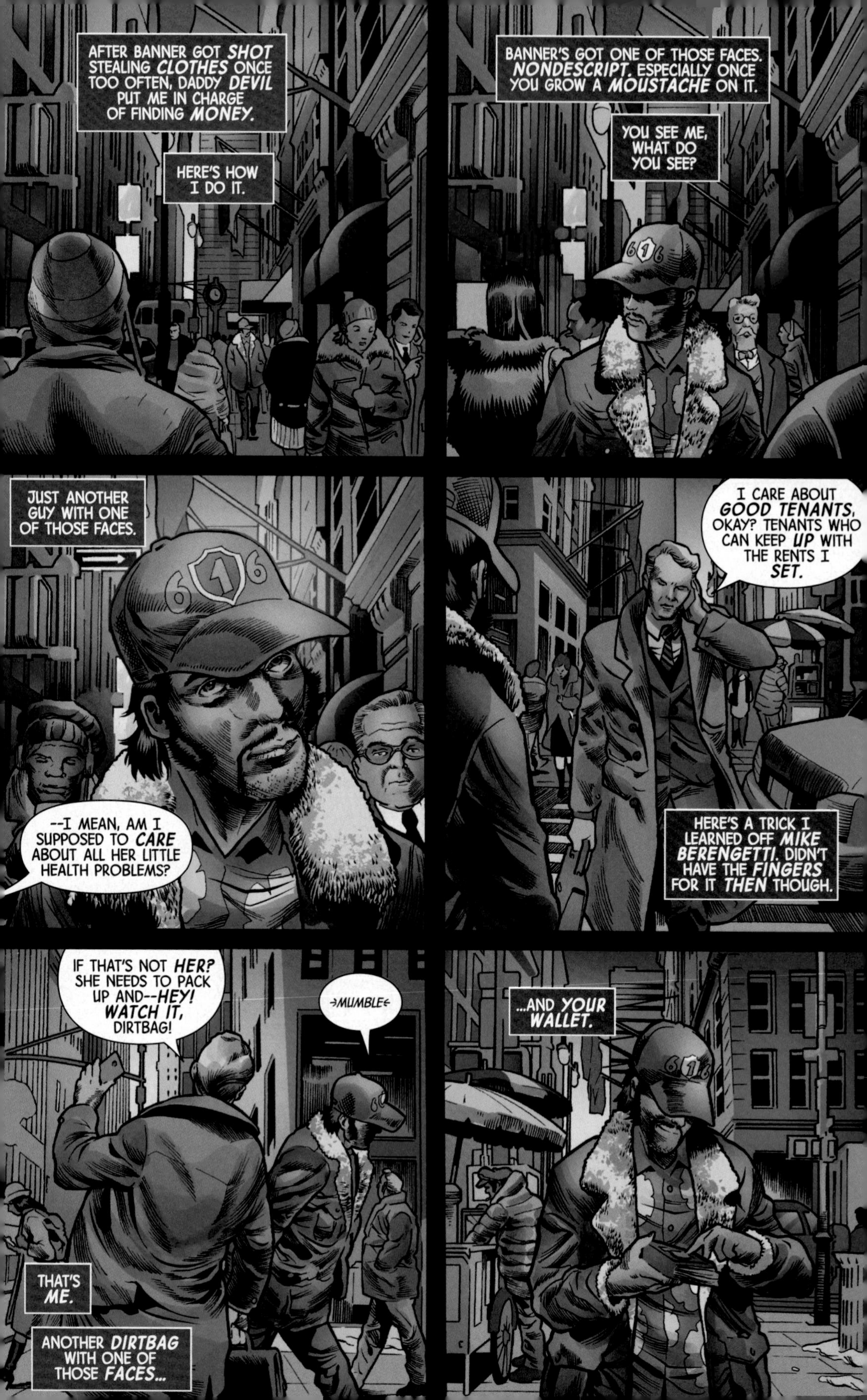
AFTER BANNER GOT SHOT STEALING CLOTHES ONCE TOO OFTEN, DADDY DEVIL PUT ME IN CHARGE OF FINDING MONEY.
HERE'S HOW I DO IT.
BANNER'S GOT ONE OF THOSE FACES. NONDESCRIPT. ESPECIALLY ONCE YOU GROW A MOUSTACHE ON IT.
YOU SEE ME, WHAT DO YOU SEE?
JUST ANOTHER GUY WITH ONE OF THOSE FACES.
--I MEAN, AM I SUPPOSED TO CARE ABOUT ALL HER LITTLE HEALTH PROBLEMS?
I CARE ABOUT GOOD TENANTS, OKAY? TENANTS WHO CAN KEEP UP WITH THE RENTS I SET.
HERE'S A TRICK I LEARNED OFF MIKE BERENGETTI. DIDN'T HAVE THE FINGERS FOR IT THEN THOUGH.
IF THAT'S NOT HER? SHE NEEDS TO PACK UP AND--HEY! WATCH IT, DIRTBAG!
MUMBLE
THAT'S ME.
ANOTHER DIRTBAG WITH ONE OF THOSE FACES...
...AND YOUR WALLET.

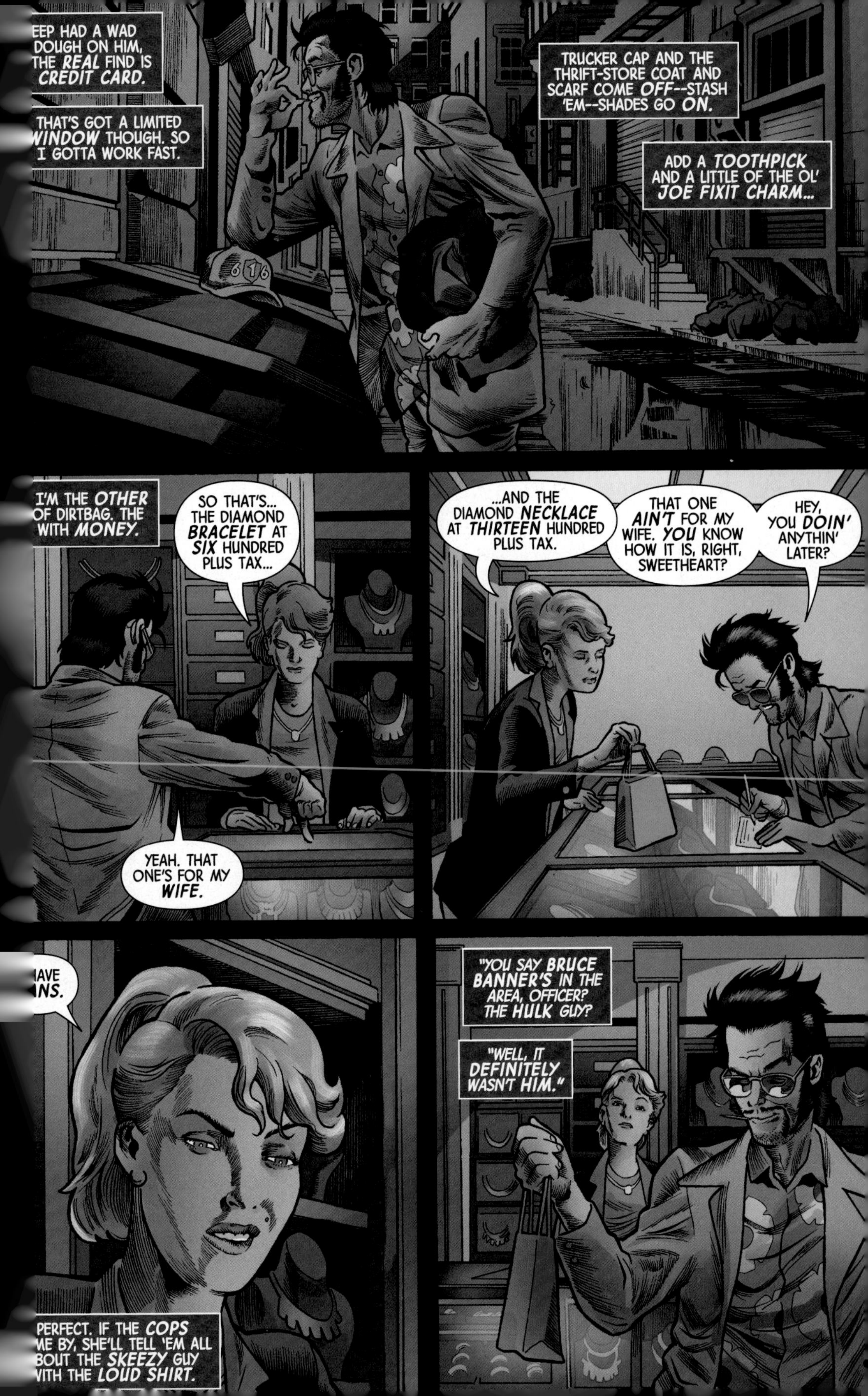

EEP HAD A WAD DOUGH ON HIM, THE REAL FIND IS CREDIT CARD.
THAT'S GOT A LIMITED WINDOW THOUGH. SO I GOTTA WORK FAST.
TRUCKER CAP AND THE THRIFT-STORE COAT AND SCARF COME OFF--STASH 'EM--SHADES GO ON.
ADD A TOOTHPICK AND A LITTLE OF THE OL' JOE FIXIT CHARM...
I'M THE OTHER OF DIRTBAG. THE WITH MONEY.
SO THAT'S... THE DIAMOND BRACELET AT SIX HUNDRED PLUS TAX...
YEAH. THAT ONE'S FOR MY WIFE.
...AND THE DIAMOND NECKLACE AT THIRTEEN HUNDRED PLUS TAX.
THAT ONE AIN'T FOR MY WIFE. YOU KNOW HOW IT IS, RIGHT, SWEETHEART?
HEY, YOU DOIN' ANYTHIN' LATER?
HAVE NS.
PERFECT. IF THE COPS ME BY, SHE'LL TELL 'EM ALL BOUT THE SKEEZY GUY WITH THE LOUD SHIRT.
"YOU SAY BRUCE BANNER'S IN THE AREA, OFFICER? THE HULK GUY?
"WELL, IT DEFINITELY WASN'T HIM."

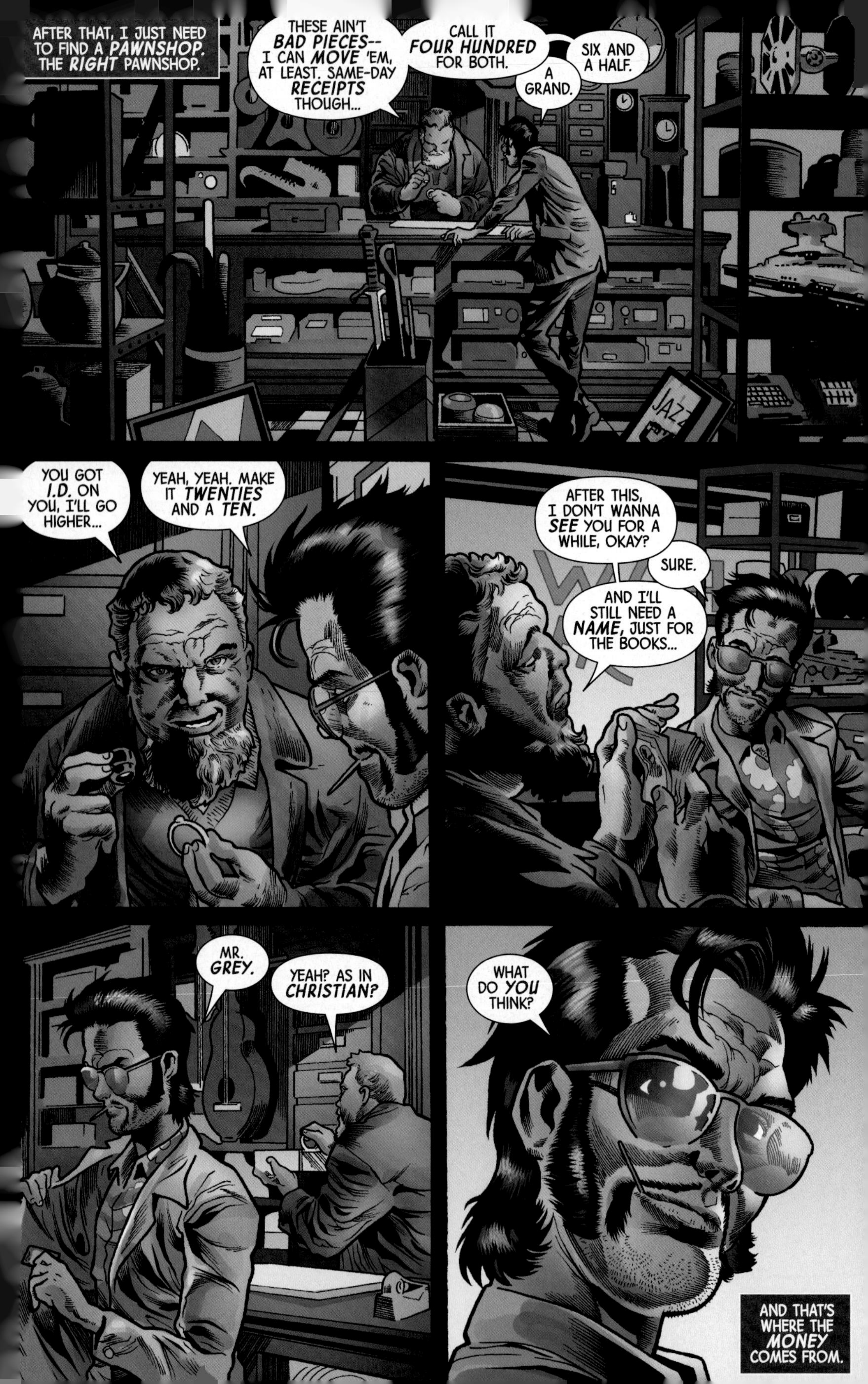
AFTER THAT, I JUST NEED TO FIND A PAWNSHOP. THE RIGHT PAWNSHOP.
THESE AIN'T BAD PIECES-- I CAN MOVE 'EM, AT LEAST. SAME-DAY RECEIPTS THOUGH...
CALL IT FOUR HUNDRED FOR BOTH.
A GRAND.
SIX AND A HALF.
YOU GOT I.D. ON YOU, I'LL GO HIGHER...
YEAH, YEAH. MAKE IT TWENTIES AND A TEN.
AFTER THIS, I DON'T WANNA SEE YOU FOR A WHILE, OKAY?
SURE.
AND I'LL STILL NEED A NAME, JUST FOR THE BOOKS...
MR. GREY.
YEAH? AS IN CHRISTIAN?
WHAT DO YOU THINK?
AND THAT'S WHERE THE MONEY COMES FROM.

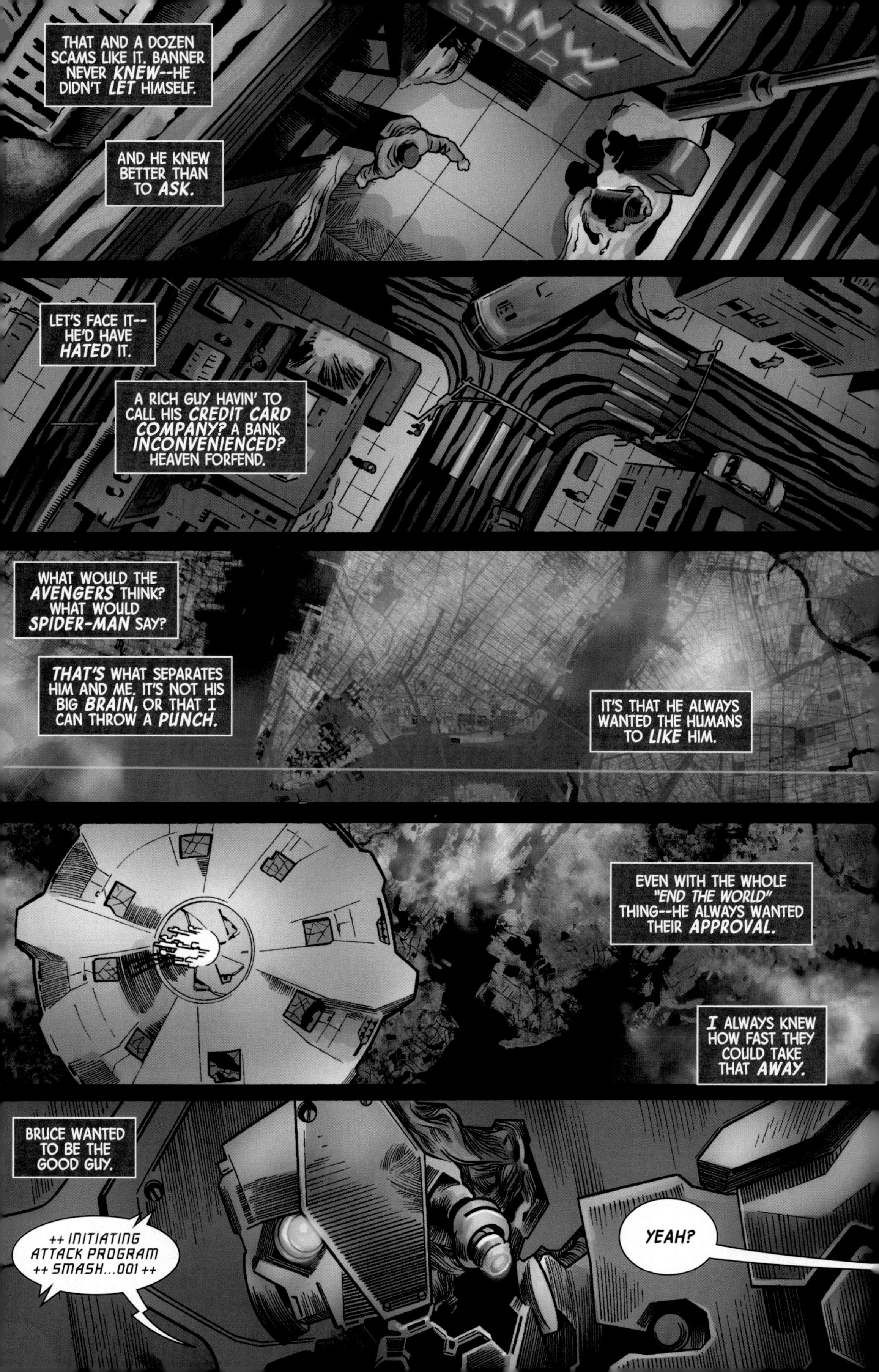

THAT AND A DOZEN SCAMS LIKE IT. BANNER NEVER KNEW--HE DIDN'T LET HIMSELF.
AND HE KNEW BETTER THAN TO ASK.
LET'S FACE IT--HE'D HAVE HATED IT.
A RICH GUY HAVIN' TO CALL HIS CREDIT CARD COMPANY? A BANK INCONVENIENCED? HEAVEN FORFEND.
WHAT WOULD THE AVENGERS THINK? WHAT WOULD SPIDER-MAN SAY?
THAT'S WHAT SEPARATES HIM AND ME. IT'S NOT HIS BIG BRAIN, OR THAT I CAN THROW A PUNCH.
IT'S THAT HE ALWAYS WANTED THE HUMANS TO LIKE HIM.
EVEN WITH THE WHOLE "END THE WORLD" THING--HE ALWAYS WANTED THEIR APPROVAL.
I ALWAYS KNEW HOW FAST THEY COULD TAKE THAT AWAY.
BRUCE WANTED TO BE THE GOOD GUY.
++ INITIATING ATTACK PROGRAM ++ SMASH...001 ++
YEAH?

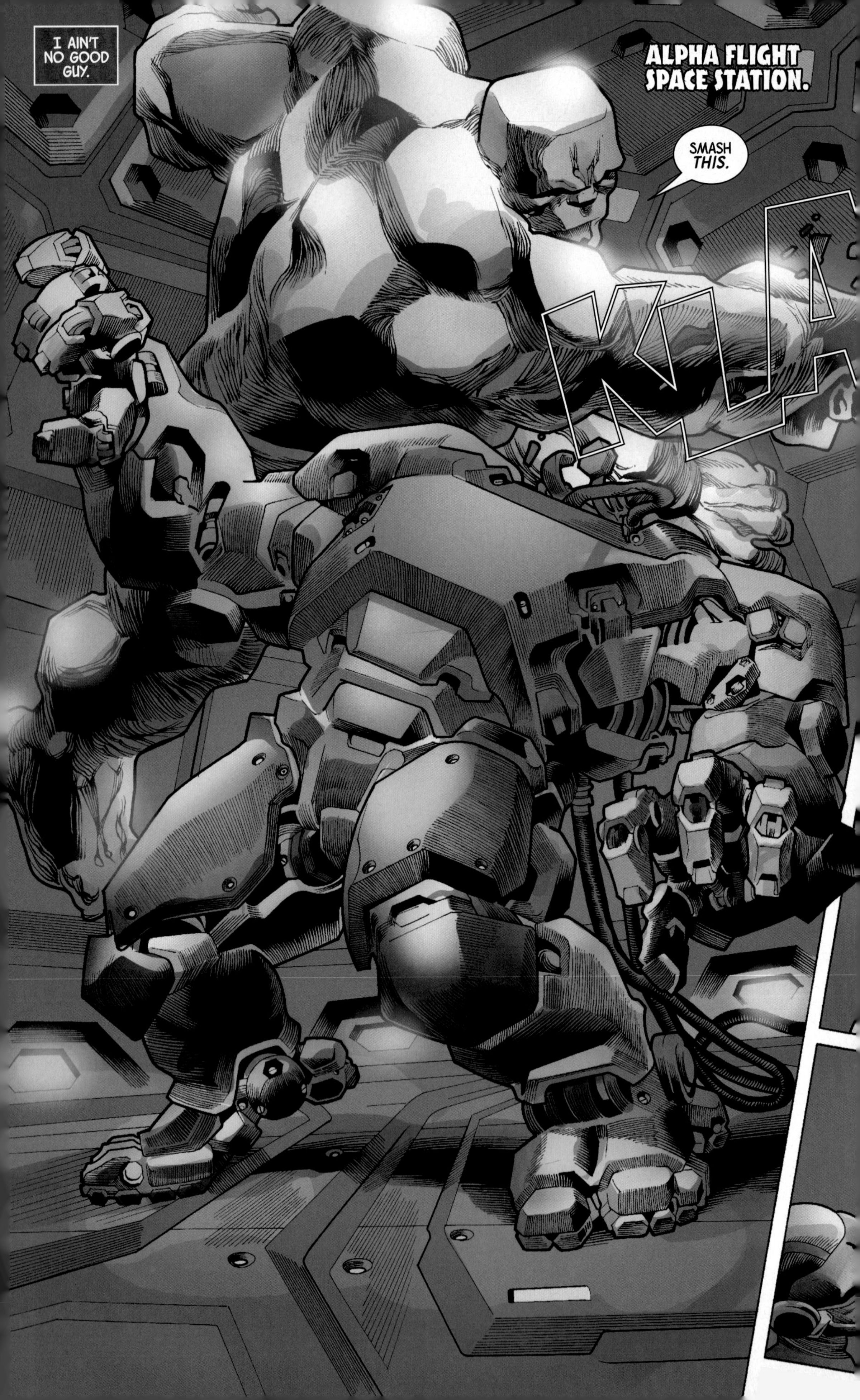
I AIN'T NO GOOD GUY.
ALPHA FLIGHT SPACE STATION.
SMASH THIS.
KRA

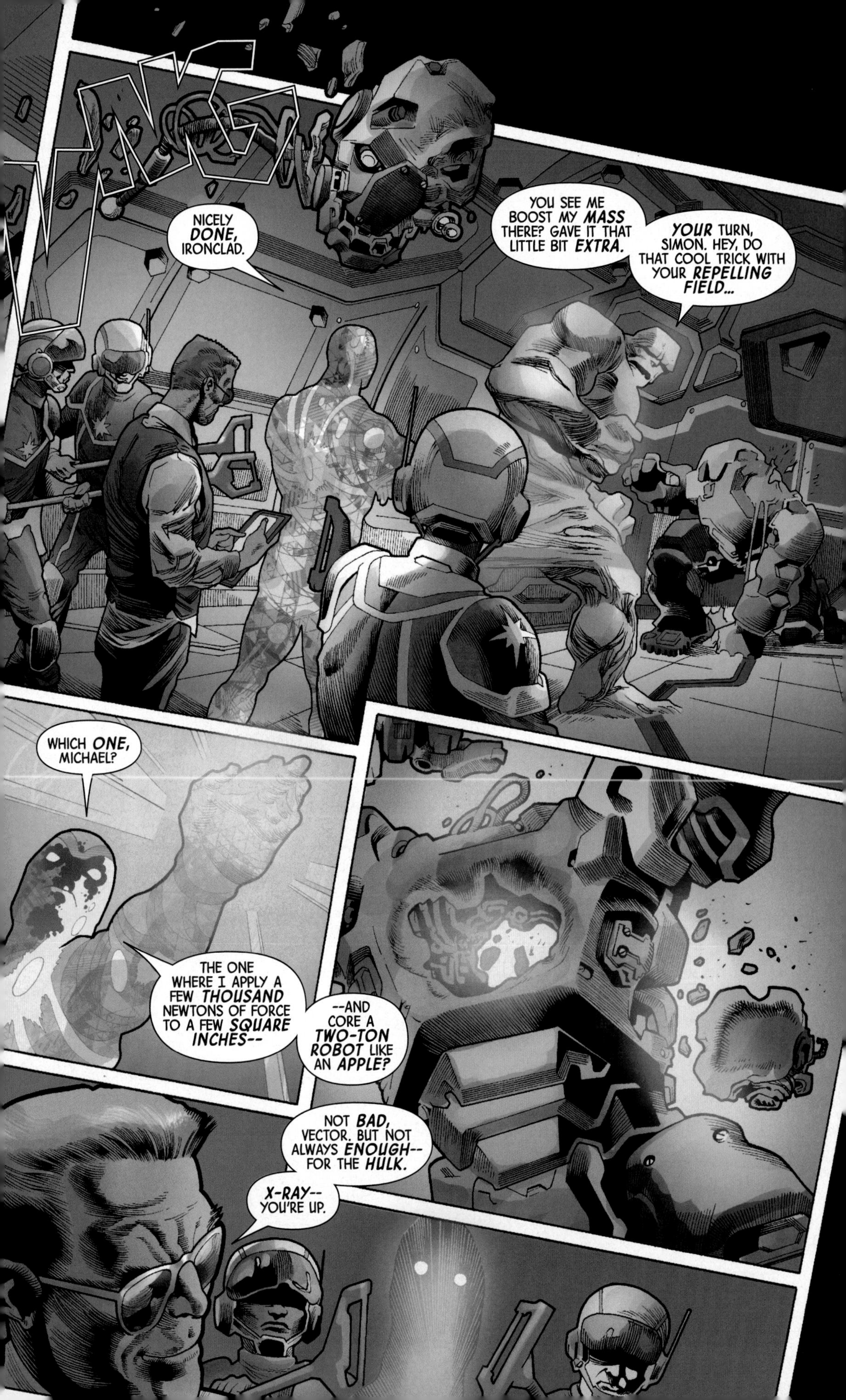
WNG
NICELY DONE, IRONCLAD.
YOU SEE ME BOOST MY MASS THERE? GAVE IT THAT LITTLE BIT EXTRA.
YOUR TURN, SIMON. HEY, DO THAT COOL TRICK WITH YOUR REPELLING FIELD...
WHICH ONE, MICHAEL?
THE ONE WHERE I APPLY A FEW THOUSAND NEWTONS OF FORCE TO A FEW SQUARE INCHES--
--AND CORE A TWO-TON ROBOT LIKE AN APPLE?
NOT BAD, VECTOR. BUT NOT ALWAYS ENOUGH-- FOR THE HULK.
X-RAY-- YOU'RE UP.

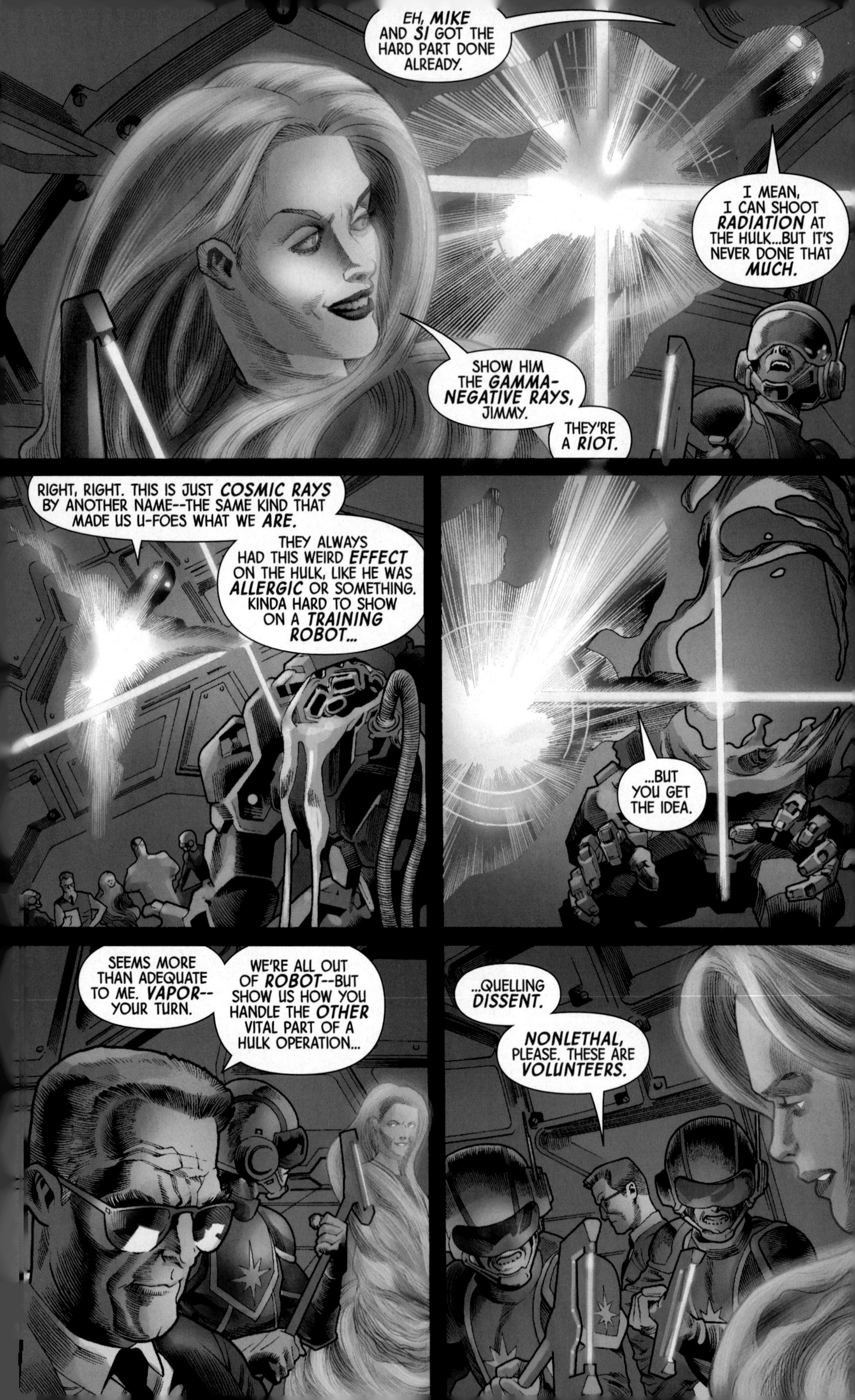
EH, MIKE AND SI GOT THE HARD PART DONE ALREADY.
I MEAN, I CAN SHOOT RADIATION AT THE HULK...BUT IT'S NEVER DONE THAT MUCH.
SHOW HIM THE GAMMA-NEGATIVE RAYS, JIMMY.
THEY'RE A RIOT.
RIGHT, RIGHT. THIS IS JUST COSMIC RAYS BY ANOTHER NAME--THE SAME KIND THAT MADE US U-FOES WHAT WE ARE.
THEY ALWAYS HAD THIS WEIRD EFFECT ON THE HULK, LIKE HE WAS ALLERGIC OR SOMETHING. KINDA HARD TO SHOW ON A TRAINING ROBOT...
...BUT YOU GET THE IDEA.
SEEMS MORE THAN ADEQUATE TO ME. VAPOR--YOUR TURN.
WE'RE ALL OUT OF ROBOT--BUT SHOW US HOW YOU HANDLE THE OTHER VITAL PART OF A HULK OPERATION...
...QUELLING DISSENT.
NONLETHAL, PLEASE. THESE ARE VOLUNTEERS.

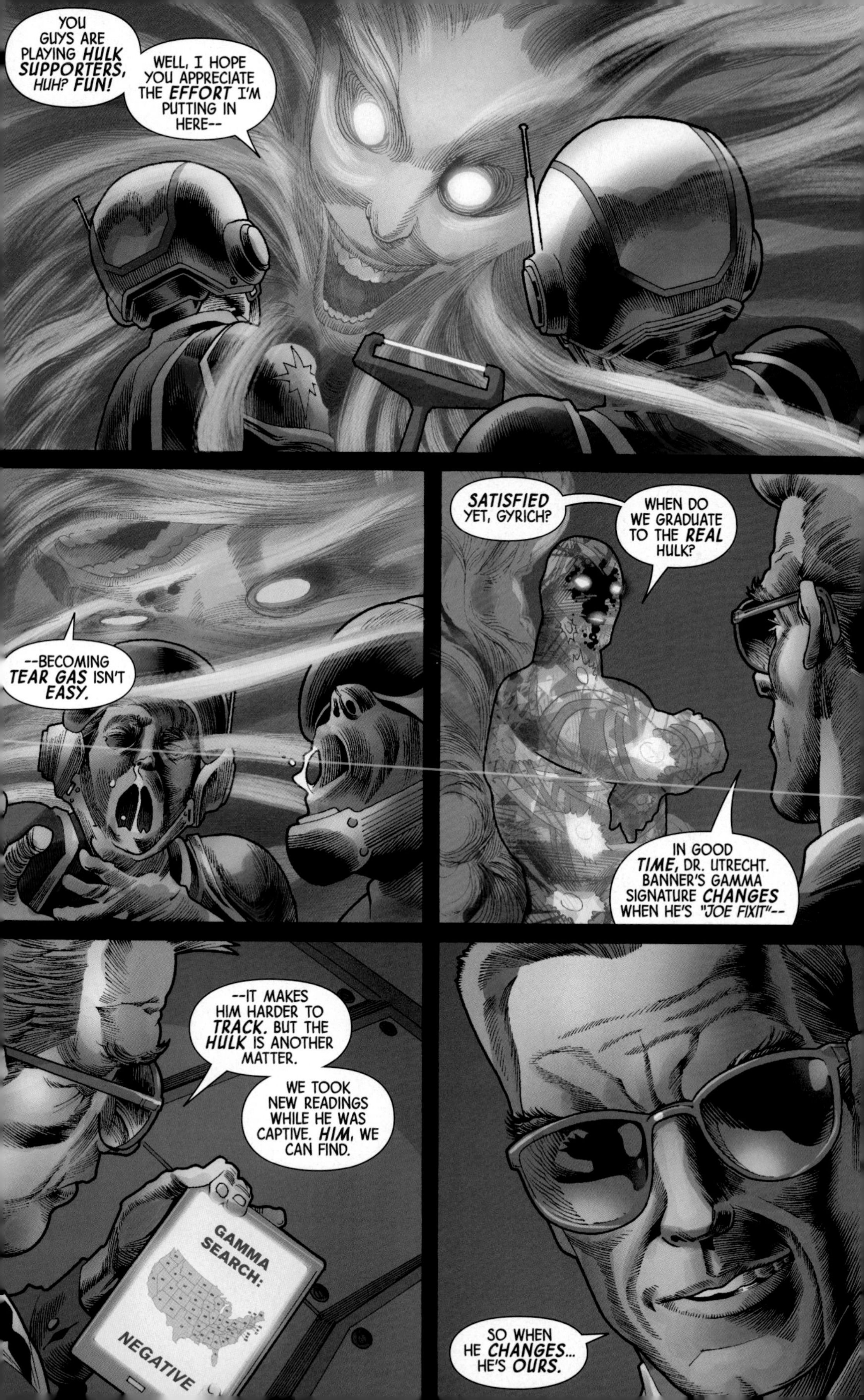
YOU GUYS ARE PLAYING HULK SUPPORTERS, HUH? FUN!
WELL, I HOPE YOU APPRECIATE THE EFFORT I'M PUTTING IN HERE--
--BECOMING TEAR GAS ISN'T EASY.
SATISFIED YET, GYRICH?
WHEN DO WE GRADUATE TO THE REAL HULK?
IN GOOD TIME, DR. UTRECHT. BANNER'S GAMMA SIGNATURE CHANGES WHEN HE'S "JOE FIXIT"--
--IT MAKES HIM HARDER TO TRACK. BUT THE HULK IS ANOTHER MATTER.
WE TOOK NEW READINGS WHILE HE WAS CAPTIVE. HIM, WE CAN FIND.
GAMMA SEARCH:
NEGATIVE
SO WHEN HE CHANGES... HE'S OURS.

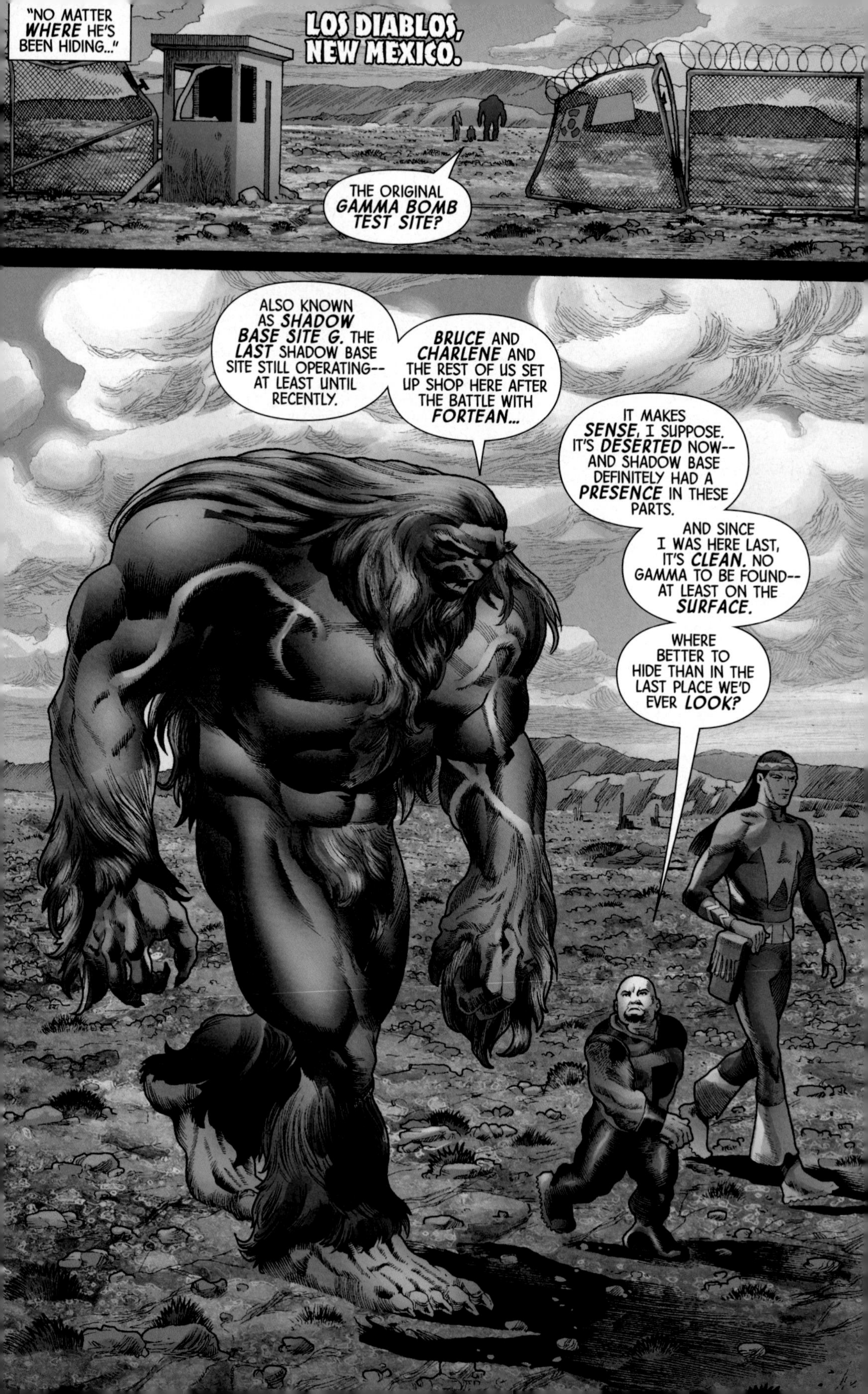
"NO MATTER WHERE HE'S BEEN HIDING..."
LOS DIABLOS, NEW MEXICO.
THE ORIGINAL GAMMA BOMB TEST SITE?
ALSO KNOWN AS SHADOW BASE SITE G. THE LAST SHADOW BASE SITE STILL OPERATING-- AT LEAST UNTIL RECENTLY.
BRUCE AND CHARLENE AND THE REST OF US SET UP SHOP HERE AFTER THE BATTLE WITH FORTEAN...
IT MAKES SENSE, I SUPPOSE. IT'S DESERTED NOW-- AND SHADOW BASE DEFINITELY HAD A PRESENCE IN THESE PARTS.
AND SINCE I WAS HERE LAST, IT'S CLEAN. NO GAMMA TO BE FOUND-- AT LEAST ON THE SURFACE.
WHERE BETTER TO HIDE THAN IN THE LAST PLACE WE'D EVER LOOK?

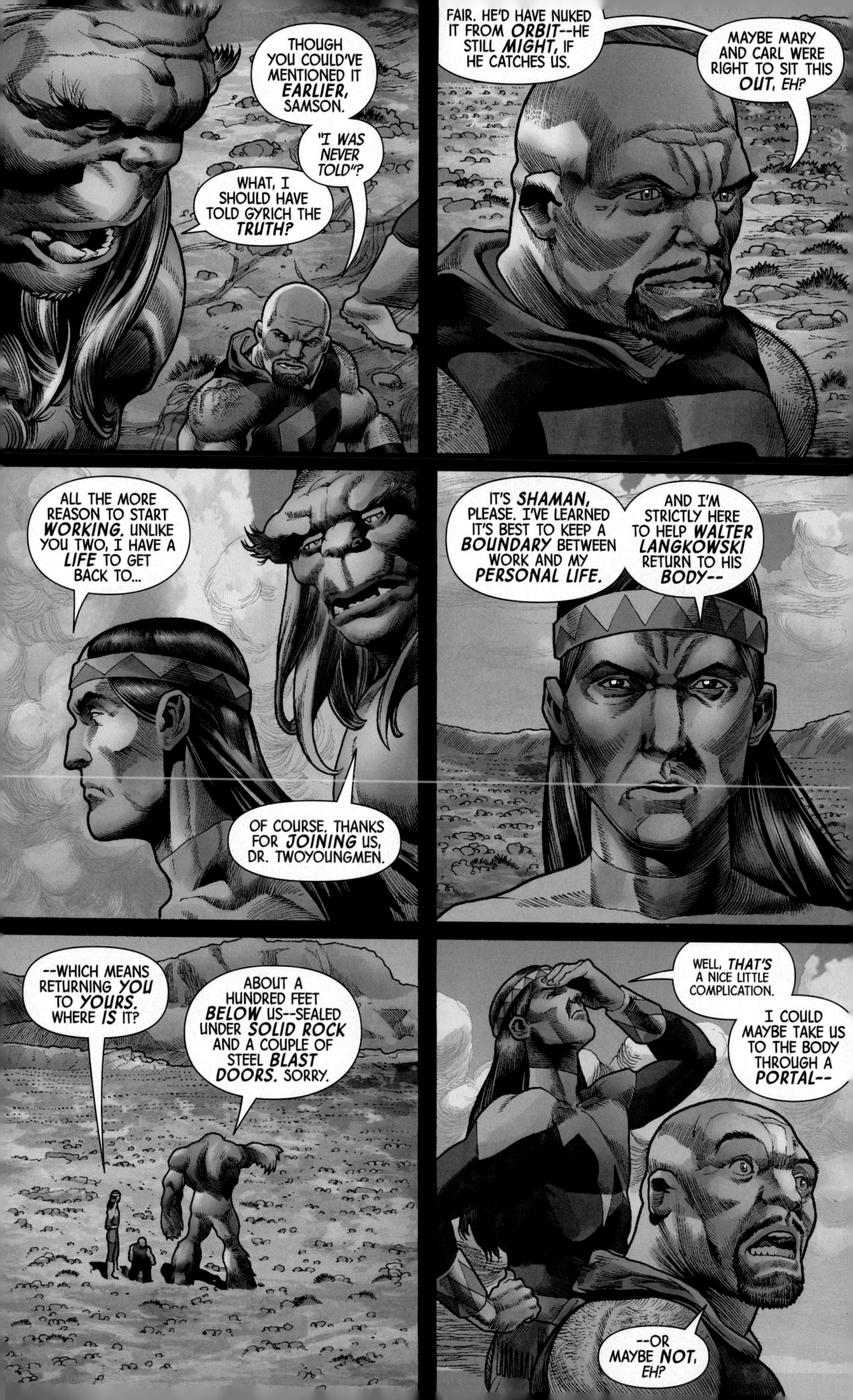
THOUGH YOU COULD'VE MENTIONED IT EARLIER, SAMSON.
"I WAS NEVER TOLD"?
WHAT, I SHOULD HAVE TOLD GYRICH THE TRUTH?
FAIR. HE'D HAVE NUKED IT FROM ORBIT--HE STILL MIGHT, IF HE CATCHES US.
MAYBE MARY AND CARL WERE RIGHT TO SIT THIS OUT, EH?
ALL THE MORE REASON TO START WORKING. UNLIKE YOU TWO, I HAVE A LIFE TO GET BACK TO...
OF COURSE. THANKS FOR JOINING US, DR. TWOYOUNGMEN.
IT'S SHAMAN, PLEASE. I'VE LEARNED IT'S BEST TO KEEP A BOUNDARY BETWEEN WORK AND MY PERSONAL LIFE.
AND I'M STRICTLY HERE TO HELP WALTER LANGKOWSKI RETURN TO HIS BODY--
--WHICH MEANS RETURNING YOU TO YOURS. WHERE IS IT?
ABOUT A HUNDRED FEET BELOW US--SEALED UNDER SOLID ROCK AND A COUPLE OF STEEL BLAST DOORS. SORRY.
WELL, THAT'S A NICE LITTLE COMPLICATION.
I COULD MAYBE TAKE US TO THE BODY THROUGH A PORTAL--
--OR MAYBE NOT, EH?

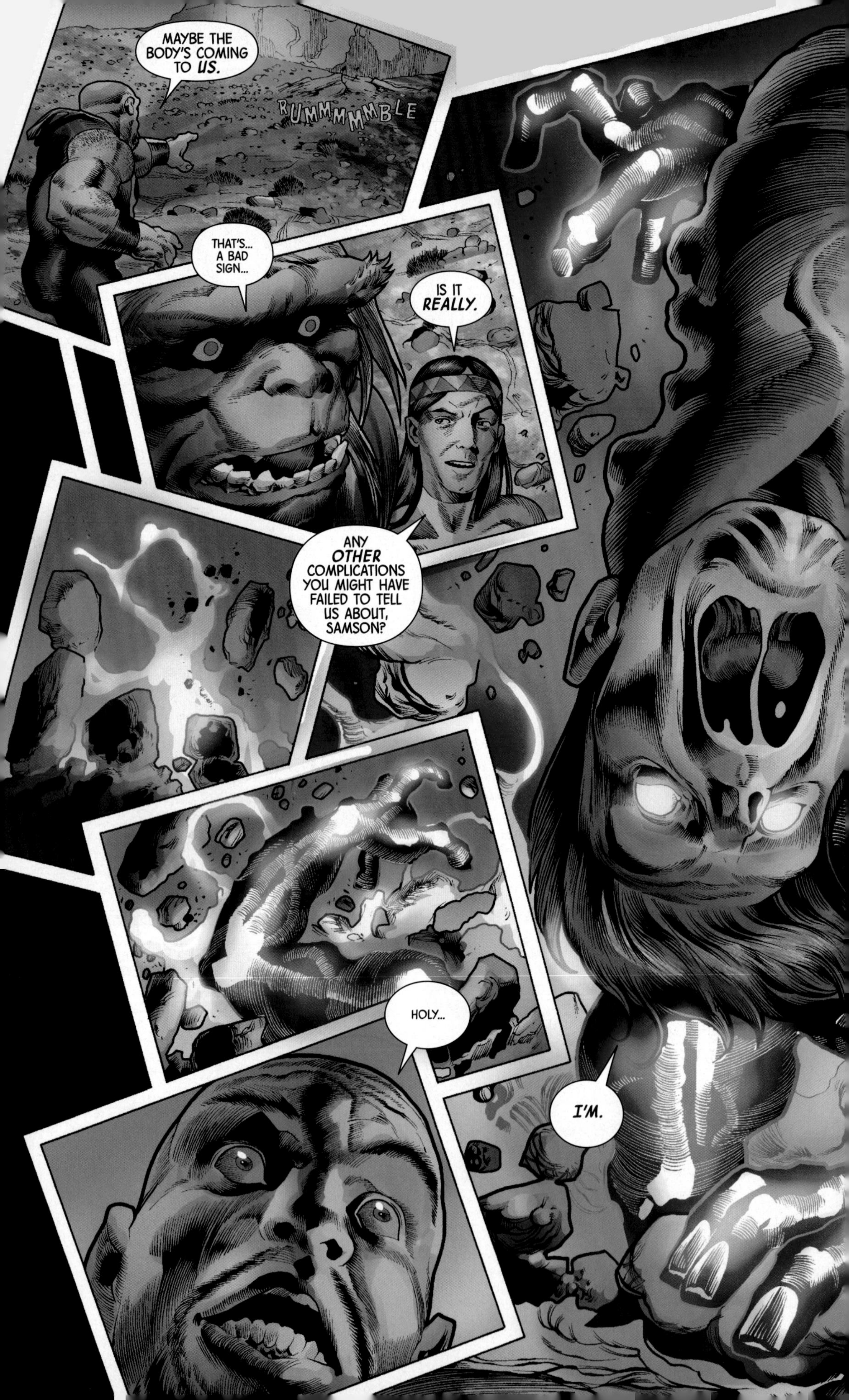
MAYBE THE BODY'S COMING TO *US.*
RUMMMMMBLE
THAT'S... A BAD SIGN...
IS IT *REALLY.*
ANY *OTHER* COMPLICATIONS YOU MIGHT HAVE FAILED TO TELL US ABOUT, SAMSON?
HOLY...
I'M.

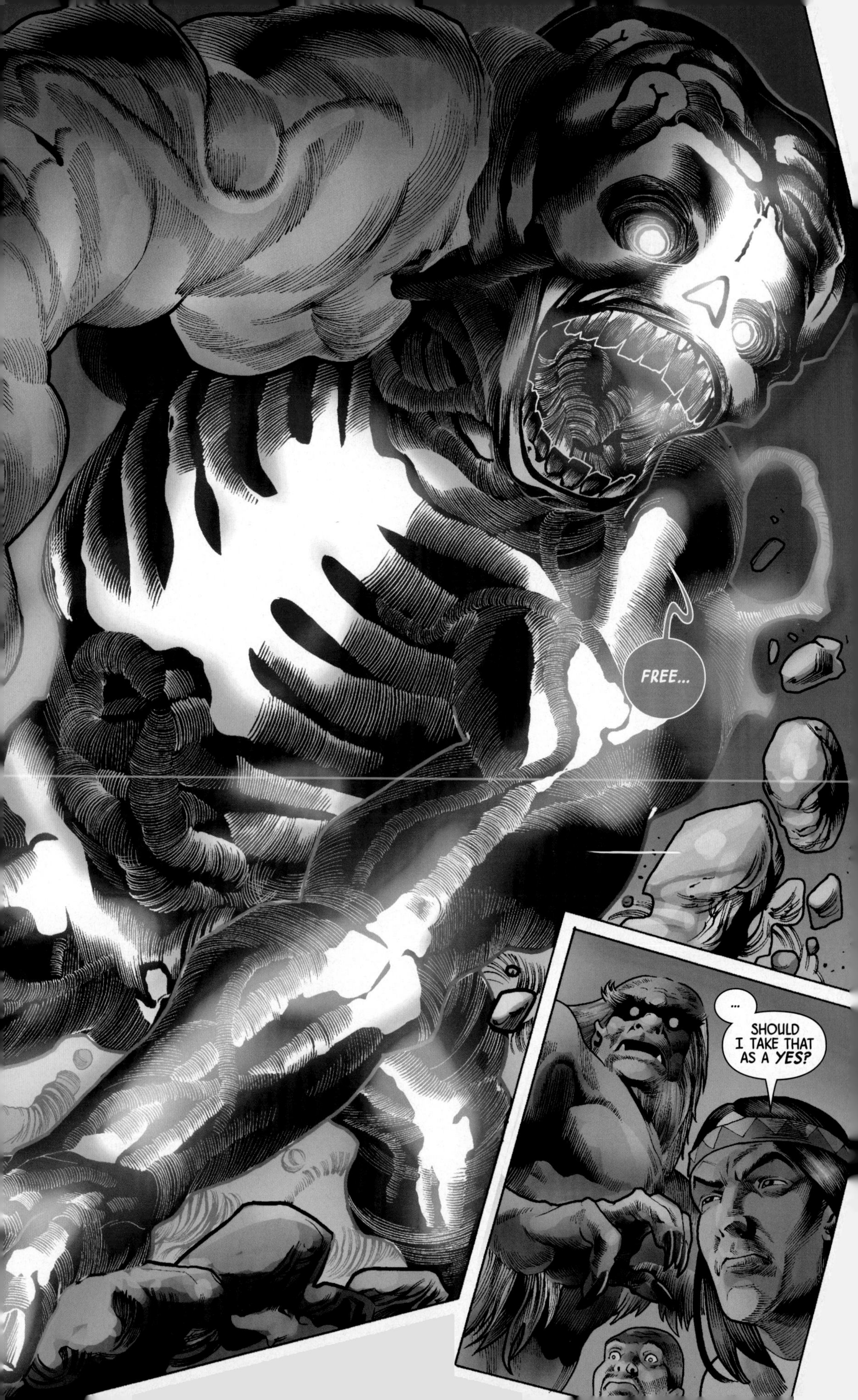
FREE...
...
SHOULD I TAKE THAT AS A *YES?*

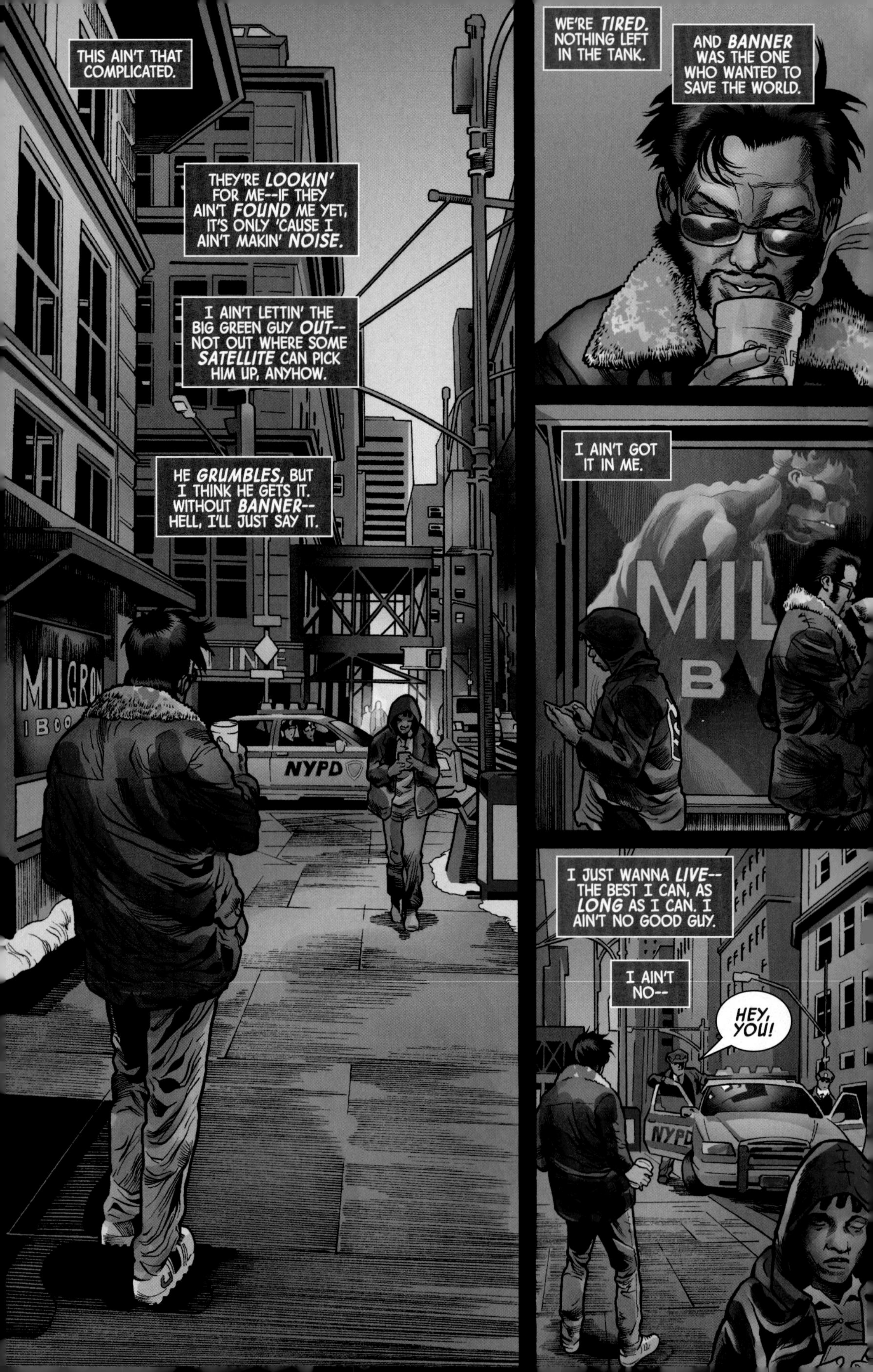

THIS AIN'T THAT COMPLICATED.
THEY'RE LOOKIN' FOR ME--IF THEY AIN'T FOUND ME YET, IT'S ONLY 'CAUSE I AIN'T MAKIN' NOISE.
I AIN'T LETTIN' THE BIG GREEN GUY OUT-- NOT OUT WHERE SOME SATELLITE CAN PICK HIM UP, ANYHOW.
HE GRUMBLES, BUT I THINK HE GETS IT. WITHOUT BANNER-- HELL, I'LL JUST SAY IT.
MILGRON
NYPD
WE'RE TIRED. NOTHING LEFT IN THE TANK.
AND BANNER WAS THE ONE WHO WANTED TO SAVE THE WORLD.
I AIN'T GOT IT IN ME.
I JUST WANNA LIVE-- THE BEST I CAN, AS LONG AS I CAN. I AIN'T NO GOOD GUY.
I AIN'T NO--
HEY, YOU!
NYPD

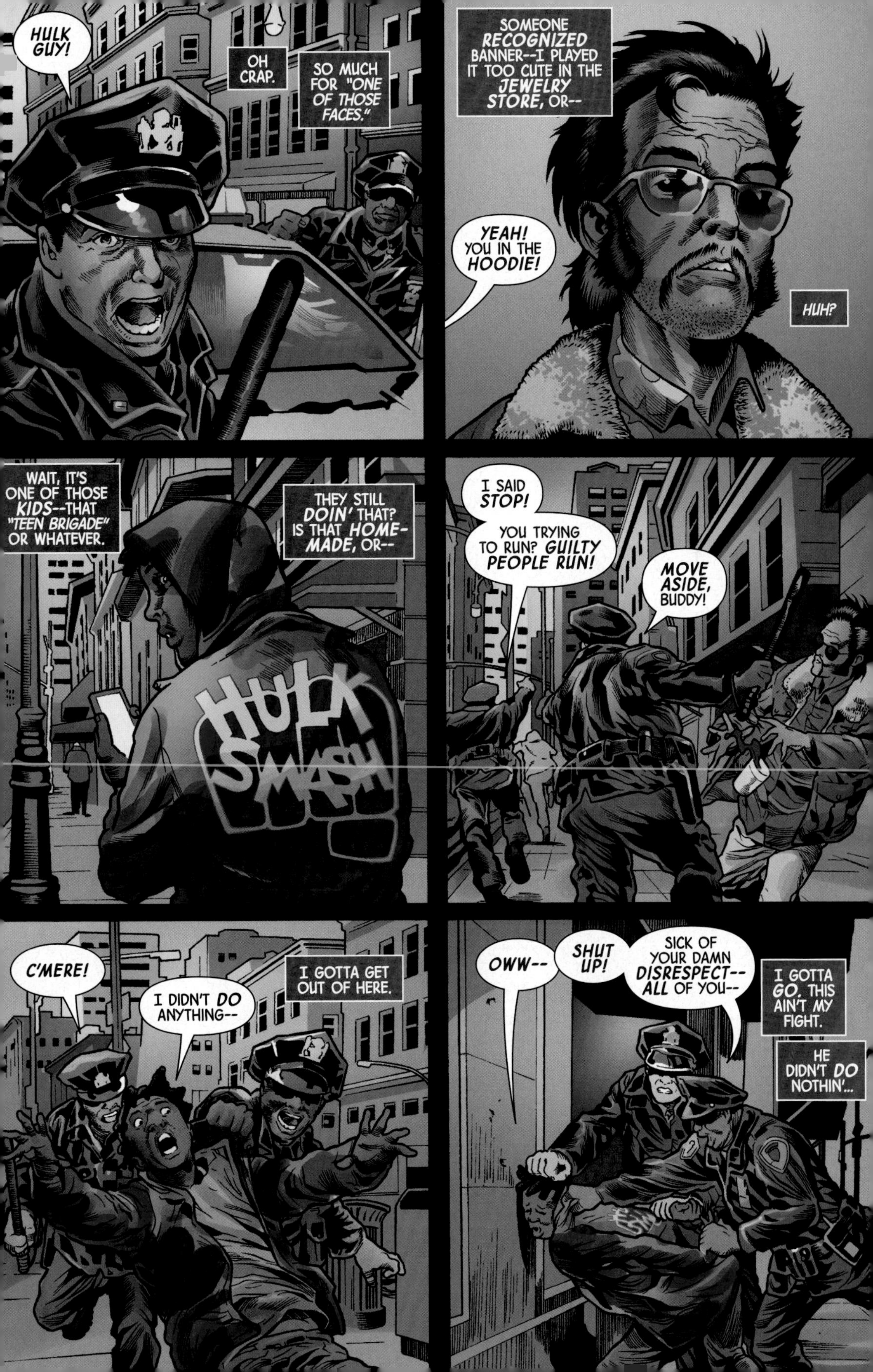
HULK GUY!
OH CRAP.
SO MUCH FOR "ONE OF THOSE FACES."
SOMEONE RECOGNIZED BANNER--I PLAYED IT TOO CUTE IN THE JEWELRY STORE, OR--
YEAH! YOU IN THE HOODIE!
HUH?
WAIT, IT'S ONE OF THOSE KIDS--THAT "TEEN BRIGADE" OR WHATEVER.
THEY STILL DOIN' THAT? IS THAT HOME-MADE, OR--
HULK SMASH
I SAID STOP!
YOU TRYING TO RUN? GUILTY PEOPLE RUN!
MOVE ASIDE, BUDDY!
C'MERE!
I DIDN'T DO ANYTHING--
I GOTTA GET OUT OF HERE.
OWW--
SHUT UP!
SICK OF YOUR DAMN DISRESPECT--ALL OF YOU--
I GOTTA GO. THIS AIN'T MY FIGHT.
HE DIDN'T DO NOTHIN'...

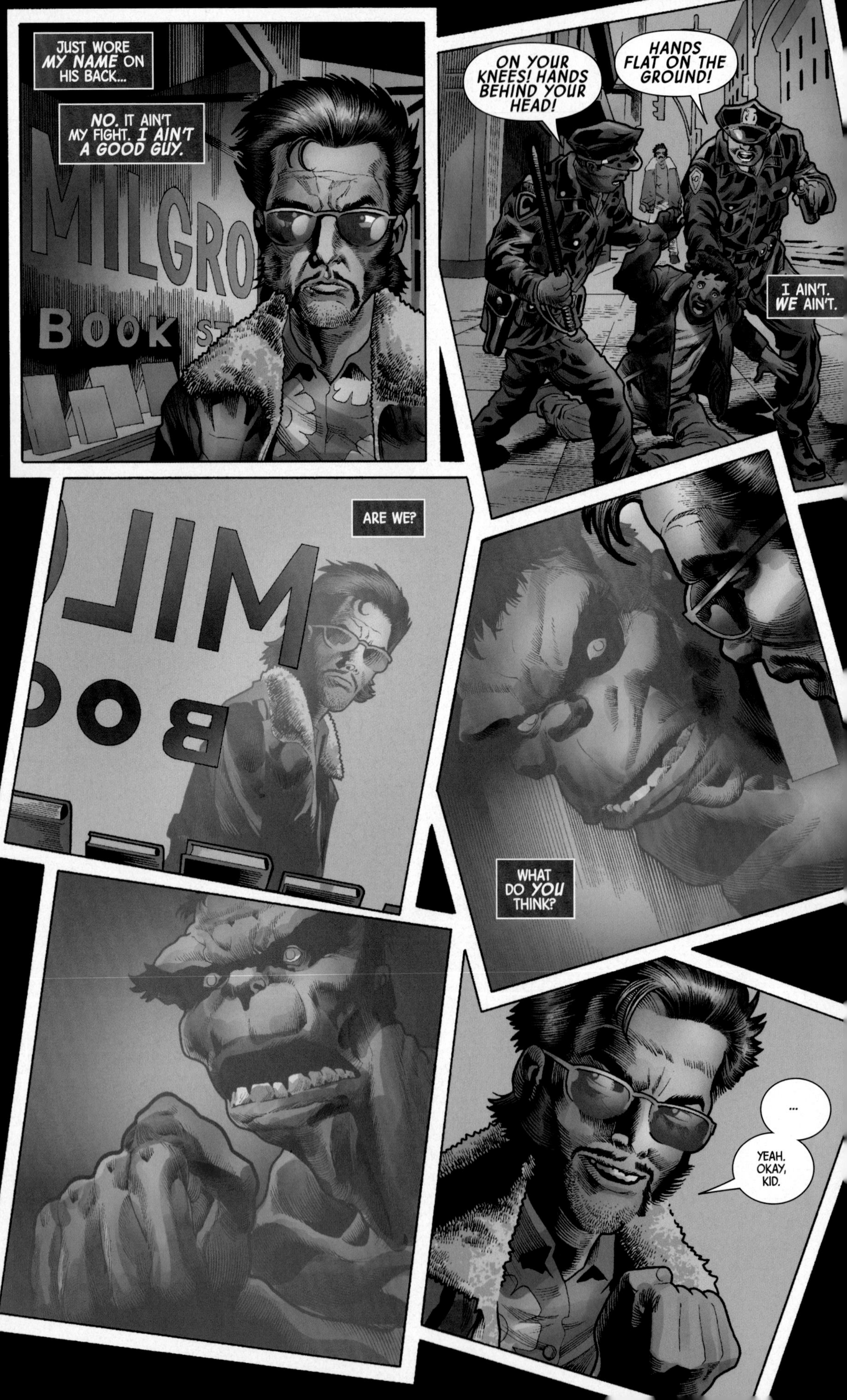

JUST WORE MY NAME ON HIS BACK...
NO. IT AIN'T MY FIGHT. I AIN'T A GOOD GUY.
MILGRO
BOOK ST
ON YOUR KNEES! HANDS BEHIND YOUR HEAD!
HANDS FLAT ON THE GROUND!
I AIN'T. WE AIN'T.
ARE WE?
WHAT DO YOU THINK?
...
YEAH. OKAY, KID.

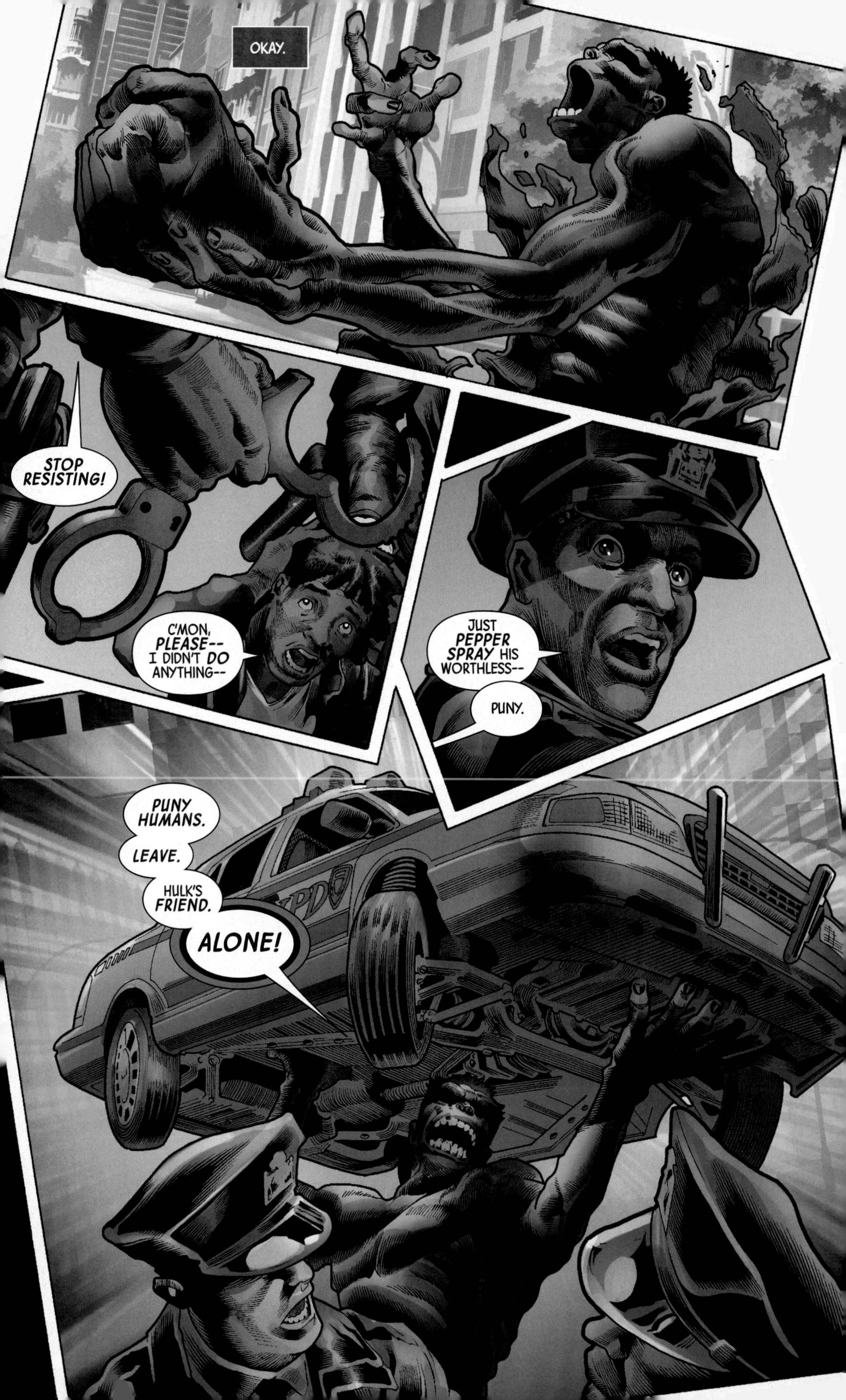
OKAY.
STOP RESISTING!
C'MON, PLEASE-- I DIDN'T DO ANYTHING--
JUST PEPPER SPRAY HIS WORTHLESS--
PUNY.
PUNY HUMANS.
LEAVE.
HULK'S FRIEND.
ALONE!

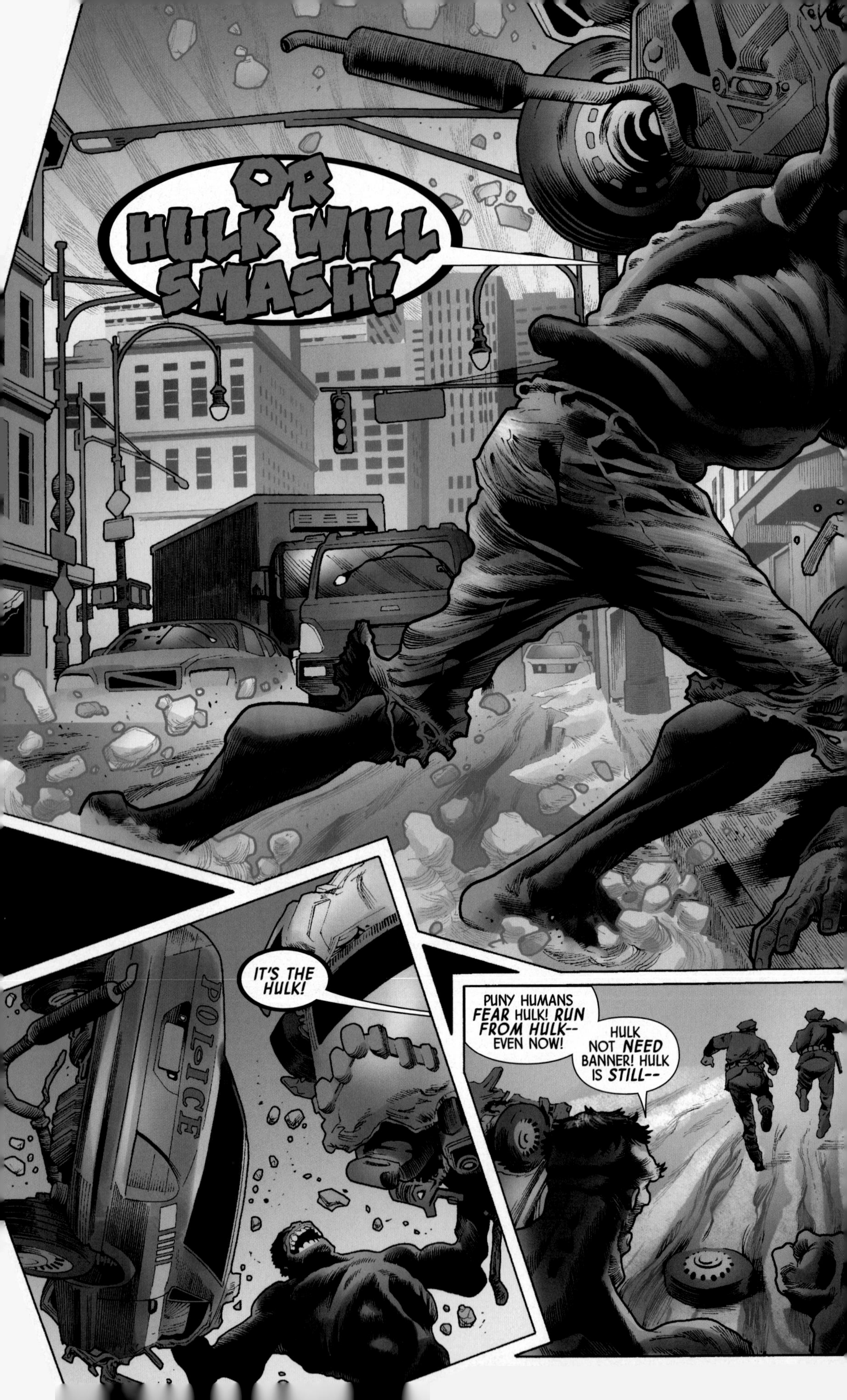
OR HULK WILL SMASH!
IT'S THE HULK!
POLICE
PUNY HUMANS FEAR HULK! RUN FROM HULK-- EVEN NOW!
HULK NOT NEED BANNER! HULK IS STILL--

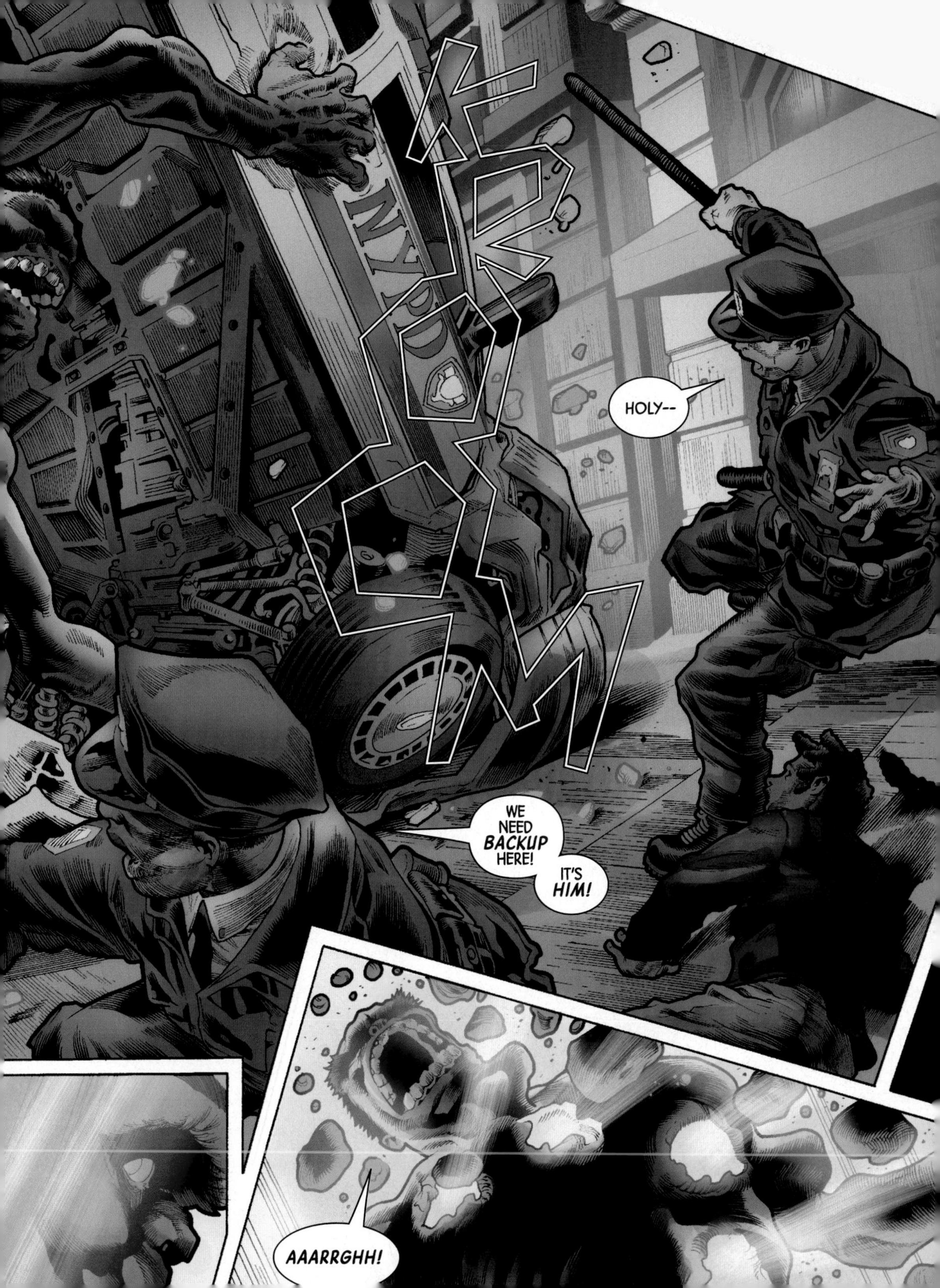

NYPD
HOLY--
WE NEED BACKUP HERE!
IT'S HIM!
AAARRGHH!

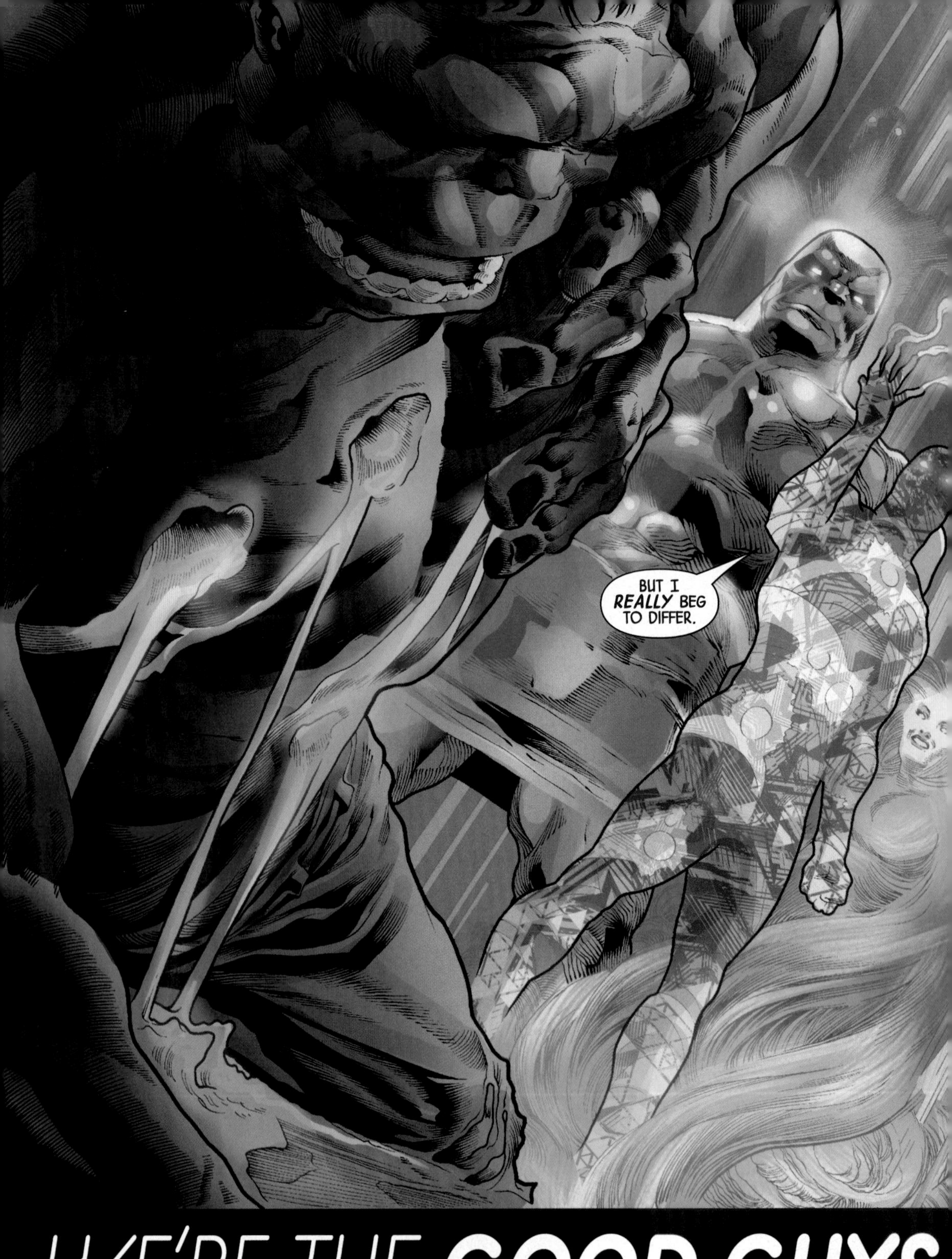
BUT I *REALLY* BEG TO DIFFER.

WE'RE THE **GOOD GUYS**

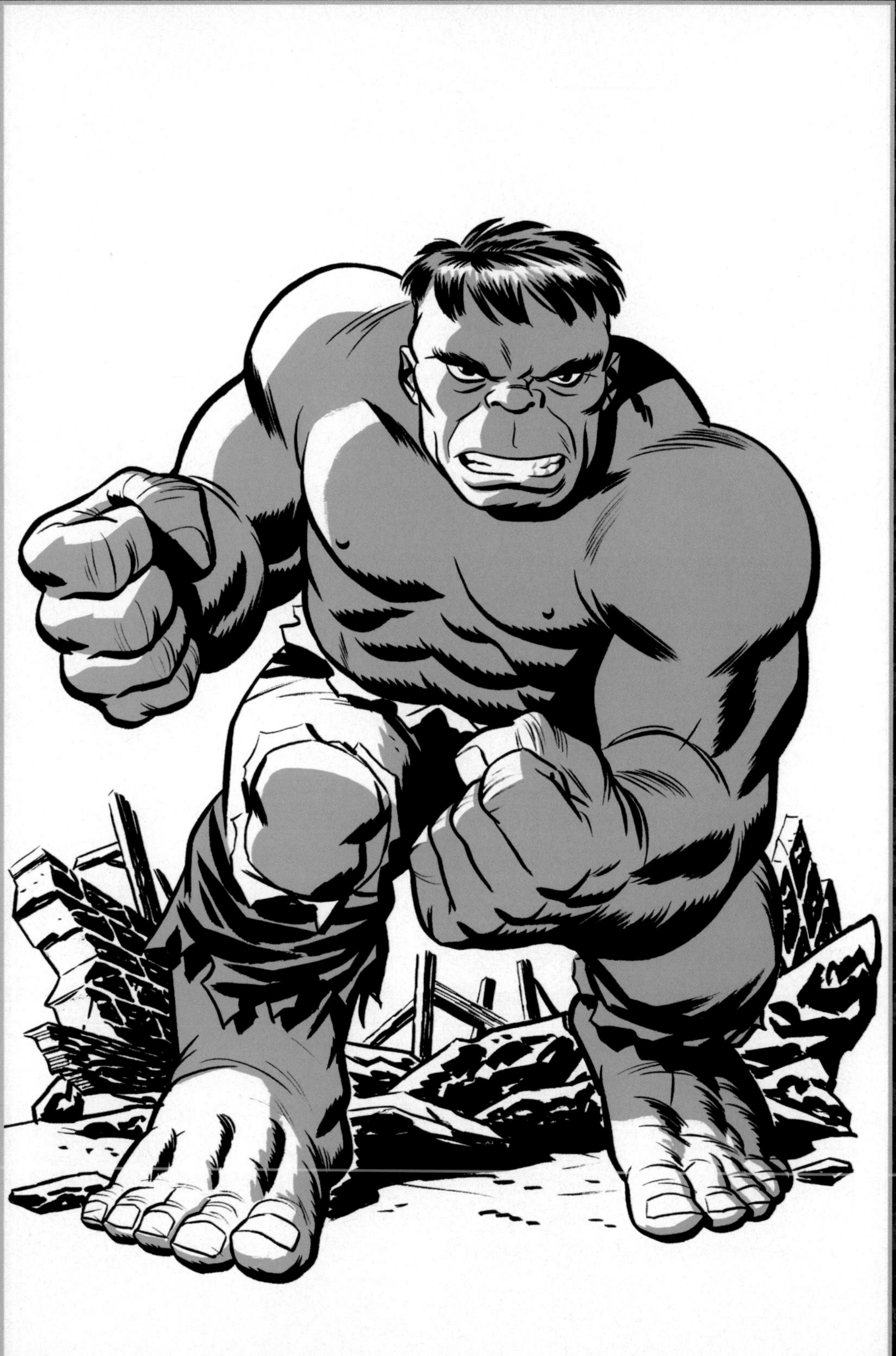

MICHAEL CHO
#44 VARIANT

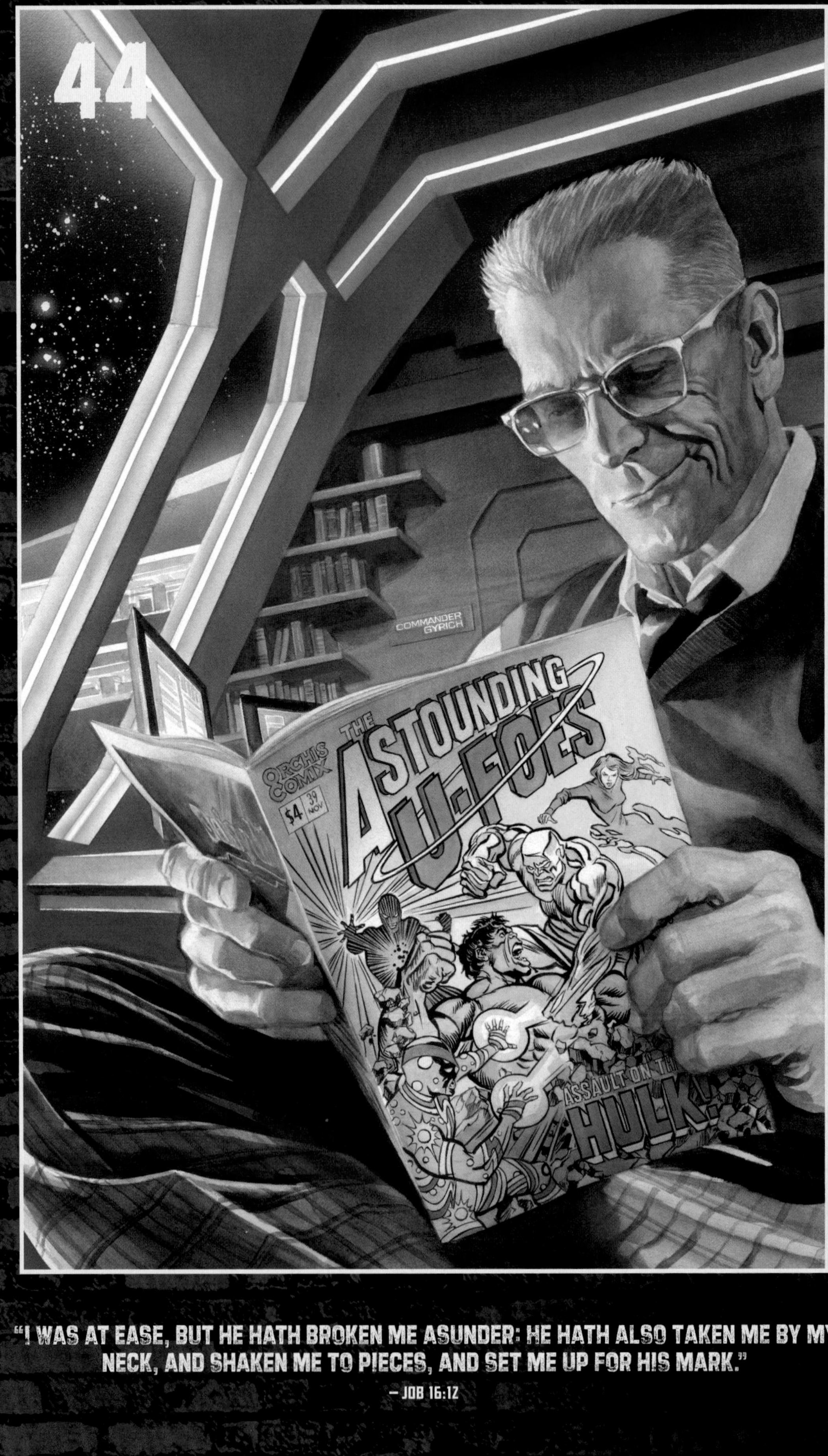
44
COMMANDER GYRICH
ORCHIS COMIX
$4 39 NOV
THE ASTOUNDING U-FOES
ASSAULT ON TH
HULK!

"I WAS AT EASE, BUT HE HATH BROKEN ME ASUNDER: HE HATH ALSO TAKEN ME BY MY NECK, AND SHAKEN ME TO PIECES, AND SET ME UP FOR HIS MARK."

– JOB 16:12

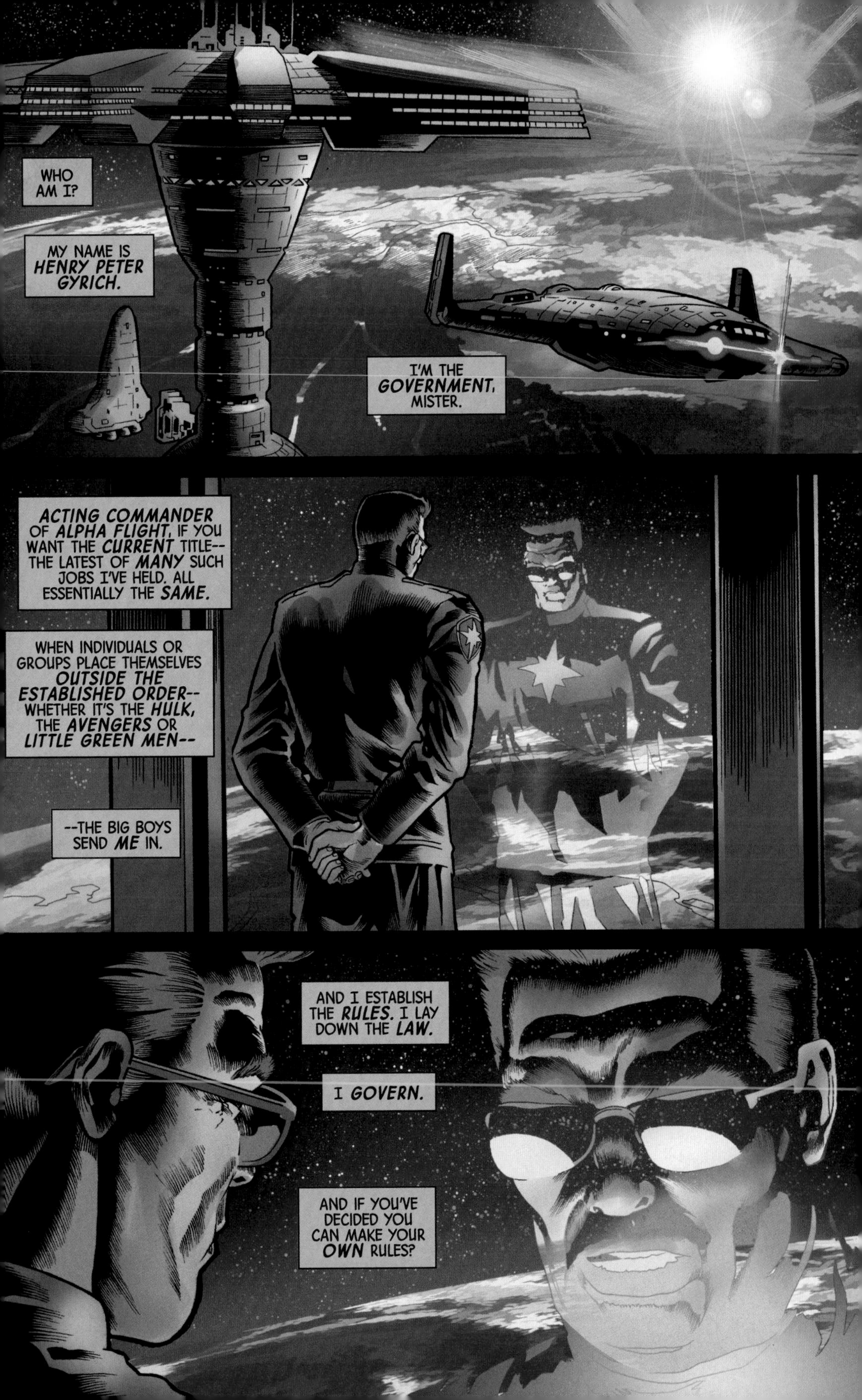
WHO AM I?
MY NAME IS HENRY PETER GYRICH.
I'M THE GOVERNMENT, MISTER.
ACTING COMMANDER OF ALPHA FLIGHT, IF YOU WANT THE CURRENT TITLE-- THE LATEST OF MANY SUCH JOBS I'VE HELD. ALL ESSENTIALLY THE SAME.
WHEN INDIVIDUALS OR GROUPS PLACE THEMSELVES OUTSIDE THE ESTABLISHED ORDER-- WHETHER IT'S THE HULK, THE AVENGERS OR LITTLE GREEN MEN--
--THE BIG BOYS SEND ME IN.
AND I ESTABLISH THE RULES. I LAY DOWN THE LAW.
I GOVERN.
AND IF YOU'VE DECIDED YOU CAN MAKE YOUR OWN RULES?

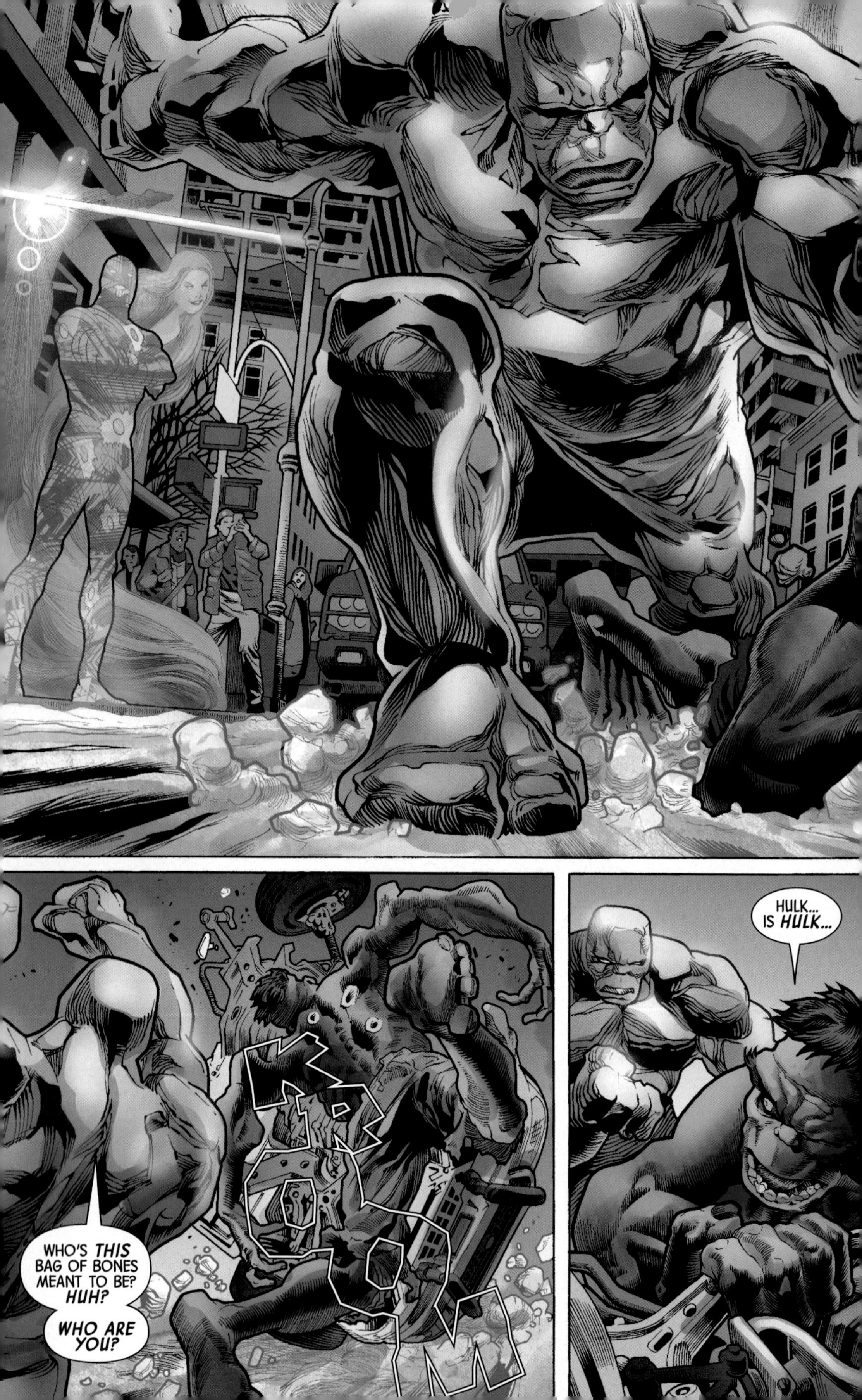
WHO'S *THIS* BAG OF BONES MEANT TO BE? *HUH?*
WHO ARE YOU?
KROOM
HULK... IS *HULK*...

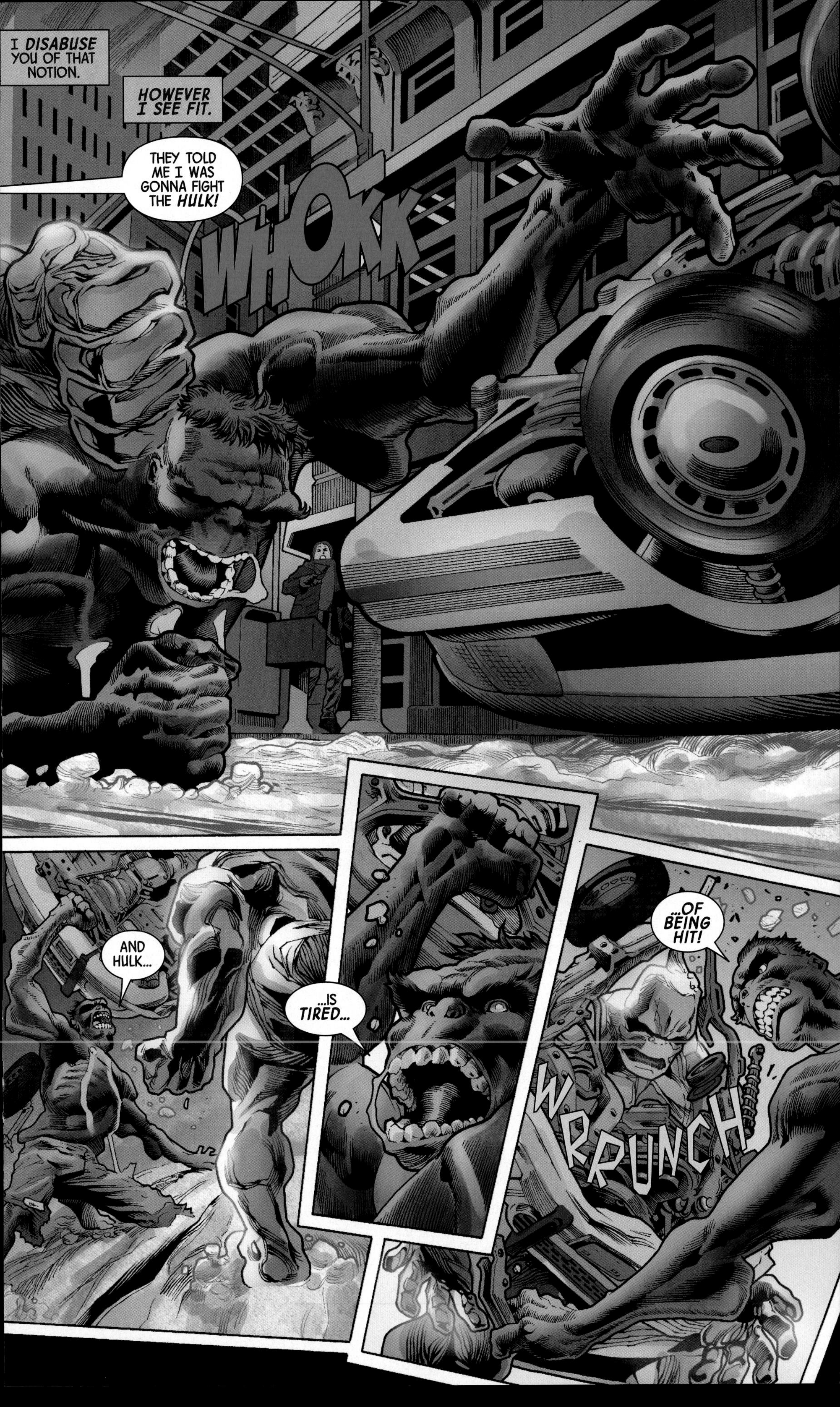

I DISABUSE YOU OF THAT NOTION.
HOWEVER I SEE FIT.
THEY TOLD ME I WAS GONNA FIGHT THE HULK!
WHOKK
AND HULK...
...IS TIRED...
...OF BEING HIT!
WRRUNCH

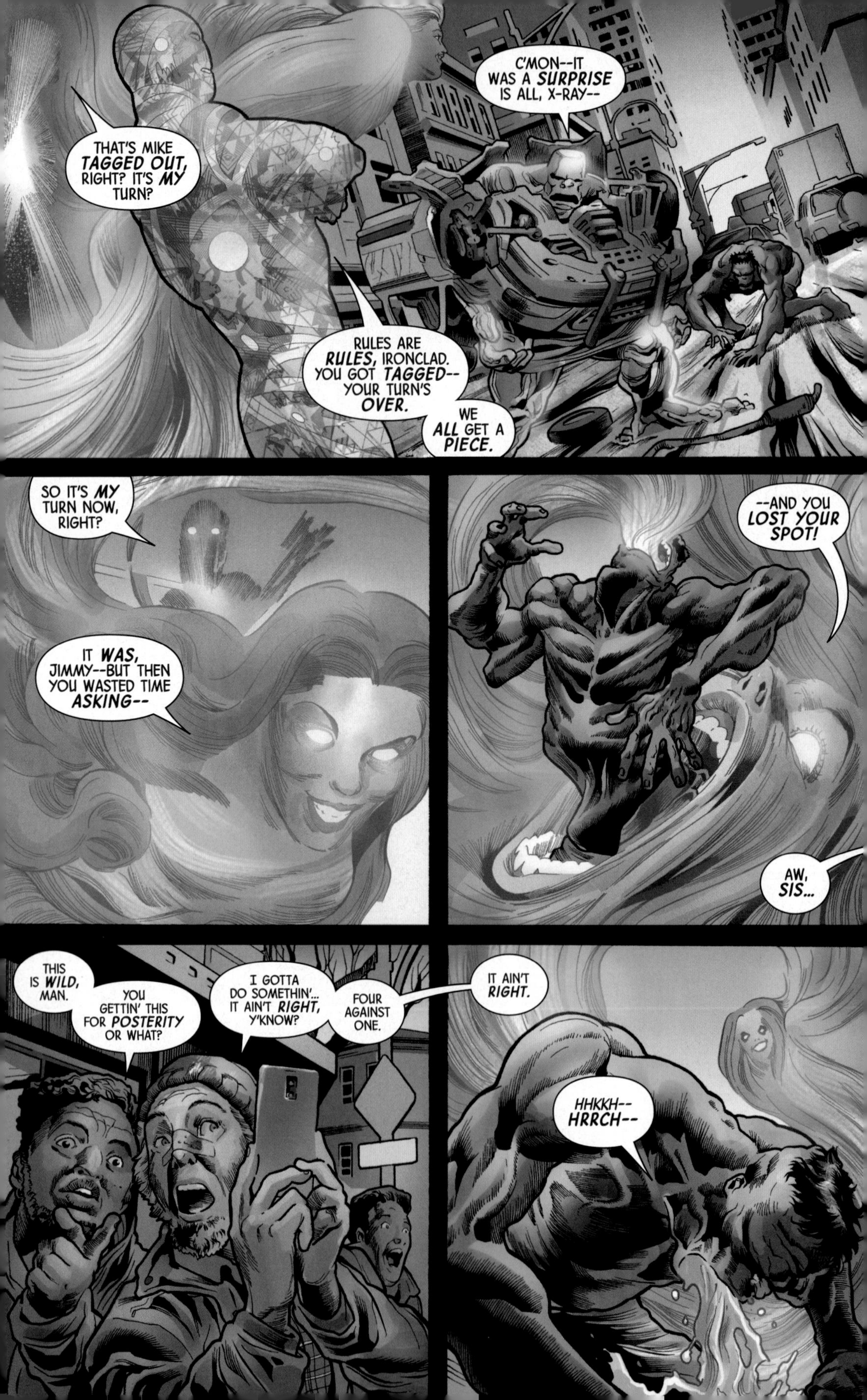
THAT'S MIKE TAGGED OUT, RIGHT? IT'S MY TURN?
C'MON--IT WAS A SURPRISE IS ALL, X-RAY--
RULES ARE RULES, IRONCLAD. YOU GOT TAGGED--YOUR TURN'S OVER.
WE ALL GET A PIECE.
SO IT'S MY TURN NOW, RIGHT?
IT WAS, JIMMY--BUT THEN YOU WASTED TIME ASKING--
--AND YOU LOST YOUR SPOT!
AW, SIS...
THIS IS WILD, MAN.
YOU GETTIN' THIS FOR POSTERITY OR WHAT?
I GOTTA DO SOMETHIN'... IT AIN'T RIGHT, Y'KNOW?
FOUR AGAINST ONE.
IT AIN'T RIGHT.
HHKKH--HRRCH--

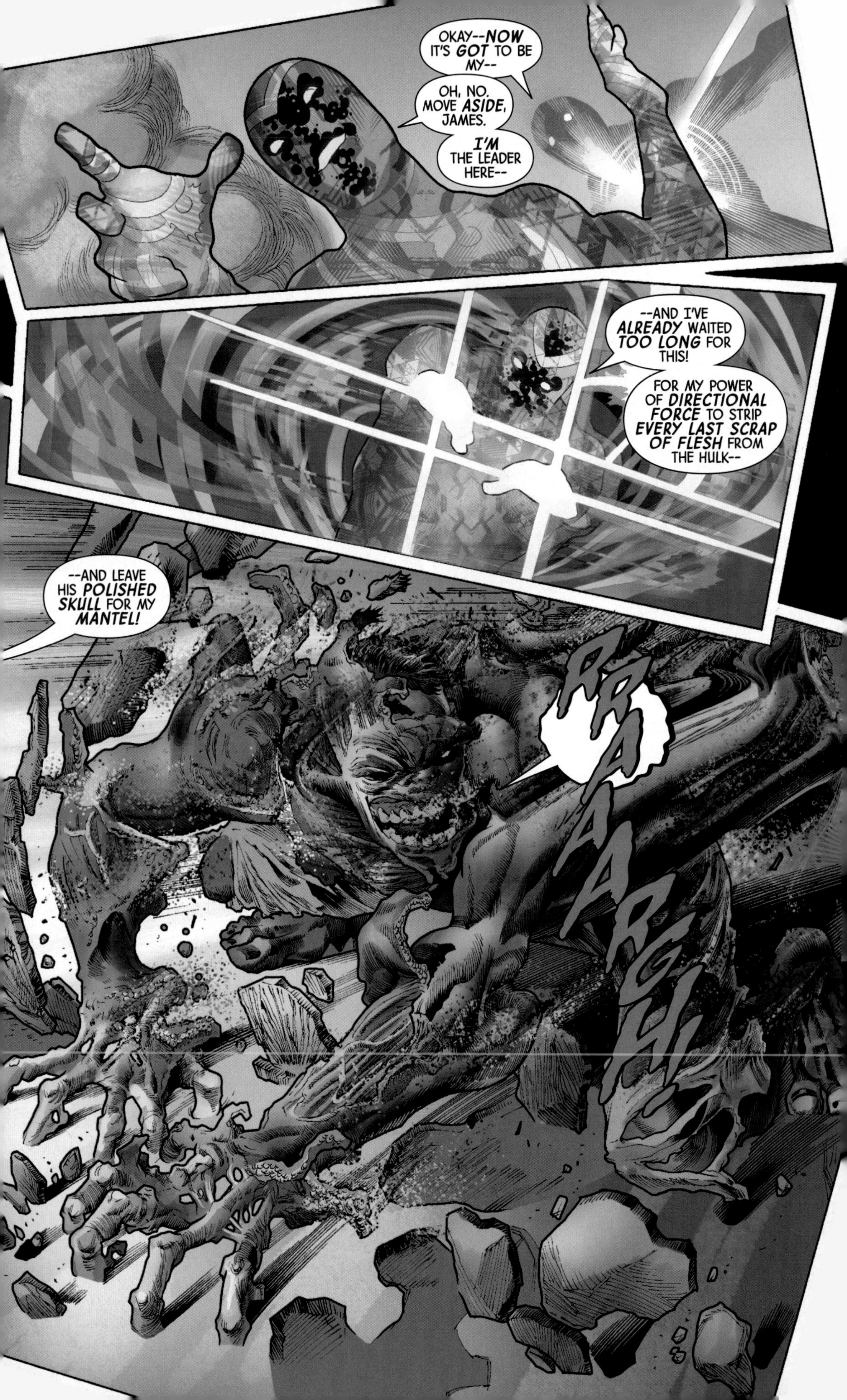
OKAY--NOW IT'S GOT TO BE MY--
OH, NO. MOVE ASIDE, JAMES.
I'M THE LEADER HERE--
--AND I'VE ALREADY WAITED TOO LONG FOR THIS!
FOR MY POWER OF DIRECTIONAL FORCE TO STRIP EVERY LAST SCRAP OF FLESH FROM THE HULK--
--AND LEAVE HIS POLISHED SKULL FOR MY MANTEL!
RRAAAARGH!

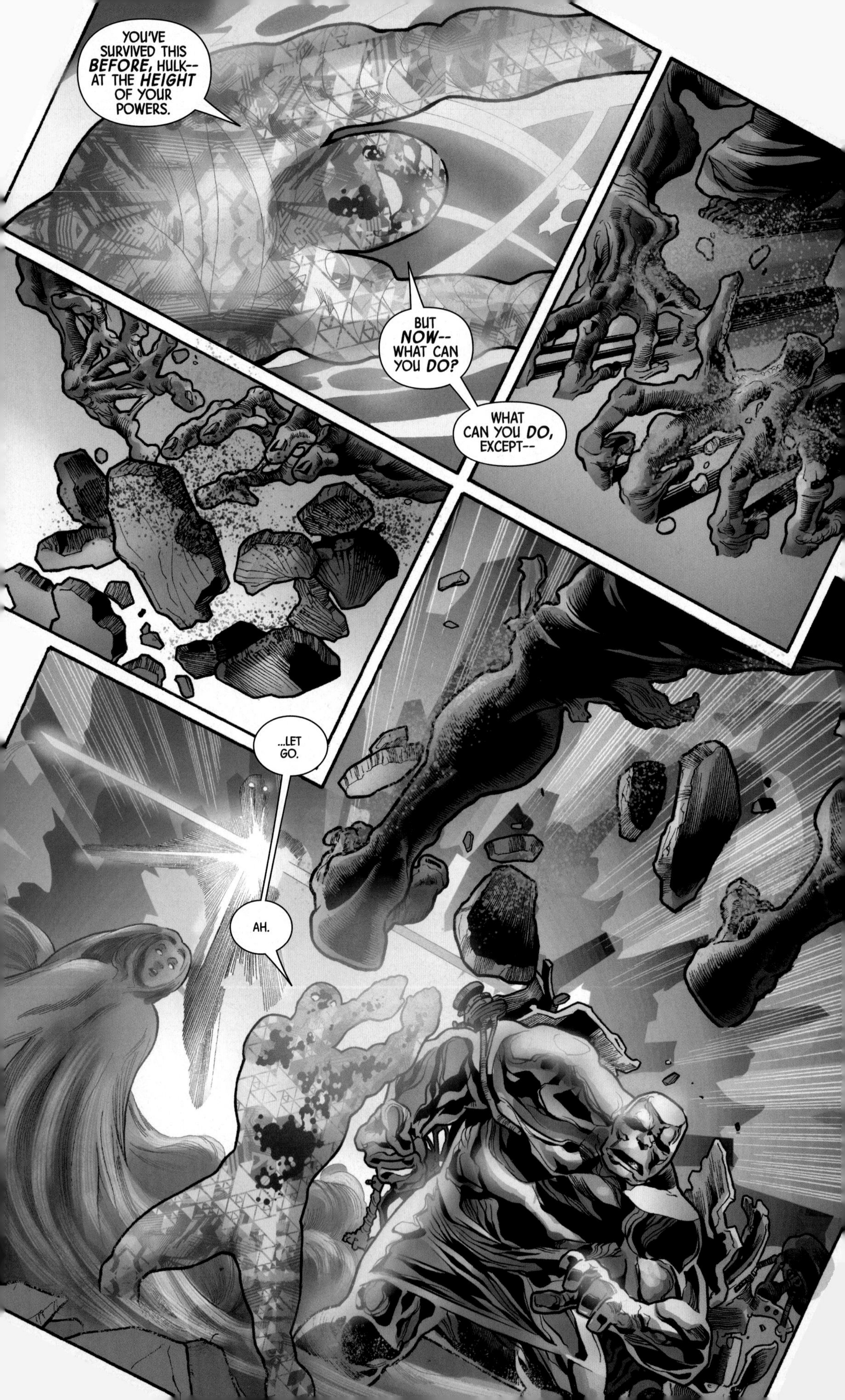

YOU'VE SURVIVED THIS *BEFORE*, HULK-- AT THE *HEIGHT* OF YOUR POWERS.
BUT *NOW*-- WHAT CAN YOU *DO?*
WHAT CAN YOU *DO*, EXCEPT--
...LET GO.
AH.

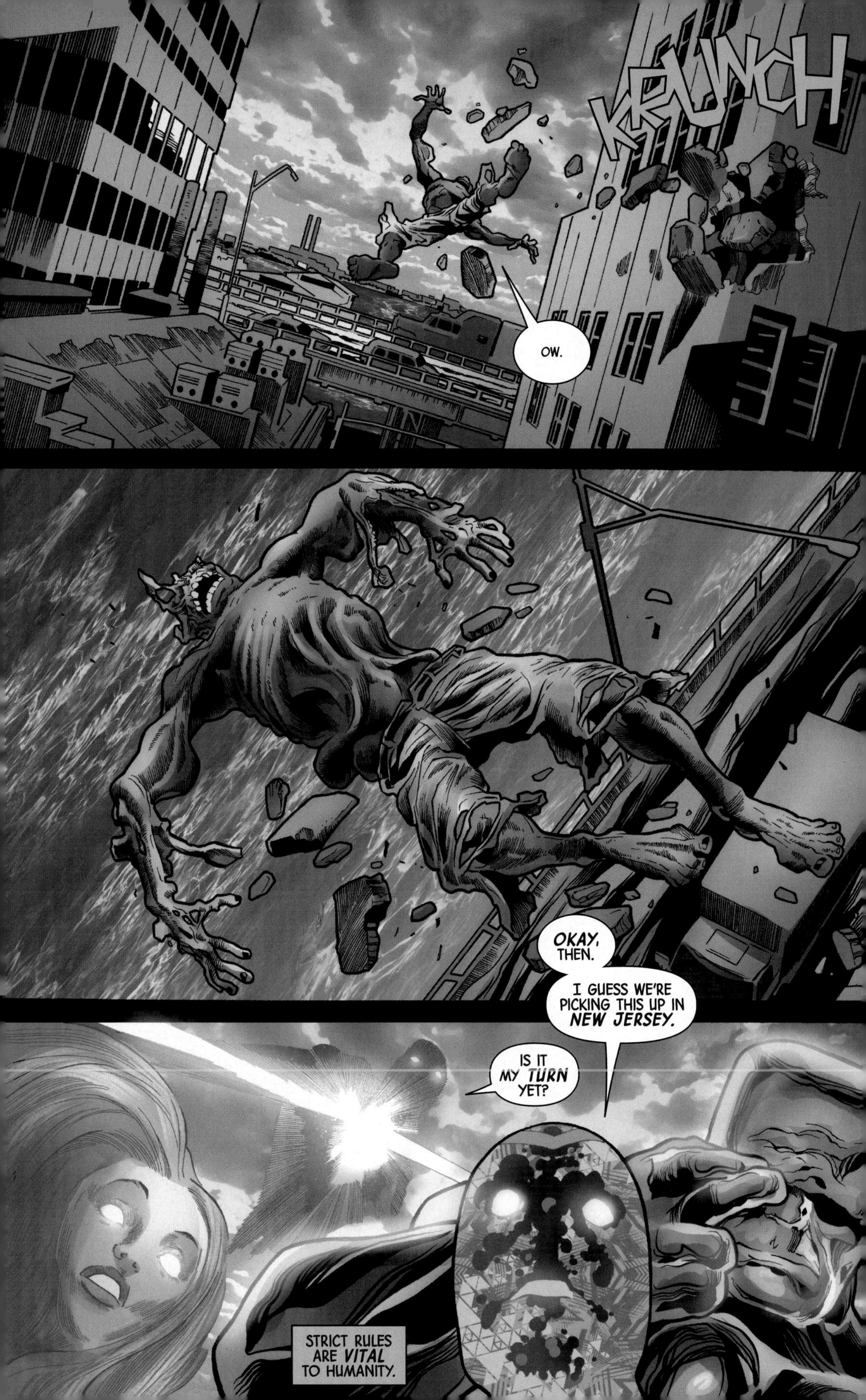
KRUNCH
OW.
OKAY, THEN.
I GUESS WE'RE PICKING THIS UP IN NEW JERSEY.
IS IT MY TURN YET?
STRICT RULES ARE VITAL TO HUMANITY.

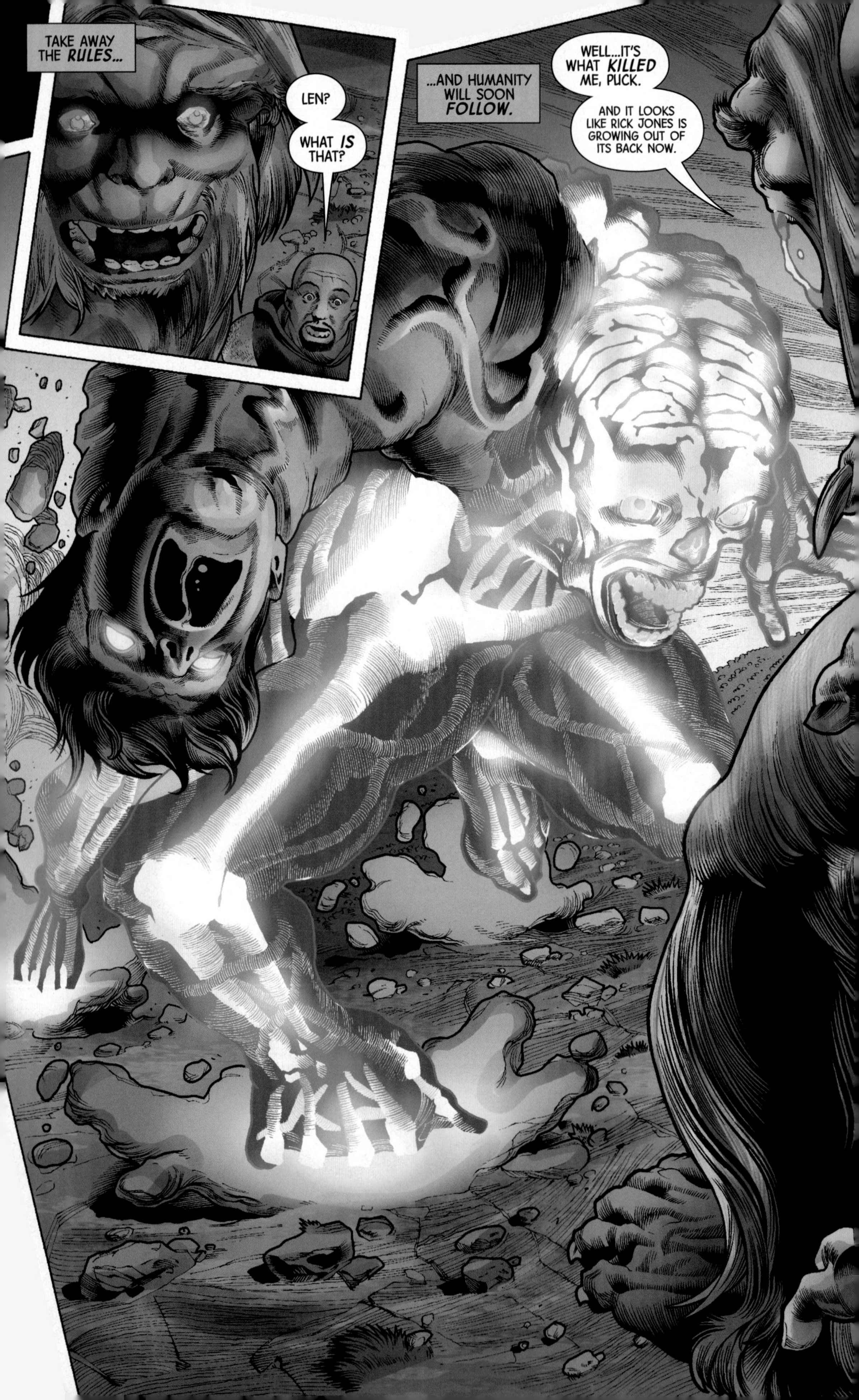
TAKE AWAY THE RULES...
LEN?
WHAT IS THAT?
...AND HUMANITY WILL SOON FOLLOW.
WELL...IT'S WHAT KILLED ME, PUCK.
AND IT LOOKS LIKE RICK JONES IS GROWING OUT OF ITS BACK NOW.

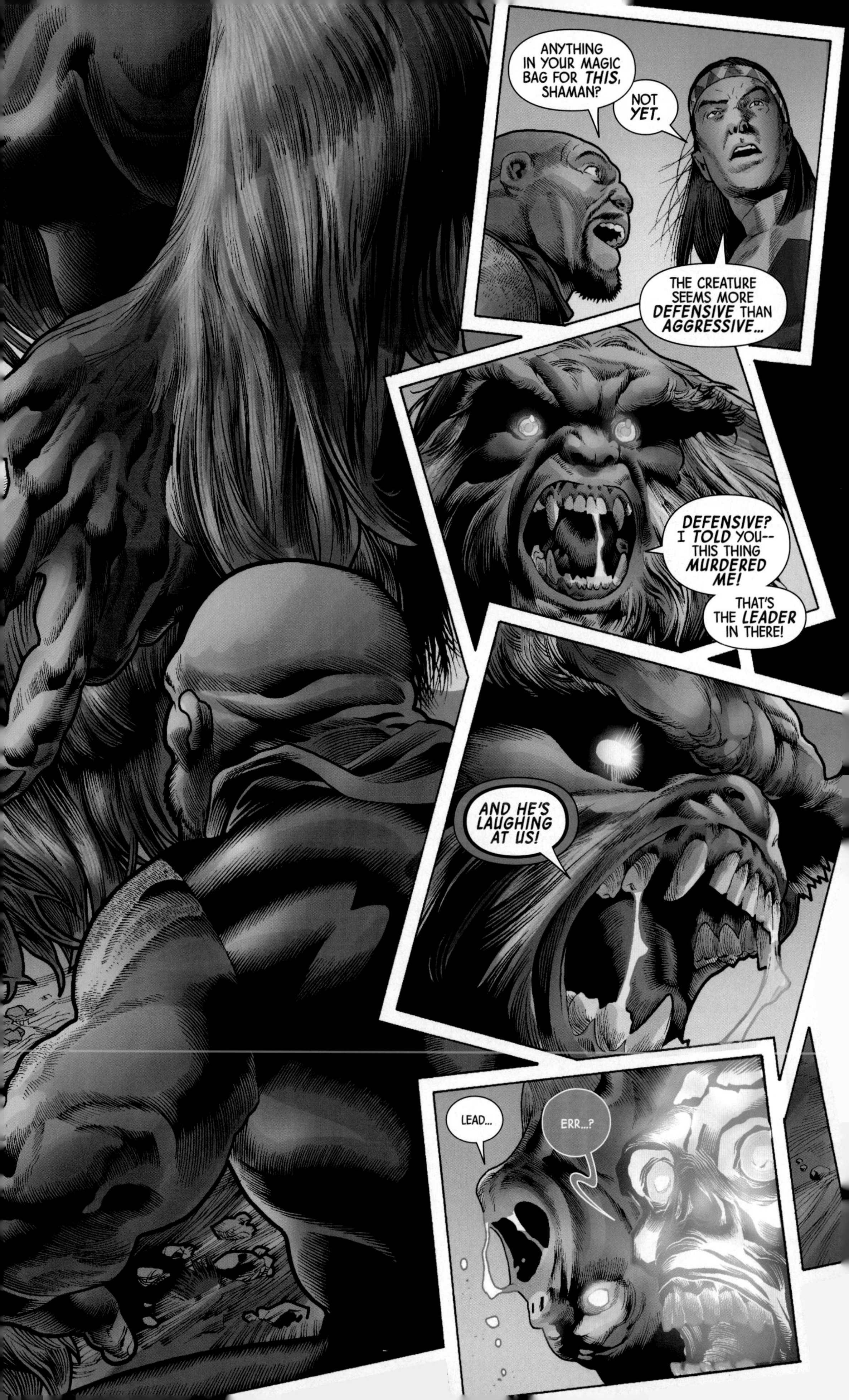
ANYTHING IN YOUR MAGIC BAG FOR *THIS*, SHAMAN?
NOT *YET.*
THE CREATURE SEEMS MORE *DEFENSIVE* THAN *AGGRESSIVE...*
DEFENSIVE? I *TOLD* YOU-- THIS THING *MURDERED ME!*
THAT'S THE *LEADER* IN THERE!
AND HE'S LAUGHING AT US!
LEAD...
ERR...?

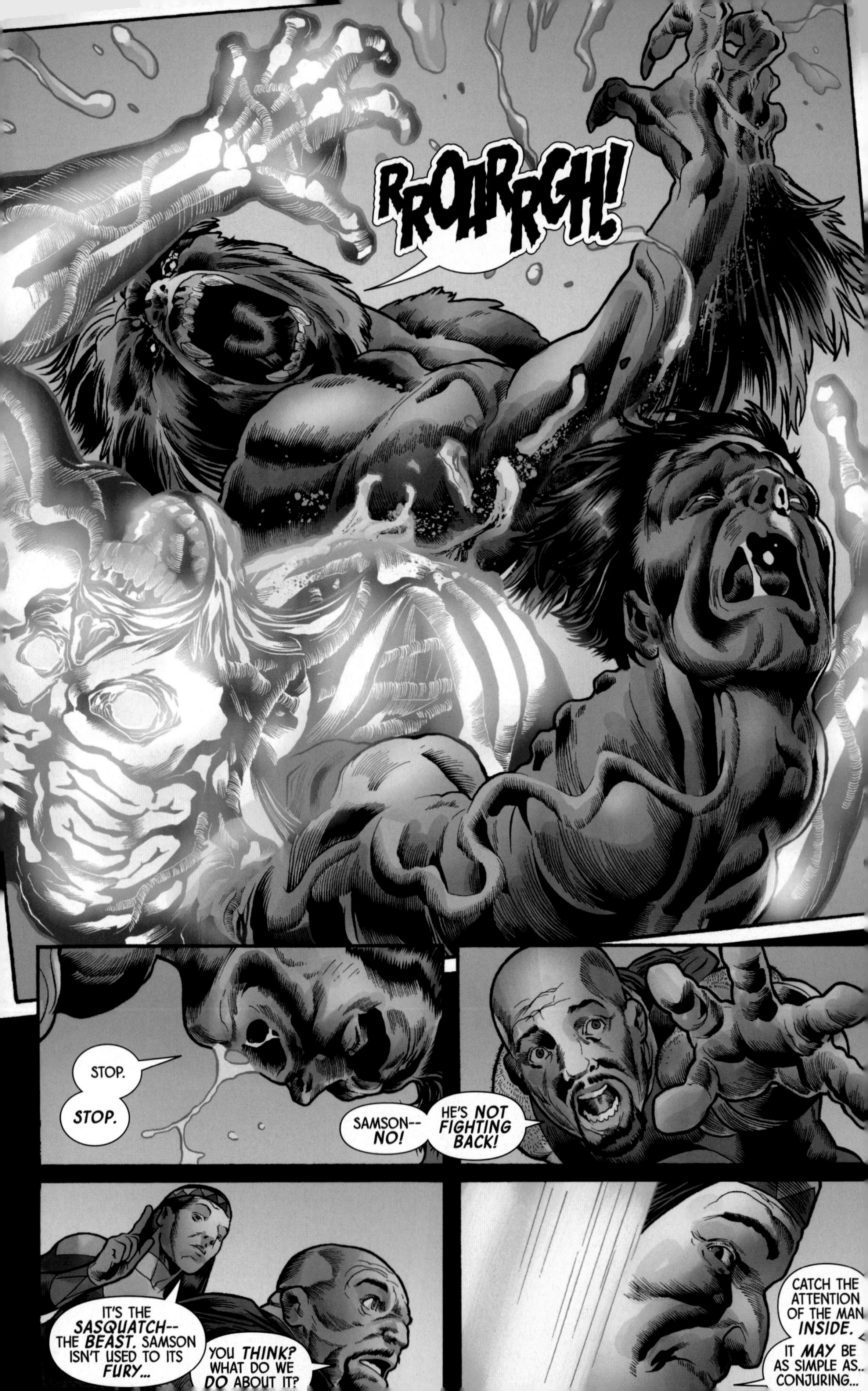
RROARRGH!
STOP.
STOP.
SAMSON-- NO!
HE'S NOT FIGHTING BACK!
IT'S THE SASQUATCH-- THE BEAST. SAMSON ISN'T USED TO ITS FURY...
YOU THINK? WHAT DO WE DO ABOUT IT?
CATCH THE ATTENTION OF THE MAN INSIDE.
IT MAY BE AS SIMPLE AS... CONJURING...

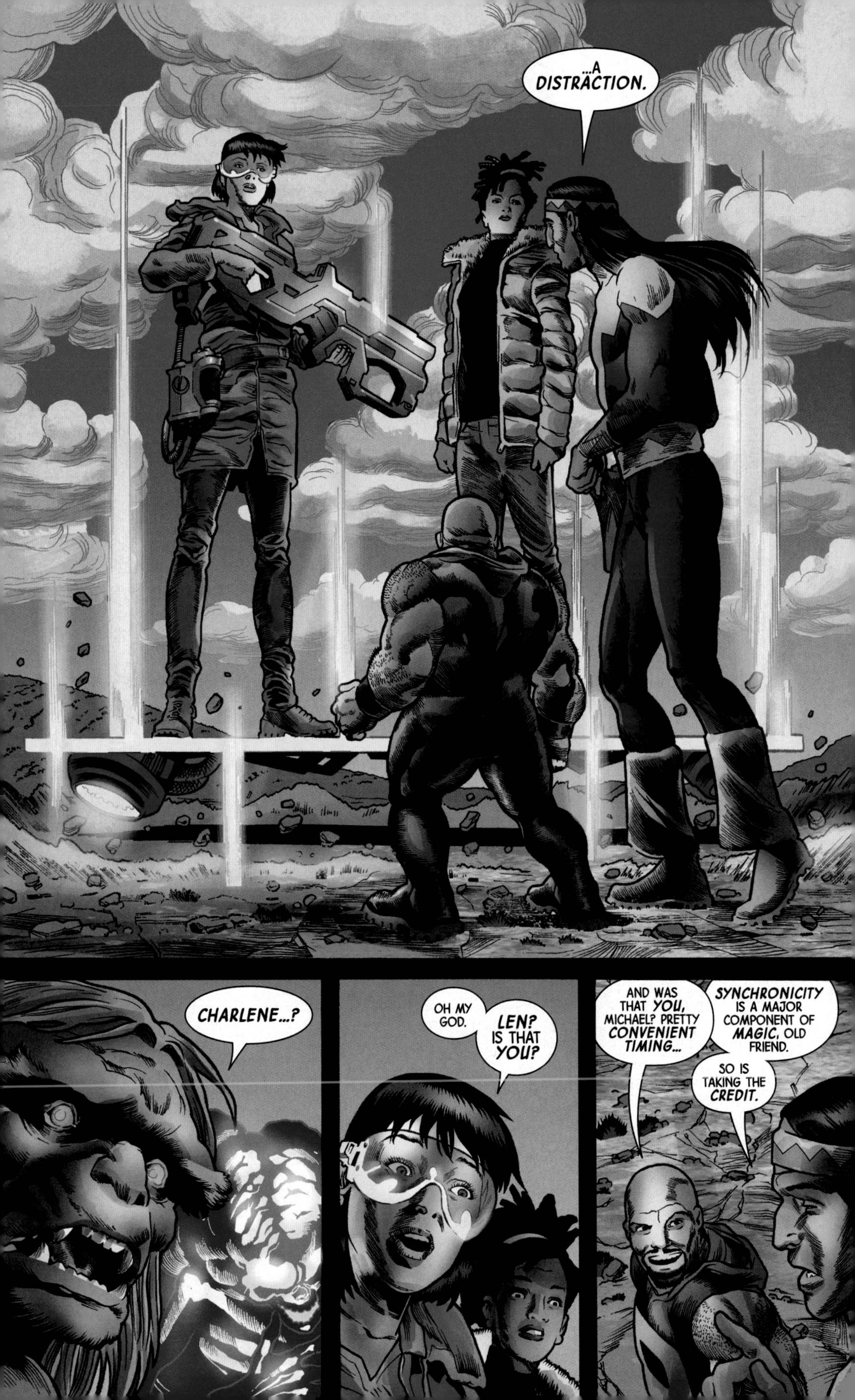
...A DISTRACTION.
CHARLENE...?
OH MY GOD.
LEN? IS THAT YOU?
AND WAS THAT YOU, MICHAEL? PRETTY CONVENIENT TIMING...
SYNCHRONICITY IS A MAJOR COMPONENT OF MAGIC, OLD FRIEND.
SO IS TAKING THE CREDIT.

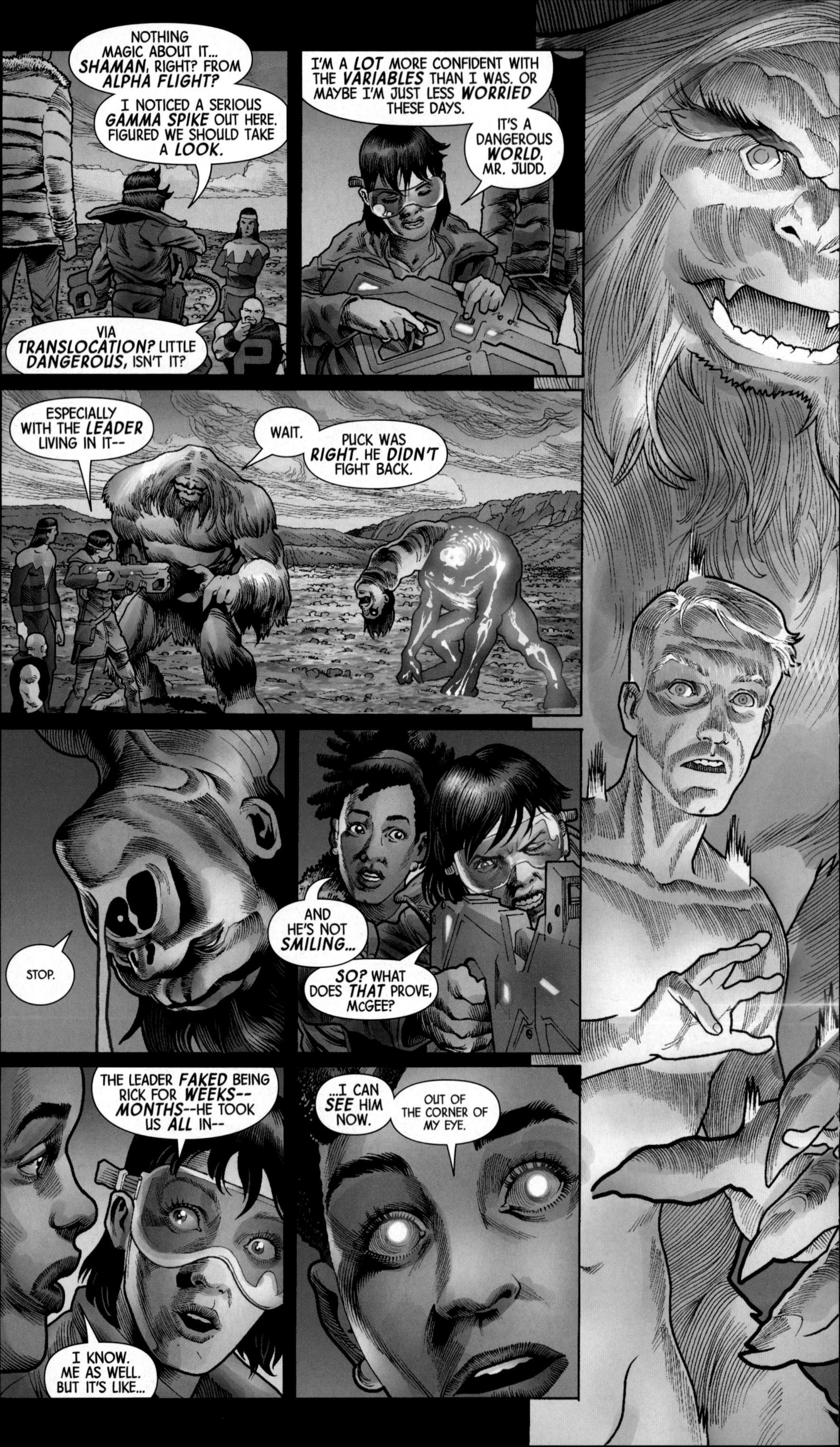
NOTHING MAGIC ABOUT IT... SHAMAN, RIGHT? FROM ALPHA FLIGHT?
I NOTICED A SERIOUS GAMMA SPIKE OUT HERE. FIGURED WE SHOULD TAKE A LOOK.
VIA TRANSLOCATION? LITTLE DANGEROUS, ISN'T IT?
I'M A LOT MORE CONFIDENT WITH THE VARIABLES THAN I WAS. OR MAYBE I'M JUST LESS WORRIED THESE DAYS.
IT'S A DANGEROUS WORLD, MR. JUDD.
ESPECIALLY WITH THE LEADER LIVING IN IT--
WAIT.
PUCK WAS RIGHT. HE DIDN'T FIGHT BACK.
STOP.
AND HE'S NOT SMILING...
SO? WHAT DOES THAT PROVE, McGEE?
THE LEADER FAKED BEING RICK FOR WEEKS--MONTHS--HE TOOK US ALL IN--
I KNOW. ME AS WELL. BUT IT'S LIKE...
...I CAN SEE HIM NOW.
OUT OF THE CORNER OF MY EYE.

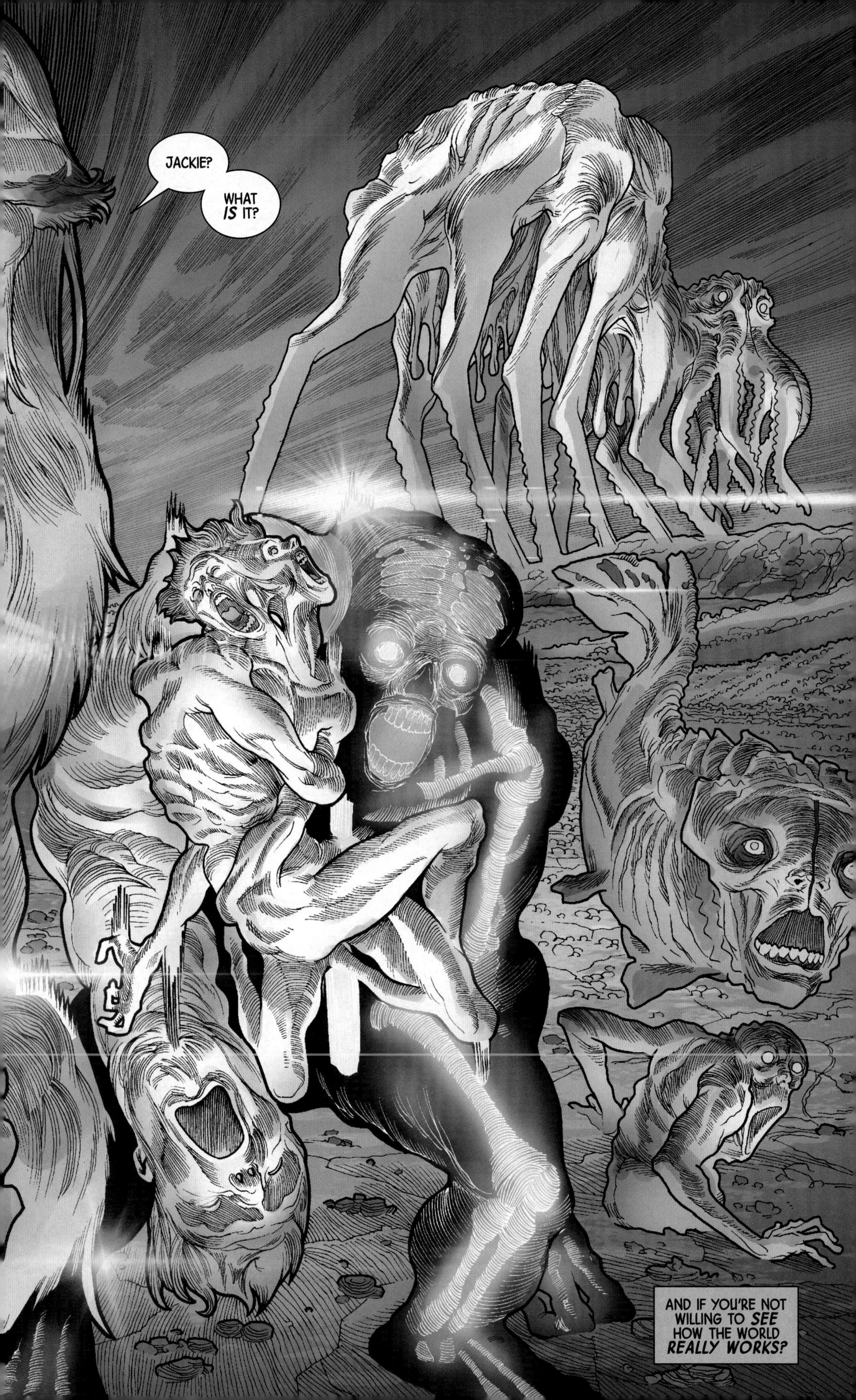
JACKIE?
WHAT IS IT?
AND IF YOU'RE NOT WILLING TO SEE HOW THE WORLD REALLY WORKS?

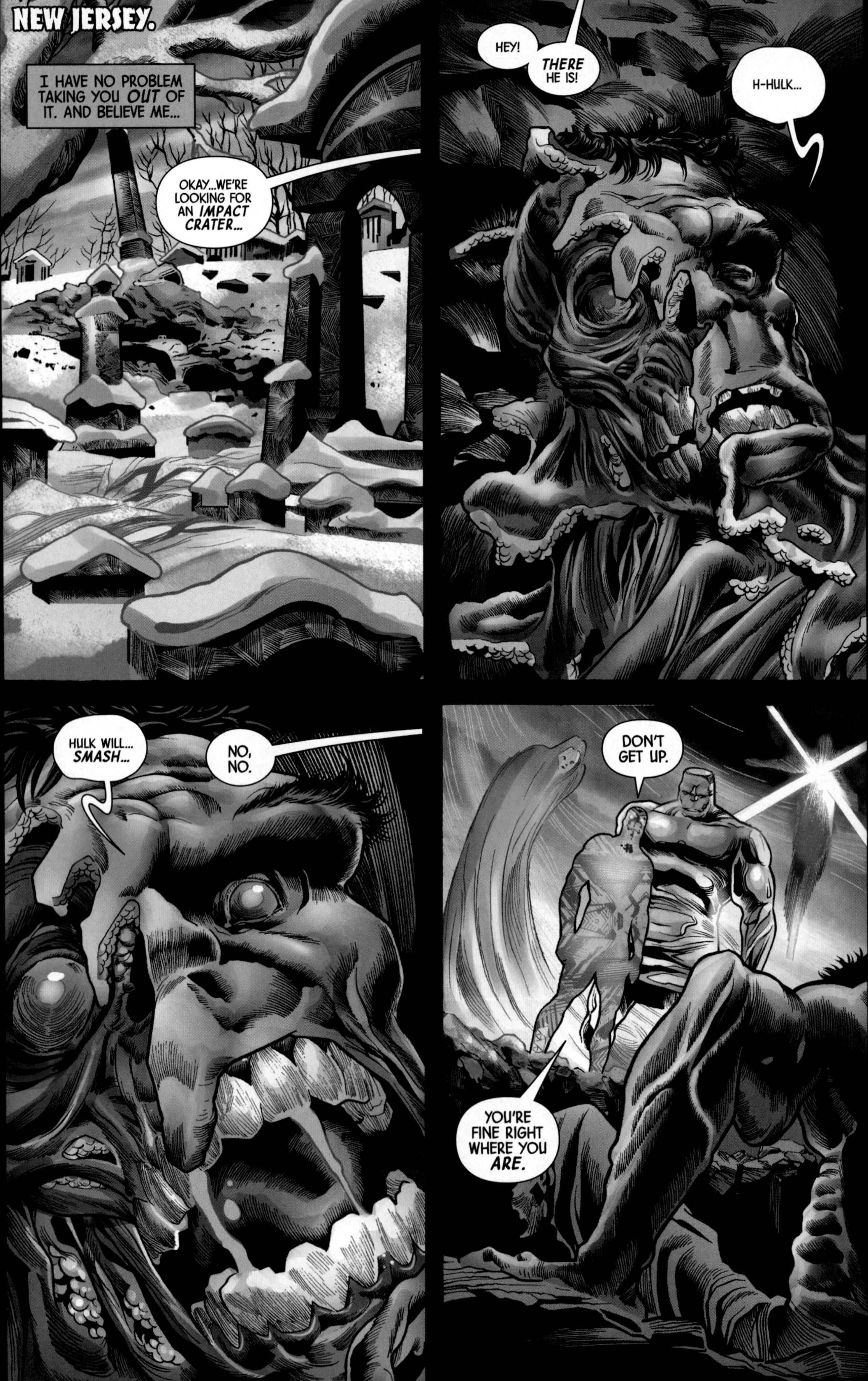
NEW JERSEY.
I HAVE NO PROBLEM TAKING YOU OUT OF IT. AND BELIEVE ME...
OKAY...WE'RE LOOKING FOR AN IMPACT CRATER...
HEY! THERE HE IS!
H-HULK...
HULK WILL... SMASH...
NO, NO.
DON'T GET UP.
YOU'RE FINE RIGHT WHERE YOU ARE.

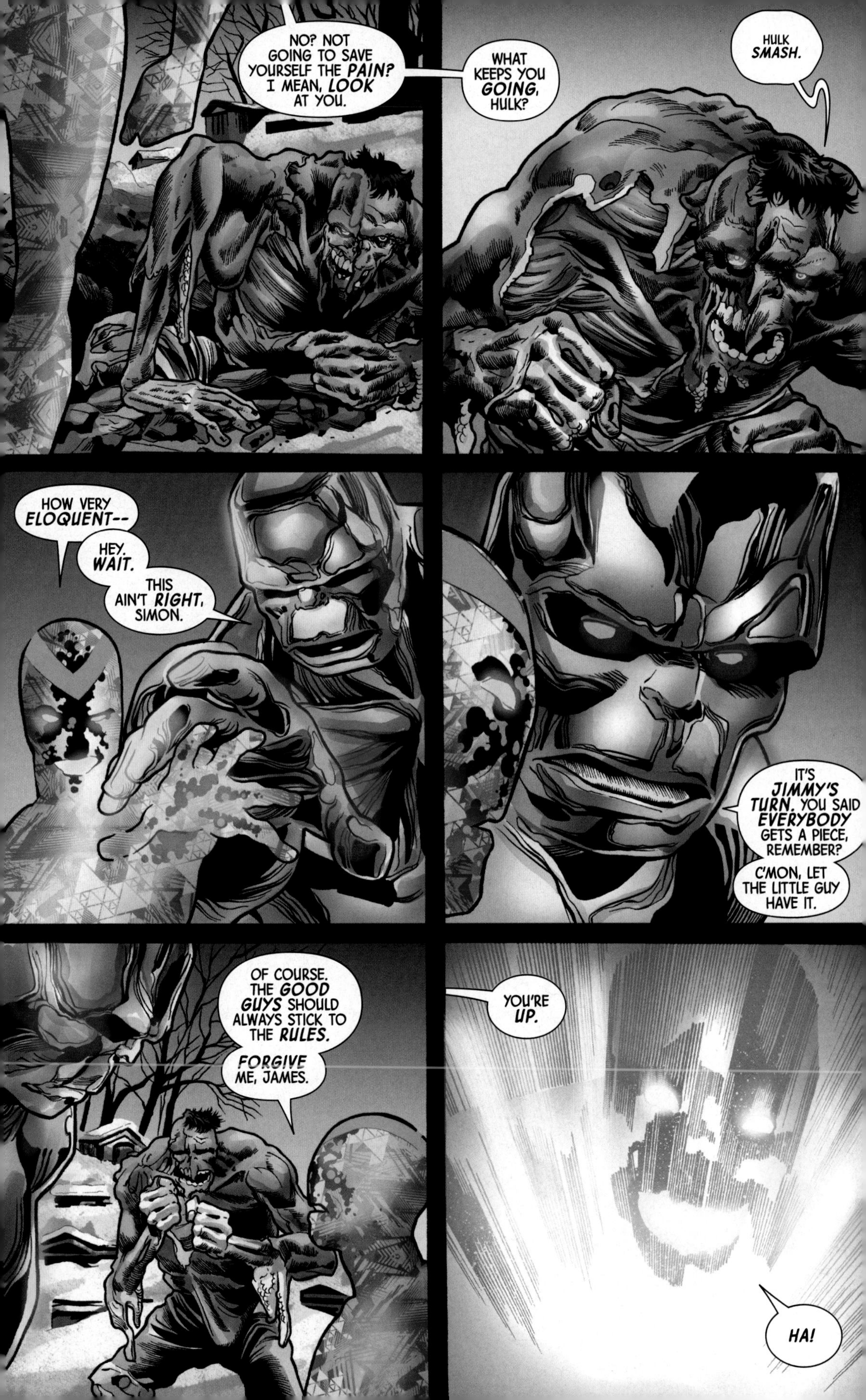
NO? NOT GOING TO SAVE YOURSELF THE PAIN? I MEAN, LOOK AT YOU.
WHAT KEEPS YOU GOING, HULK?
HULK SMASH.
HOW VERY ELOQUENT--
HEY. WAIT.
THIS AIN'T RIGHT, SIMON.
IT'S JIMMY'S TURN. YOU SAID EVERYBODY GETS A PIECE, REMEMBER?
C'MON, LET THE LITTLE GUY HAVE IT.
OF COURSE. THE GOOD GUYS SHOULD ALWAYS STICK TO THE RULES.
FORGIVE ME, JAMES.
YOU'RE UP.
HA!

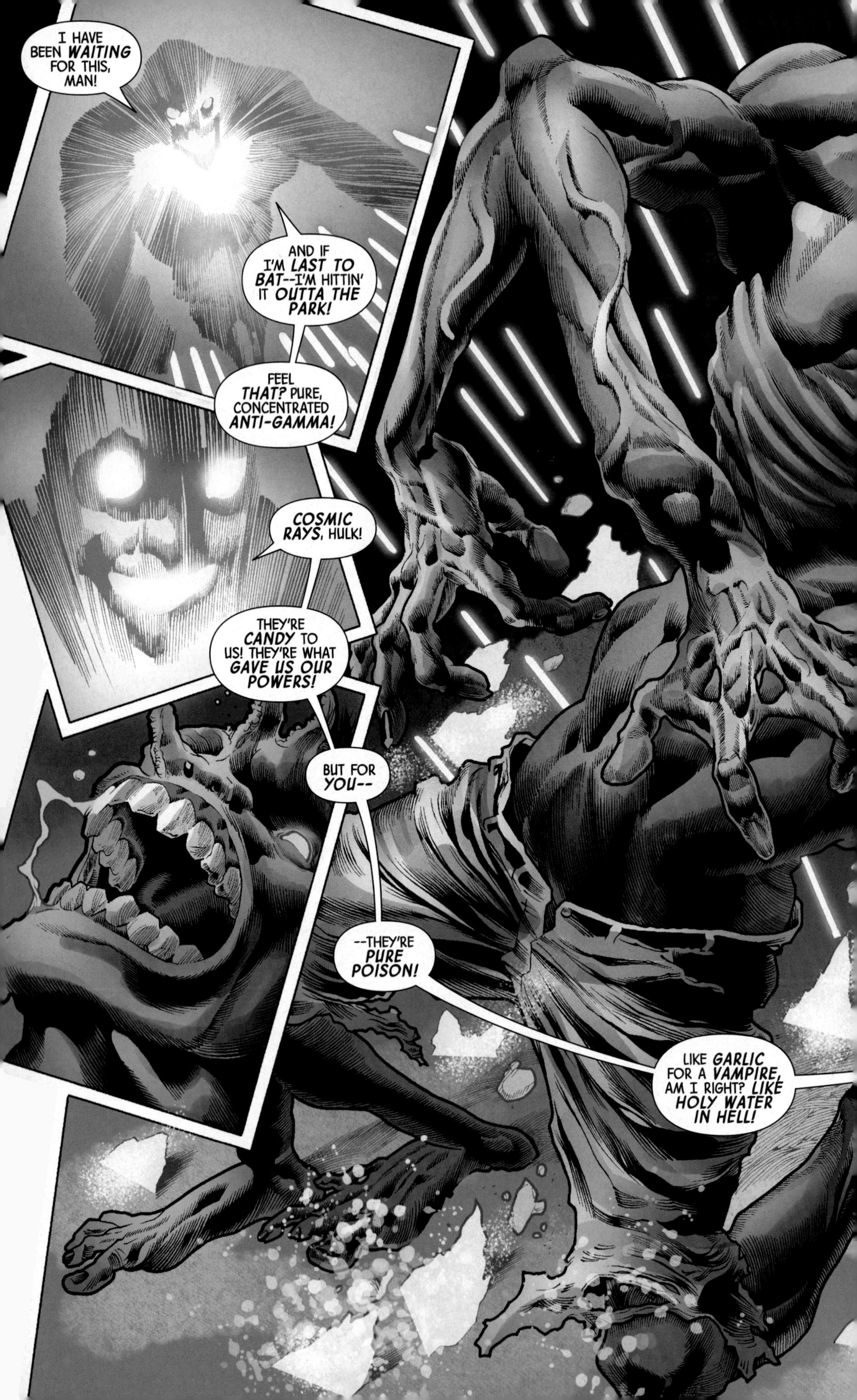
I HAVE BEEN WAITING FOR THIS, MAN!
AND IF I'M LAST TO BAT--I'M HITTIN' IT OUTTA THE PARK!
FEEL THAT? PURE, CONCENTRATED ANTI-GAMMA!
COSMIC RAYS, HULK!
THEY'RE CANDY TO US! THEY'RE WHAT GAVE US OUR POWERS!
BUT FOR YOU--
--THEY'RE PURE POISON!
LIKE GARLIC FOR A VAMPIRE, AM I RIGHT? LIKE HOLY WATER IN HELL!

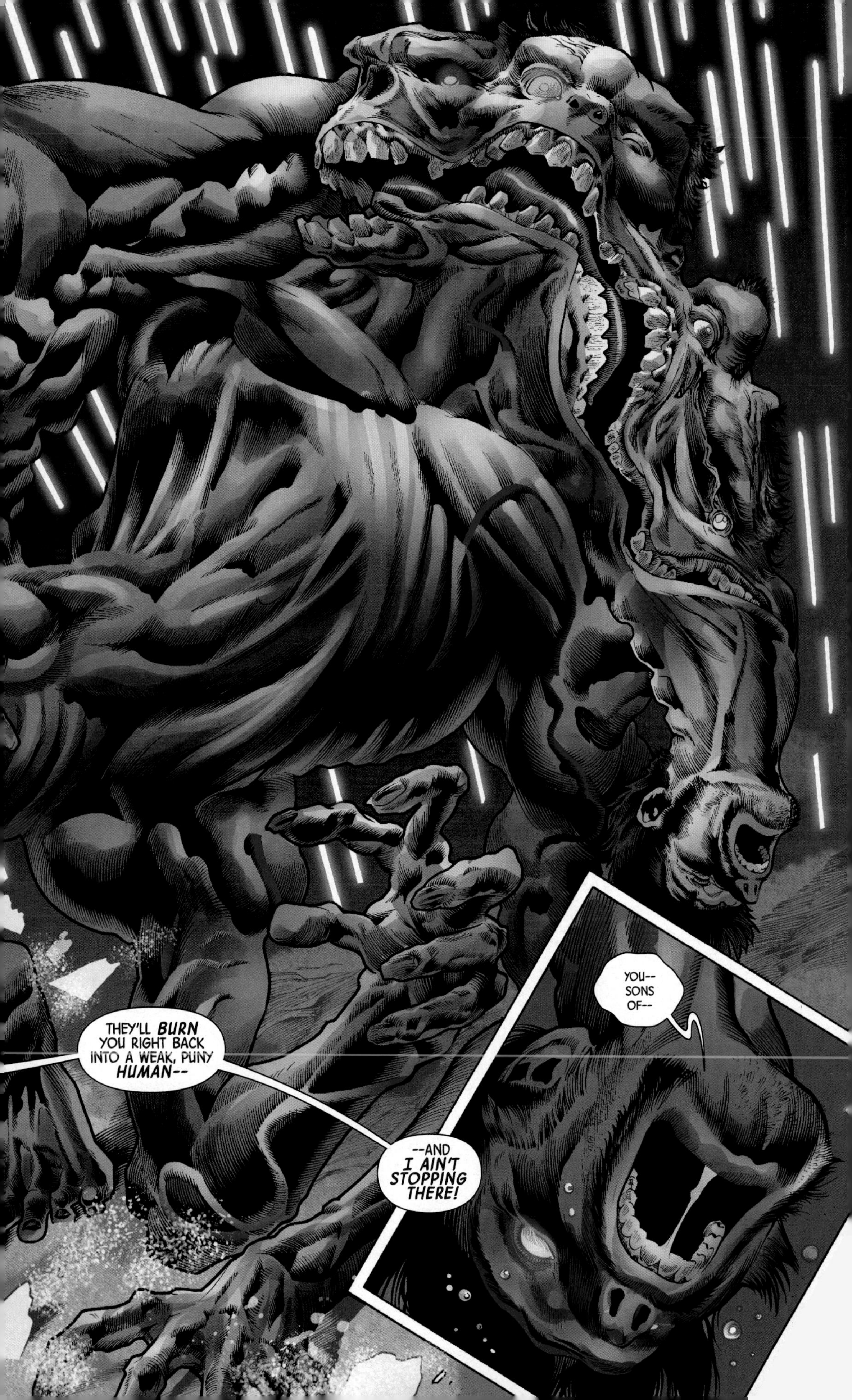
THEY'LL BURN YOU RIGHT BACK INTO A WEAK, PUNY HUMAN--
YOU-- SONS OF--
--AND I AIN'T STOPPING THERE!

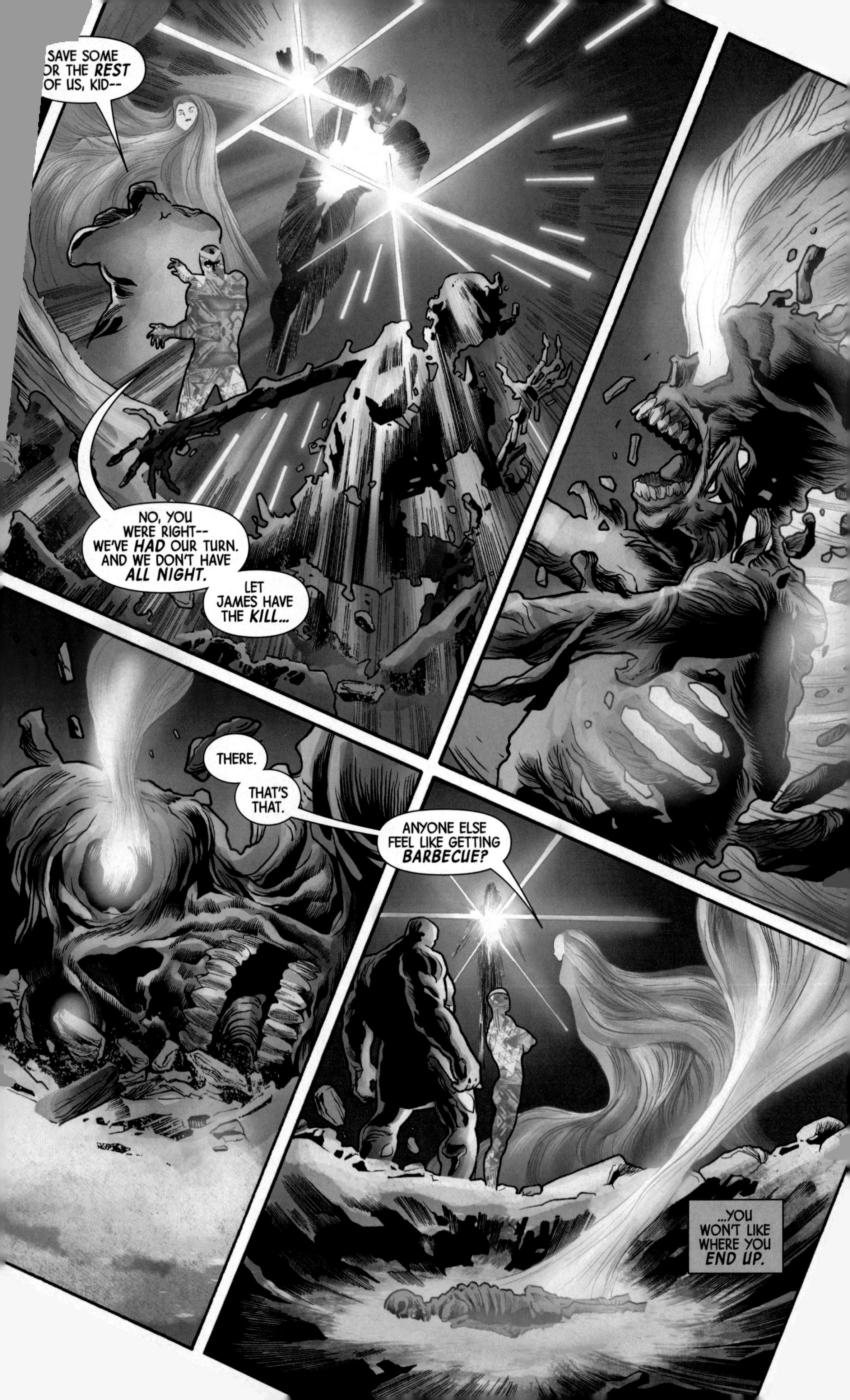
SAVE SOME
OR THE REST
OF US, KID--
NO, YOU WERE RIGHT-- WE'VE HAD OUR TURN. AND WE DON'T HAVE ALL NIGHT.
LET JAMES HAVE THE KILL...
THERE.
THAT'S THAT.
ANYONE ELSE FEEL LIKE GETTING BARBECUE?
...YOU WON'T LIKE WHERE YOU END UP.

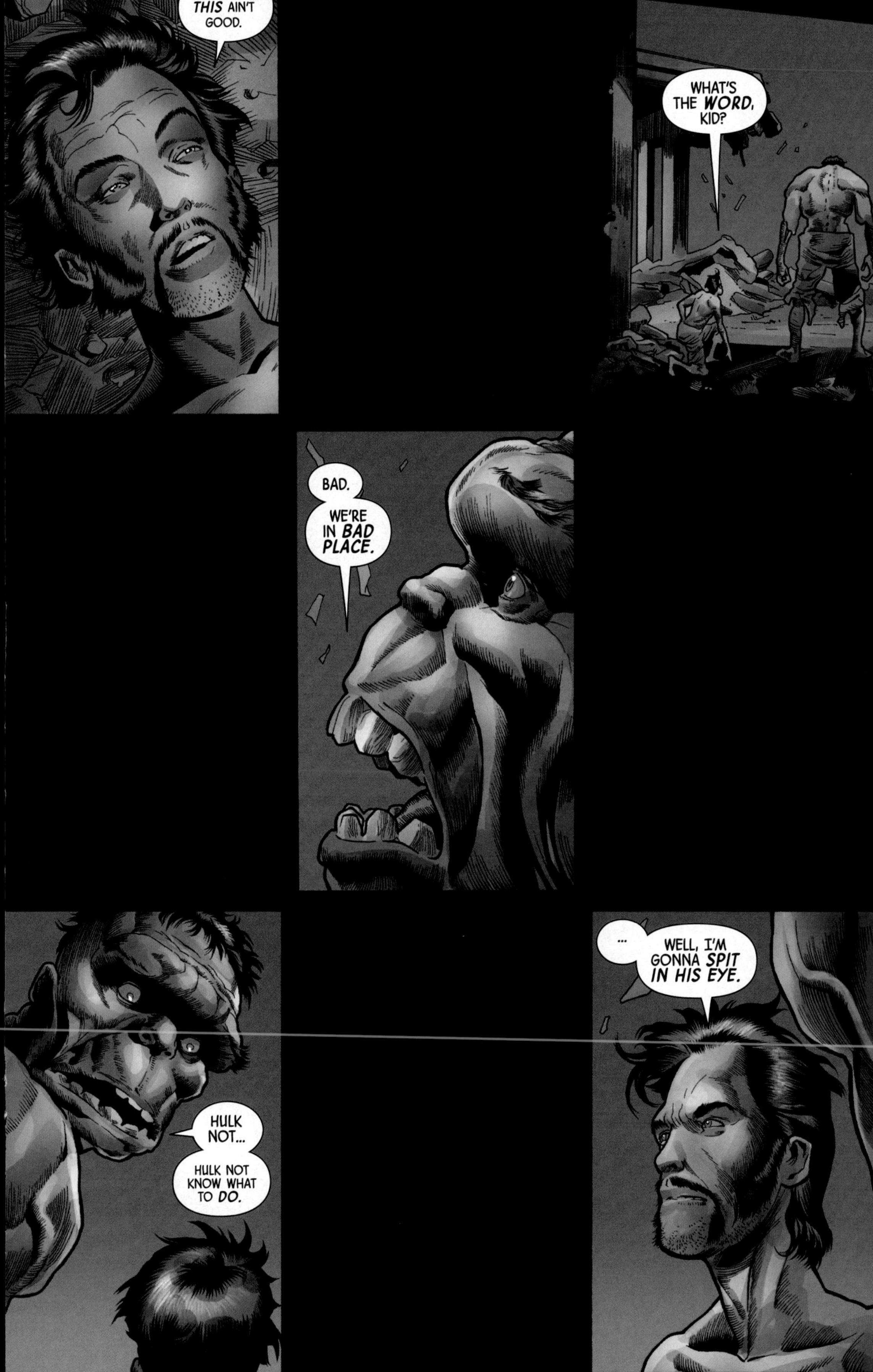
THIS AIN'T GOOD.
WHAT'S THE WORD, KID?
BAD.
WE'RE IN BAD PLACE.
HULK NOT...
HULK NOT KNOW WHAT TO DO.
...
WELL, I'M GONNA SPIT IN HIS EYE.

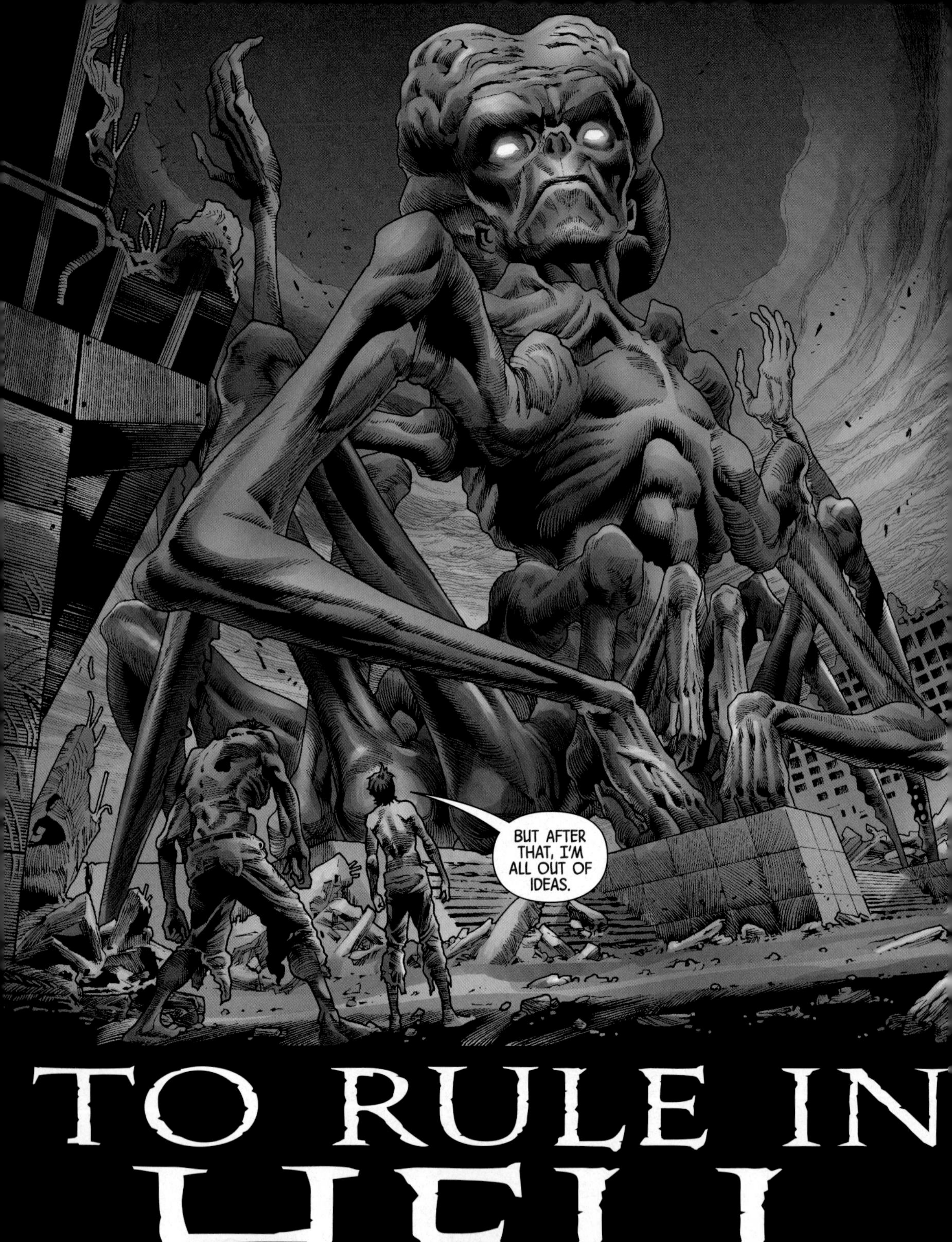
BUT AFTER THAT, I'M ALL OUT OF IDEAS.

TO RULE IN HELL

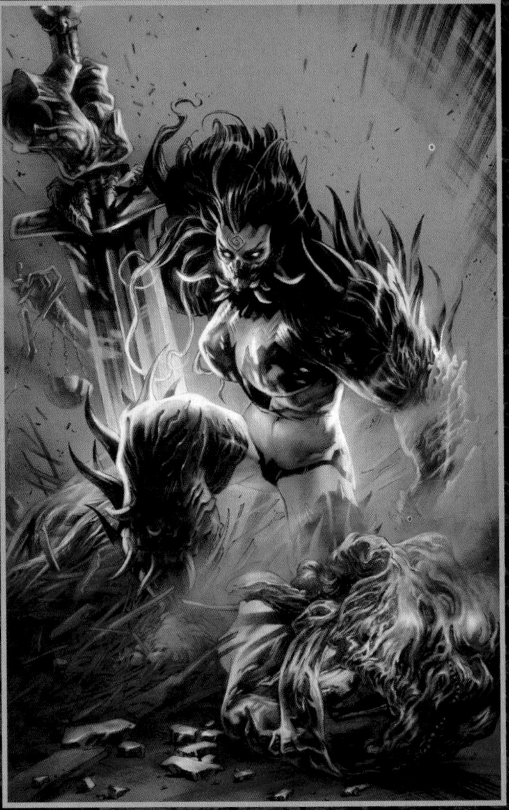

ALEXANDER LOZANO
#42 KNULLIFIED VARIANT

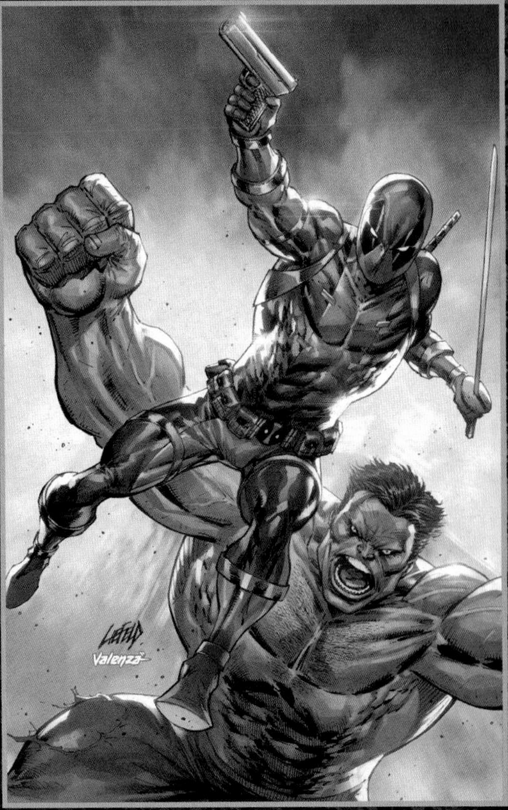

ROB LIEFELD
#45 DEADPOOL 30TH ANNIVERSARY VARIANT

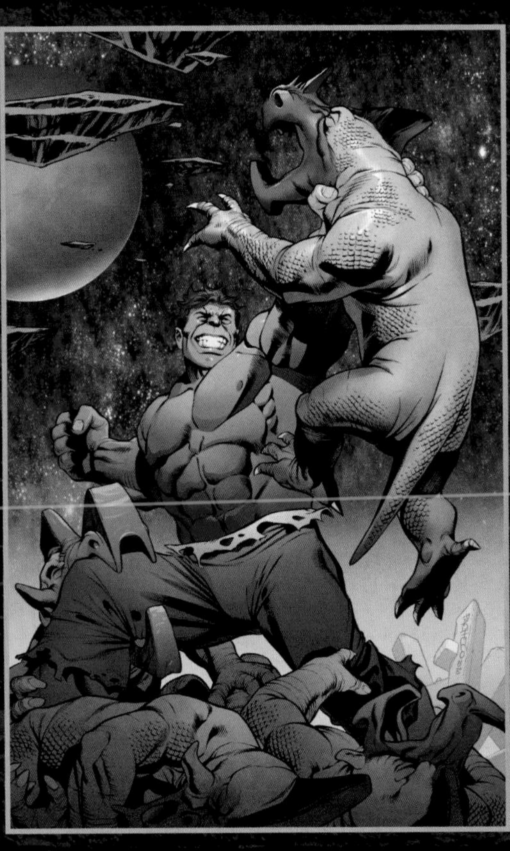

CARLOS PACHECO, RAFAEL FONTERIZ & MATT MILLA

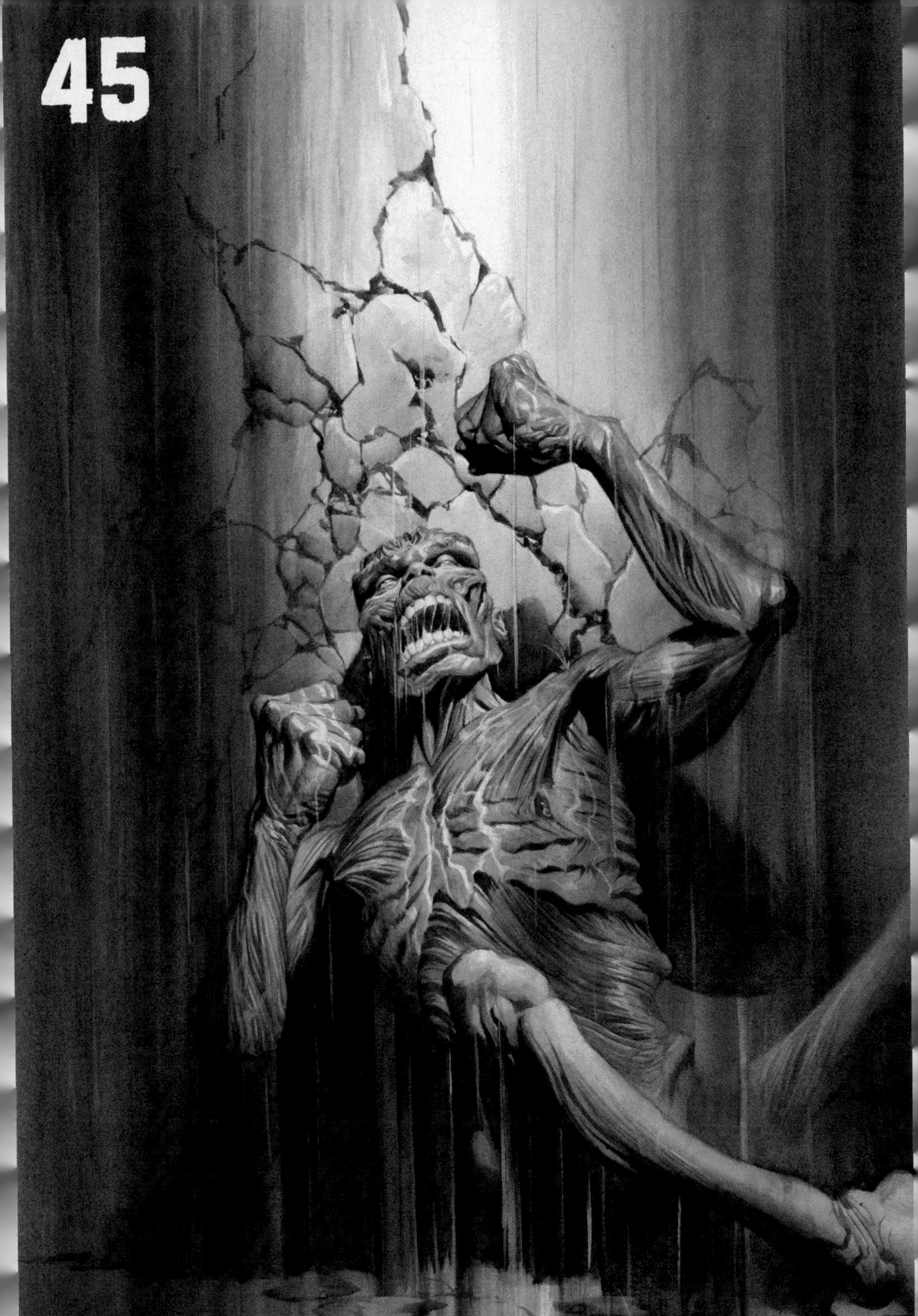
45

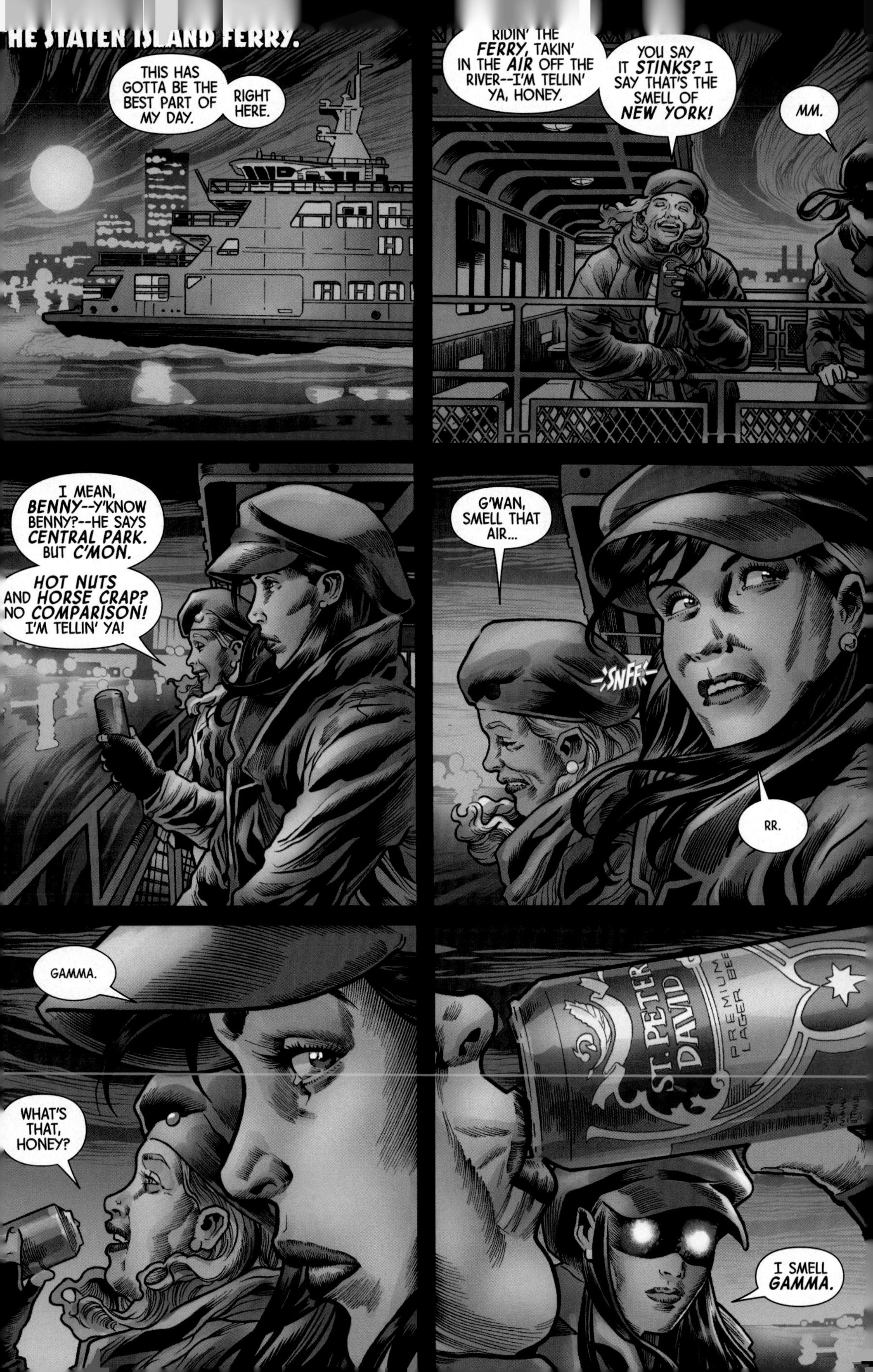
HE STATEN ISLAND FERRY.
THIS HAS GOTTA BE THE BEST PART OF MY DAY.
RIGHT HERE.
RIDIN' THE FERRY, TAKIN' IN THE AIR OFF THE RIVER--I'M TELLIN' YA, HONEY.
YOU SAY IT STINKS? I SAY THAT'S THE SMELL OF NEW YORK!
MM.
I MEAN, BENNY--Y'KNOW BENNY?--HE SAYS CENTRAL PARK. BUT C'MON.
HOT NUTS AND HORSE CRAP? NO COMPARISON! I'M TELLIN' YA!
G'WAN, SMELL THAT AIR...
SNFF
RR.
GAMMA.
WHAT'S THAT, HONEY?
ST. PETER DAVID
PREMIUM LAGER BEE
I SMELL GAMMA.

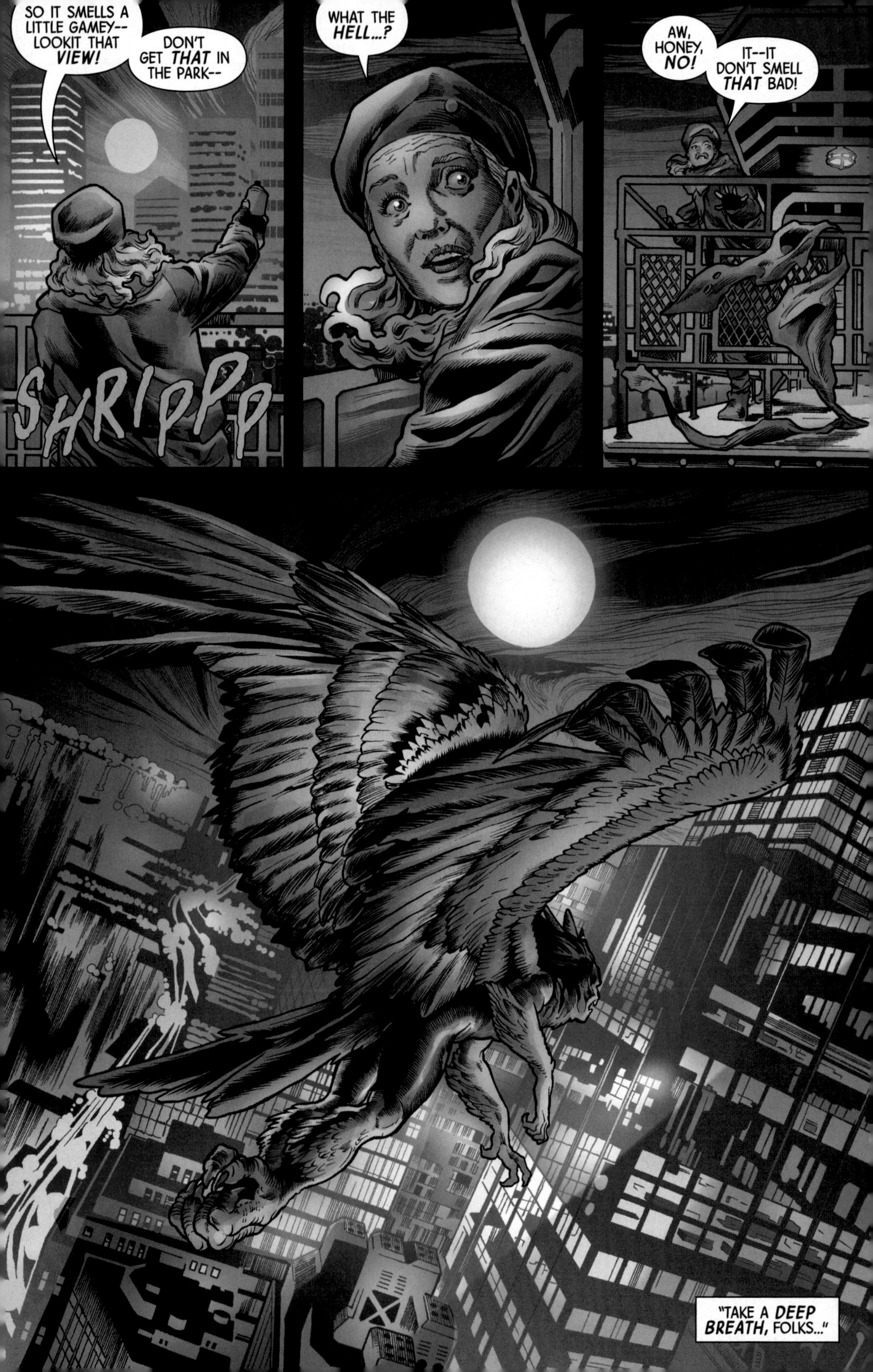
SO IT SMELLS A LITTLE GAMEY-- LOOKIT THAT VIEW!
DON'T GET THAT IN THE PARK--
SHRIPPP
WHAT THE HELL...?
AW, HONEY, NO!
IT--IT DON'T SMELL THAT BAD!
"TAKE A DEEP BREATH, FOLKS..."

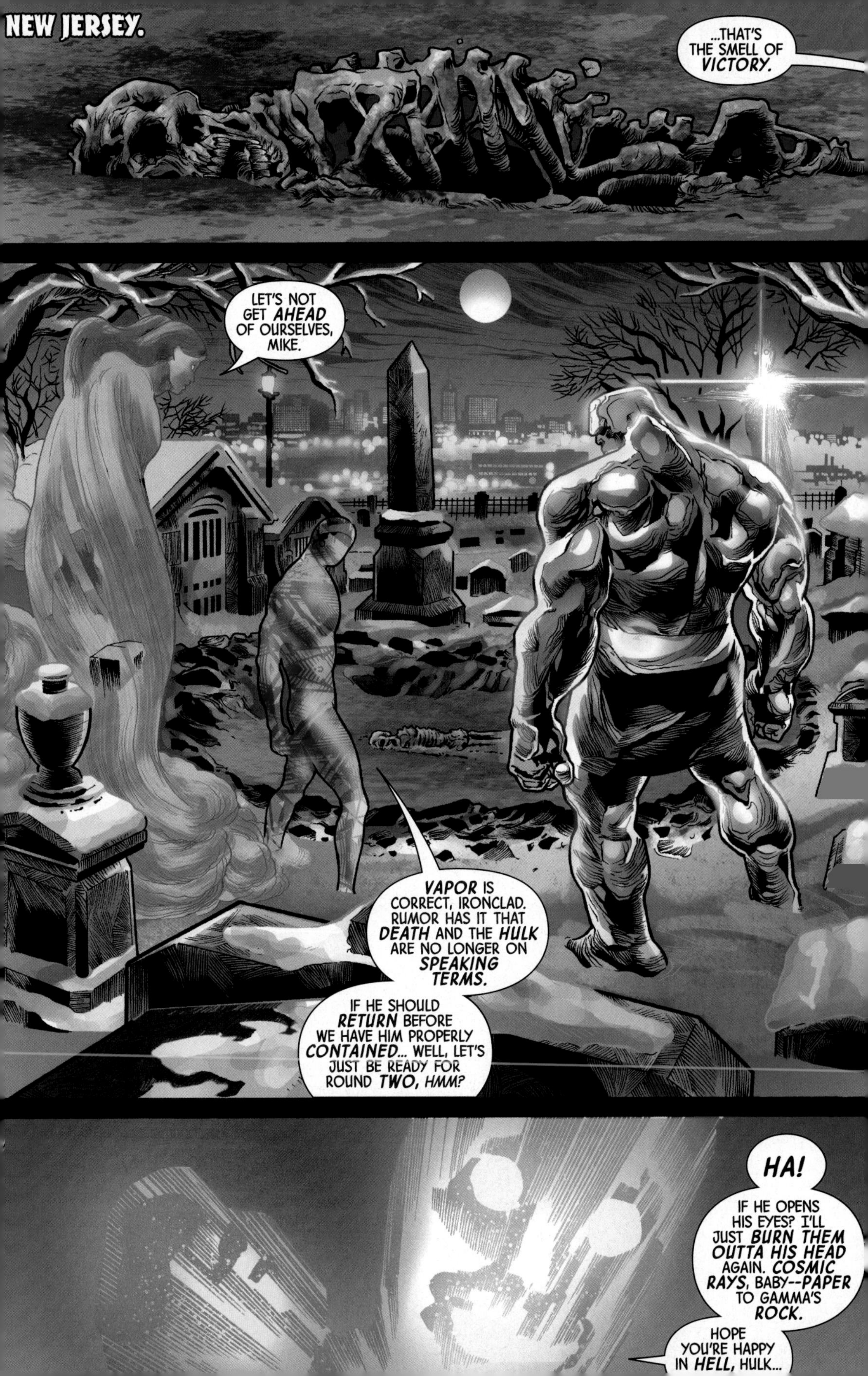
NEW JERSEY.
...THAT'S THE SMELL OF VICTORY.
LET'S NOT GET AHEAD OF OURSELVES, MIKE.
VAPOR IS CORRECT, IRONCLAD. RUMOR HAS IT THAT DEATH AND THE HULK ARE NO LONGER ON SPEAKING TERMS.
IF HE SHOULD RETURN BEFORE WE HAVE HIM PROPERLY CONTAINED... WELL, LET'S JUST BE READY FOR ROUND TWO, HMM?
HA!
IF HE OPENS HIS EYES? I'LL JUST BURN THEM OUTTA HIS HEAD AGAIN. COSMIC RAYS, BABY--PAPER TO GAMMA'S ROCK.
HOPE YOU'RE HAPPY IN HELL, HULK...

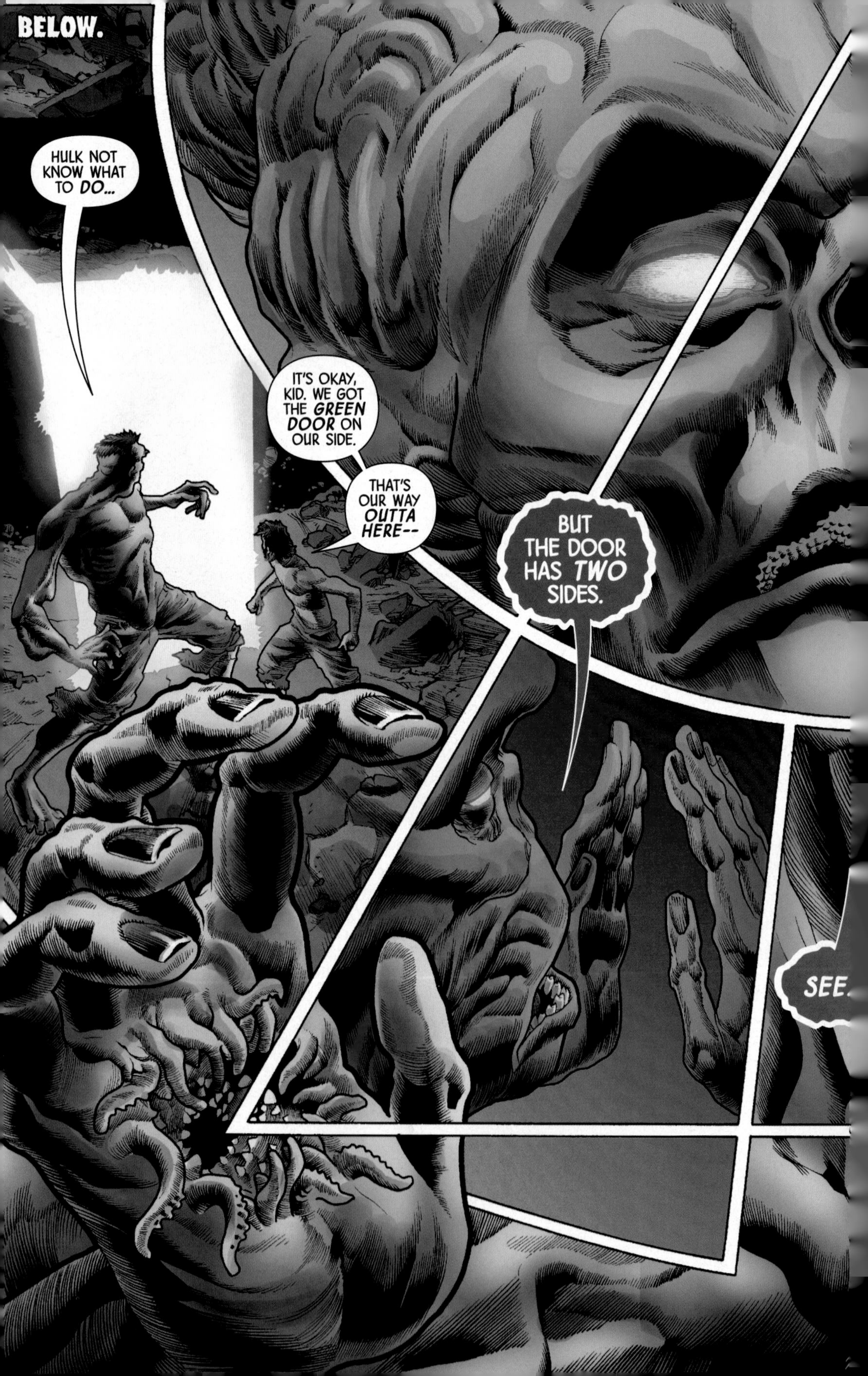
BELOW.
HULK NOT KNOW WHAT TO DO...
IT'S OKAY, KID. WE GOT THE GREEN DOOR ON OUR SIDE.
THAT'S OUR WAY OUTTA HERE--
BUT THE DOOR HAS TWO SIDES.
SEE.

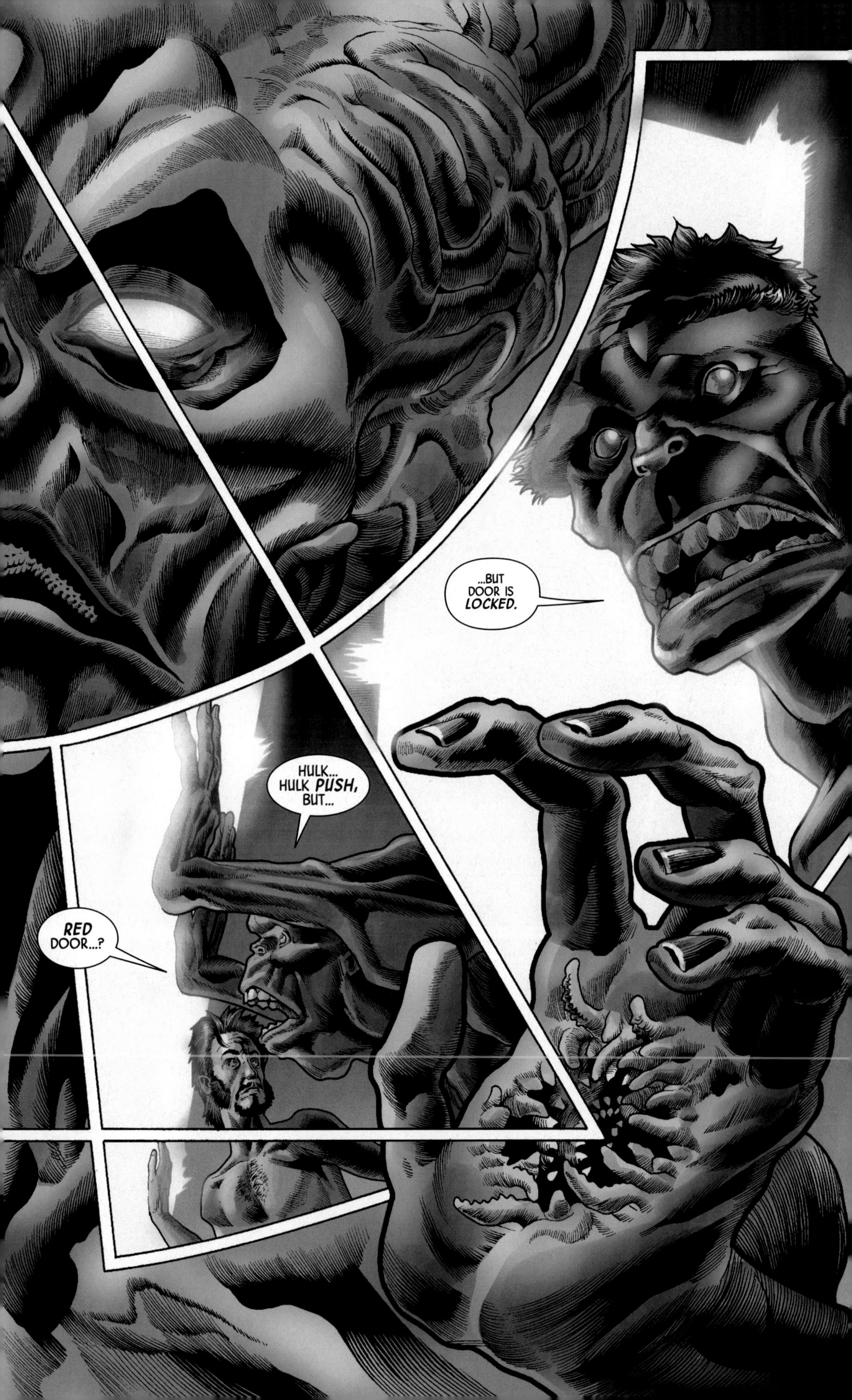
HULK... HULK PUSH, BUT...
...BUT DOOR IS LOCKED.
RED DOOR...?

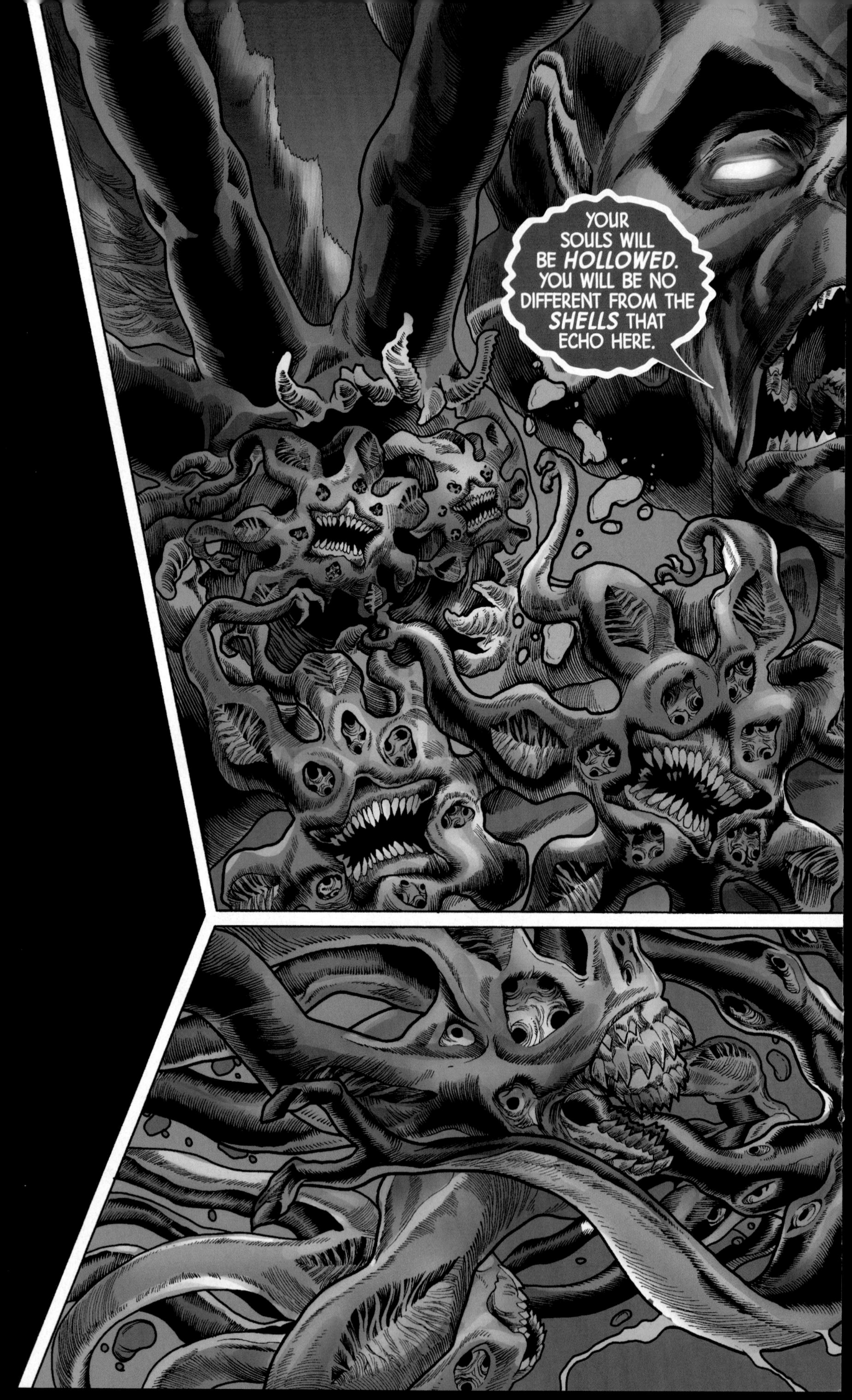
YOUR SOULS WILL BE *HOLLOWED.* YOU WILL BE NO DIFFERENT FROM THE *SHELLS* THAT ECHO HERE.

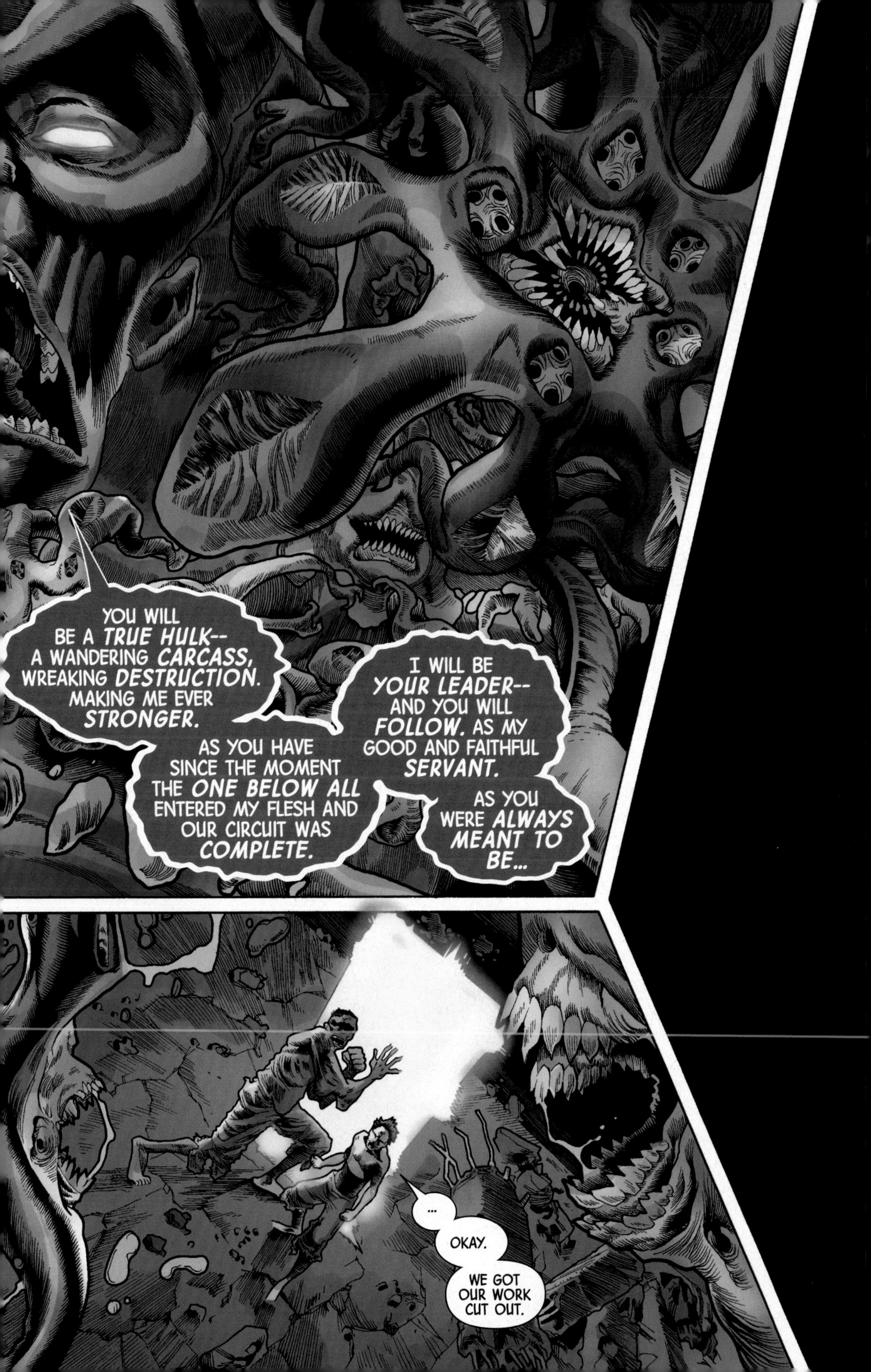
YOU WILL BE A TRUE HULK-- A WANDERING CARCASS, WREAKING DESTRUCTION. MAKING ME EVER STRONGER.
AS YOU HAVE SINCE THE MOMENT THE ONE BELOW ALL ENTERED MY FLESH AND OUR CIRCUIT WAS COMPLETE.
I WILL BE YOUR LEADER-- AND YOU WILL FOLLOW. AS MY GOOD AND FAITHFUL SERVANT.
AS YOU WERE ALWAYS MEANT TO BE...
...
OKAY.
WE GOT OUR WORK CUT OUT.

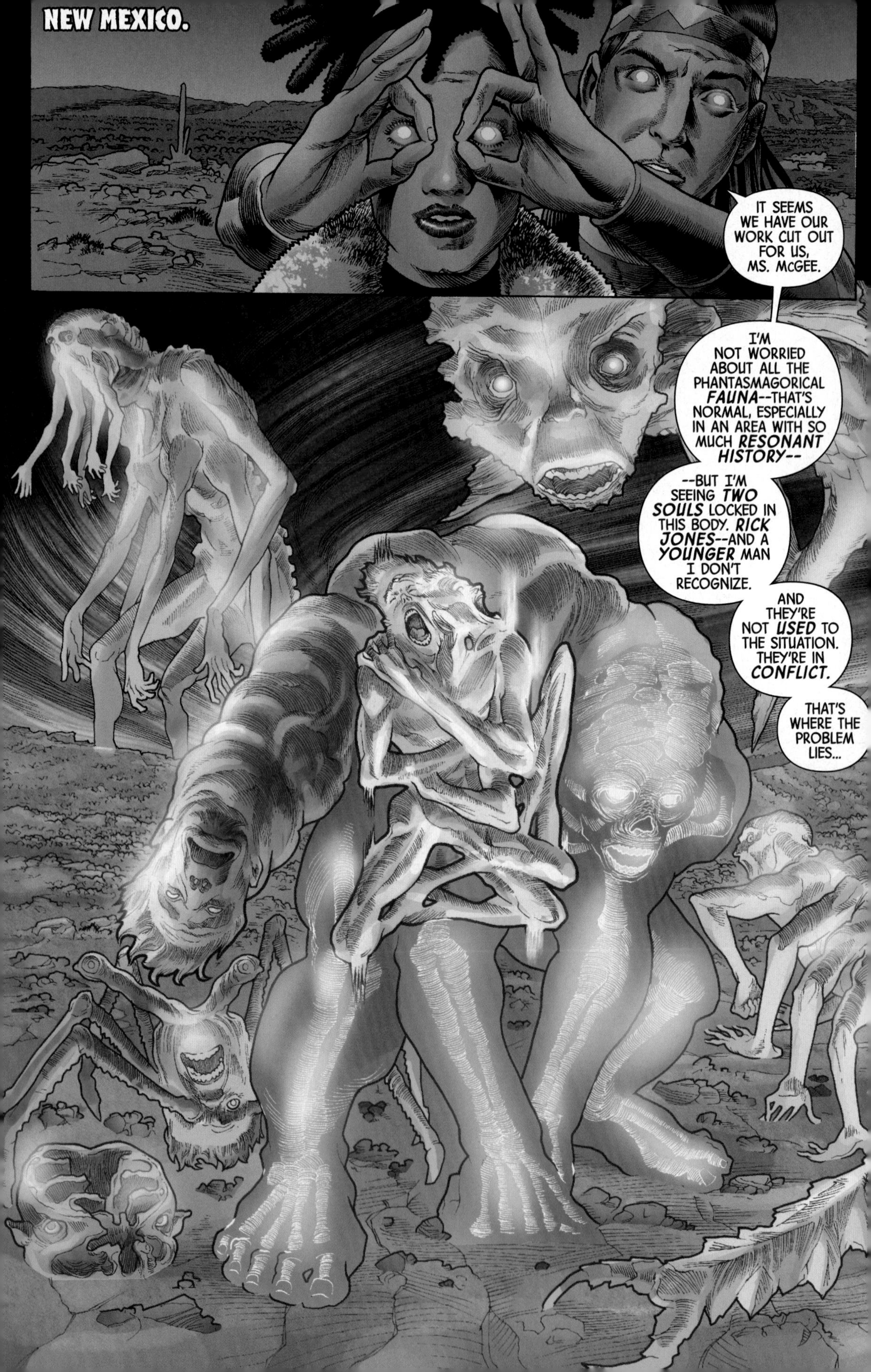
NEW MEXICO.
IT SEEMS WE HAVE OUR WORK CUT OUT FOR US, MS. McGEE.
I'M NOT WORRIED ABOUT ALL THE PHANTASMAGORICAL FAUNA--THAT'S NORMAL, ESPECIALLY IN AN AREA WITH SO MUCH RESONANT HISTORY--
--BUT I'M SEEING TWO SOULS LOCKED IN THIS BODY. RICK JONES--AND A YOUNGER MAN I DON'T RECOGNIZE.
AND THEY'RE NOT USED TO THE SITUATION. THEY'RE IN CONFLICT.
THAT'S WHERE THE PROBLEM LIES...

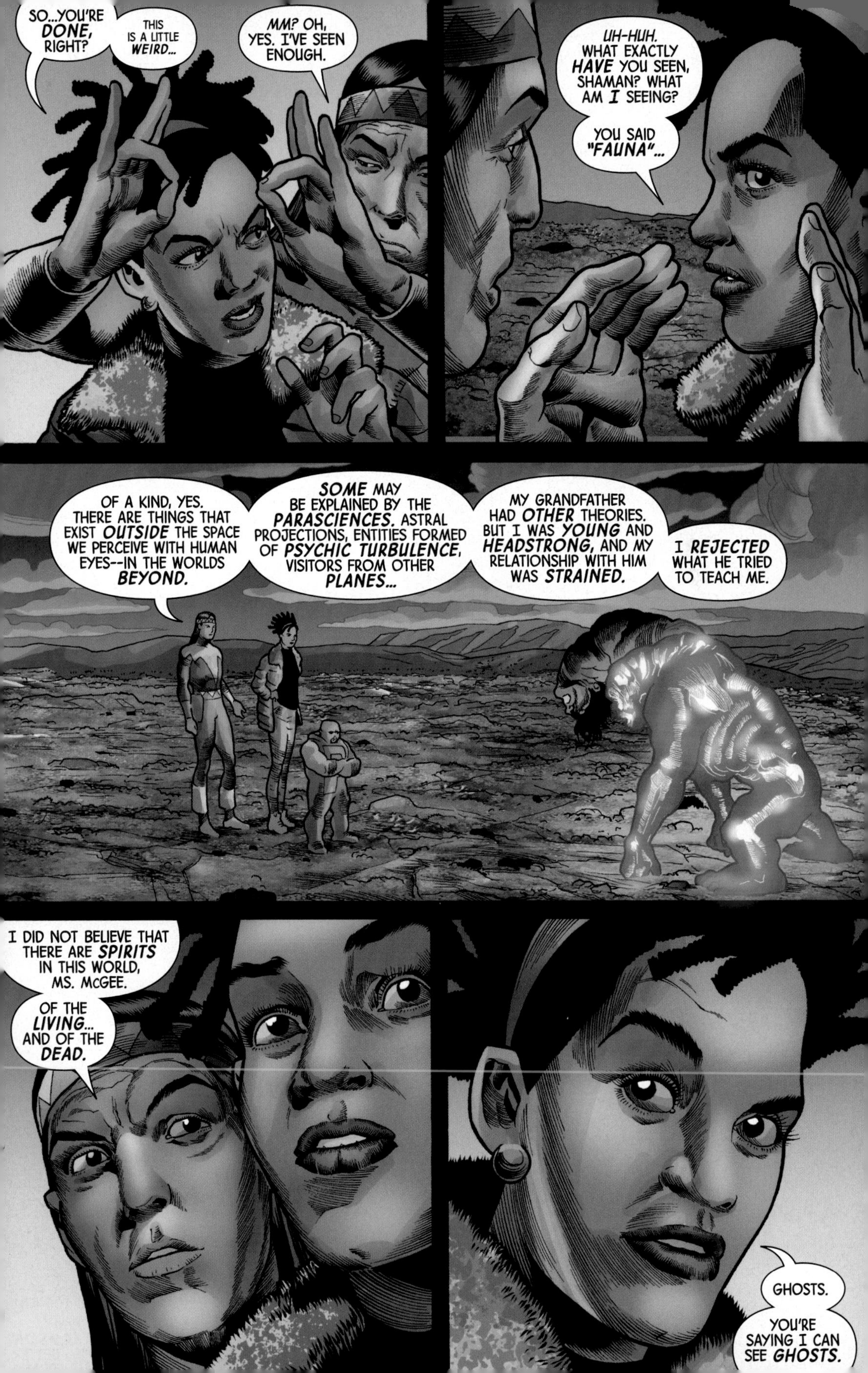
SO...YOU'RE DONE, RIGHT?
THIS IS A LITTLE WEIRD...
MM? OH, YES. I'VE SEEN ENOUGH.
UH-HUH. WHAT EXACTLY HAVE YOU SEEN, SHAMAN? WHAT AM I SEEING?
YOU SAID "FAUNA"...
OF A KIND, YES. THERE ARE THINGS THAT EXIST OUTSIDE THE SPACE WE PERCEIVE WITH HUMAN EYES--IN THE WORLDS BEYOND.
SOME MAY BE EXPLAINED BY THE PARASCIENCES. ASTRAL PROJECTIONS, ENTITIES FORMED OF PSYCHIC TURBULENCE, VISITORS FROM OTHER PLANES...
MY GRANDFATHER HAD OTHER THEORIES. BUT I WAS YOUNG AND HEADSTRONG, AND MY RELATIONSHIP WITH HIM WAS STRAINED.
I REJECTED WHAT HE TRIED TO TEACH ME.
I DID NOT BELIEVE THAT THERE ARE SPIRITS IN THIS WORLD, MS. McGEE.
OF THE LIVING... AND OF THE DEAD.
GHOSTS.
YOU'RE SAYING I CAN SEE GHOSTS.

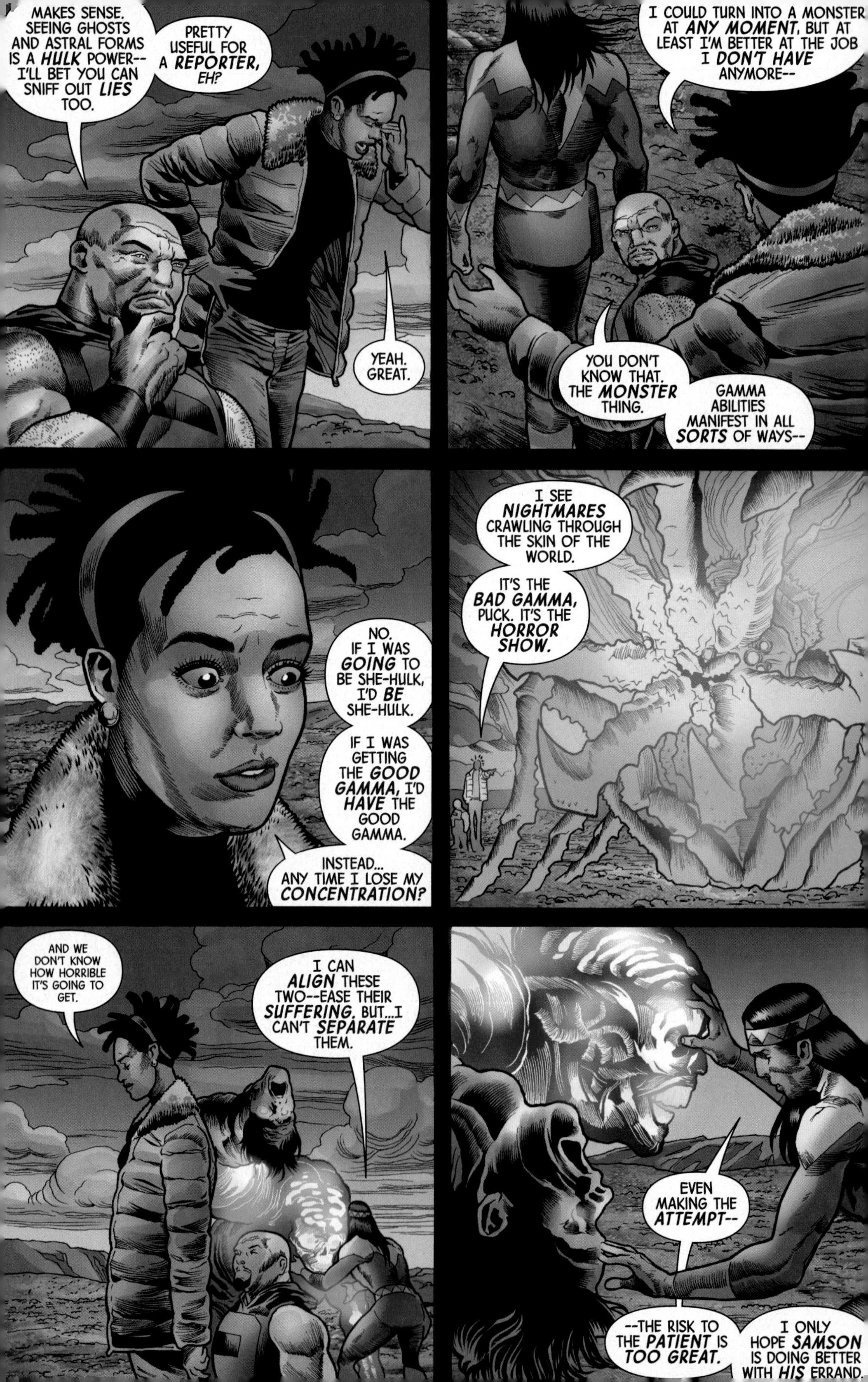

MAKES SENSE. SEEING GHOSTS AND ASTRAL FORMS IS A HULK POWER-- I'LL BET YOU CAN SNIFF OUT LIES TOO.
PRETTY USEFUL FOR A REPORTER, EH?
YEAH. GREAT.
I COULD TURN INTO A MONSTER AT ANY MOMENT, BUT AT LEAST I'M BETTER AT THE JOB I DON'T HAVE ANYMORE--
YOU DON'T KNOW THAT. THE MONSTER THING.
GAMMA ABILITIES MANIFEST IN ALL SORTS OF WAYS--
NO. IF I WAS GOING TO BE SHE-HULK, I'D BE SHE-HULK.
IF I WAS GETTING THE GOOD GAMMA, I'D HAVE THE GOOD GAMMA.
INSTEAD... ANY TIME I LOSE MY CONCENTRATION?
I SEE NIGHTMARES CRAWLING THROUGH THE SKIN OF THE WORLD.
IT'S THE BAD GAMMA, PUCK. IT'S THE HORROR SHOW.
AND WE DON'T KNOW HOW HORRIBLE IT'S GOING TO GET.
I CAN ALIGN THESE TWO--EASE THEIR SUFFERING. BUT...I CAN'T SEPARATE THEM.
EVEN MAKING THE ATTEMPT--
--THE RISK TO THE PATIENT IS TOO GREAT.
I ONLY HOPE SAMSON IS DOING BETTER WITH HIS ERRAND.

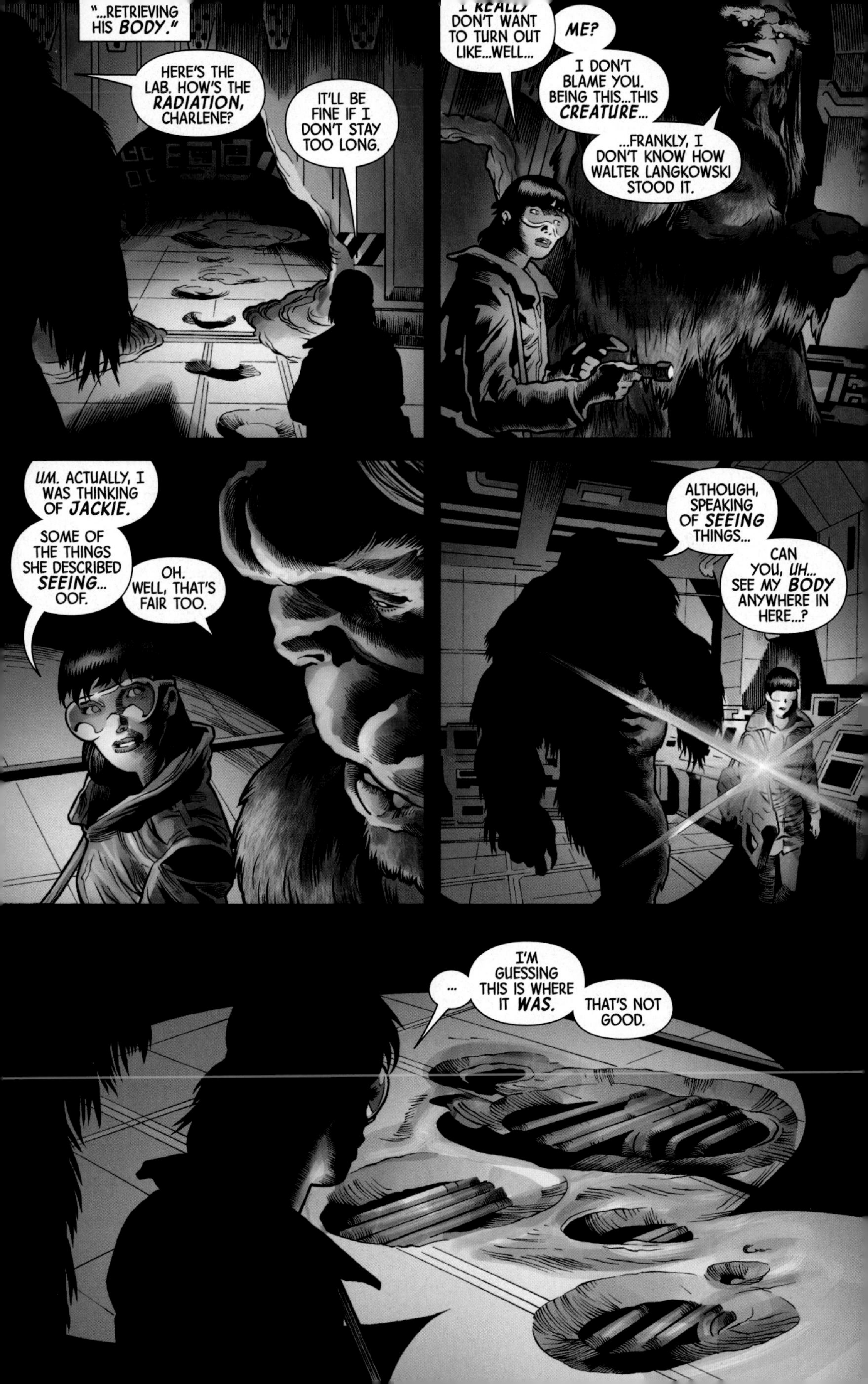

"...RETRIEVING HIS BODY."
HERE'S THE LAB. HOW'S THE RADIATION, CHARLENE?
IT'LL BE FINE IF I DON'T STAY TOO LONG.
I REALLY DON'T WANT TO TURN OUT LIKE...WELL...
ME?
I DON'T BLAME YOU. BEING THIS...THIS CREATURE...
...FRANKLY, I DON'T KNOW HOW WALTER LANGKOWSKI STOOD IT.
UM. ACTUALLY, I WAS THINKING OF JACKIE.
SOME OF THE THINGS SHE DESCRIBED SEEING... OOF.
OH. WELL, THAT'S FAIR TOO.
ALTHOUGH, SPEAKING OF SEEING THINGS...
CAN YOU, UH... SEE MY BODY ANYWHERE IN HERE...?
...
I'M GUESSING THIS IS WHERE IT WAS.
THAT'S NOT GOOD.

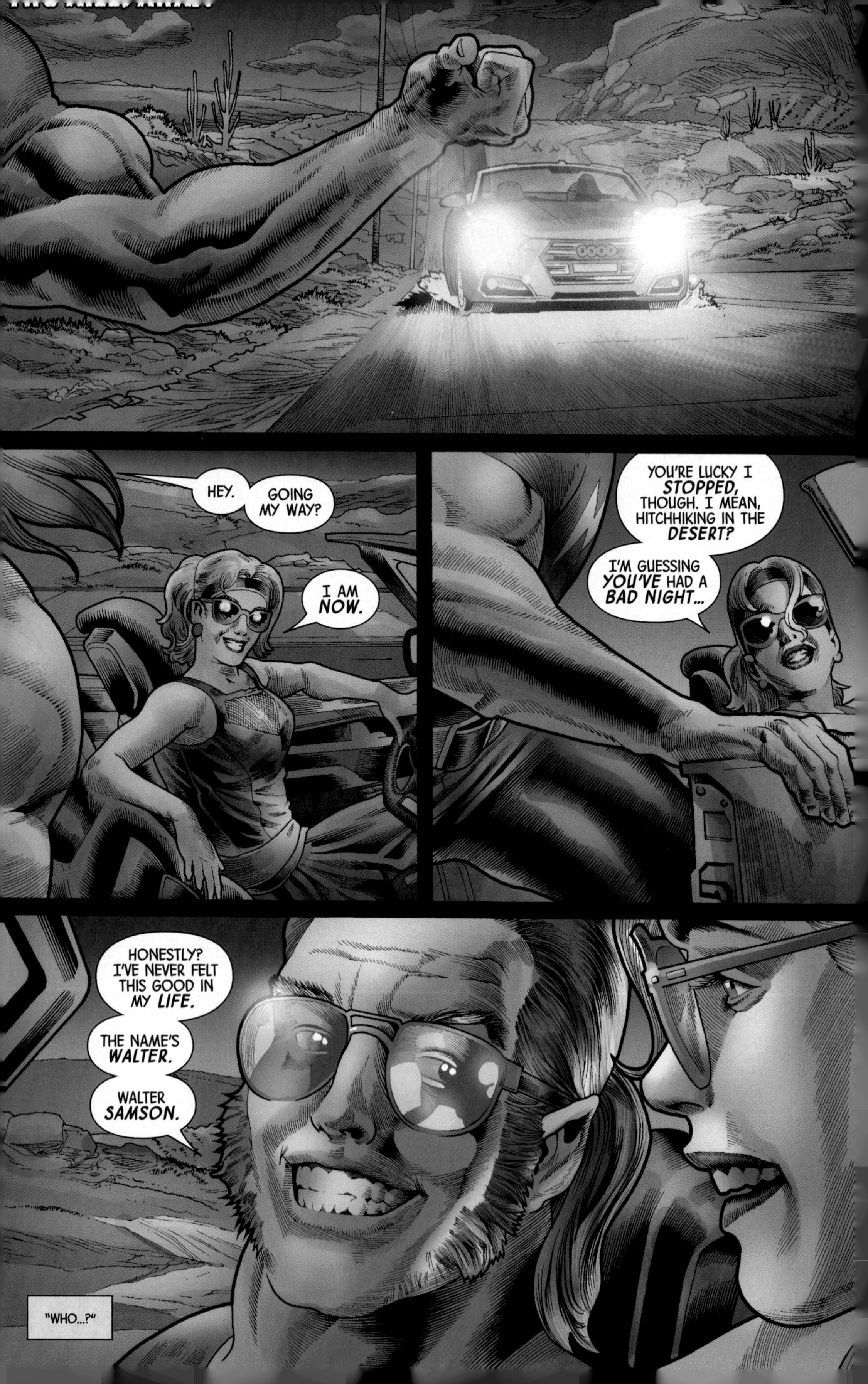
HEY.
GOING MY WAY?
I AM NOW.
YOU'RE LUCKY I STOPPED, THOUGH. I MEAN, HITCHHIKING IN THE DESERT?
I'M GUESSING YOU'VE HAD A BAD NIGHT...
HONESTLY? I'VE NEVER FELT THIS GOOD IN MY LIFE.
THE NAME'S WALTER.
WALTER SAMSON.
"WHO...?"

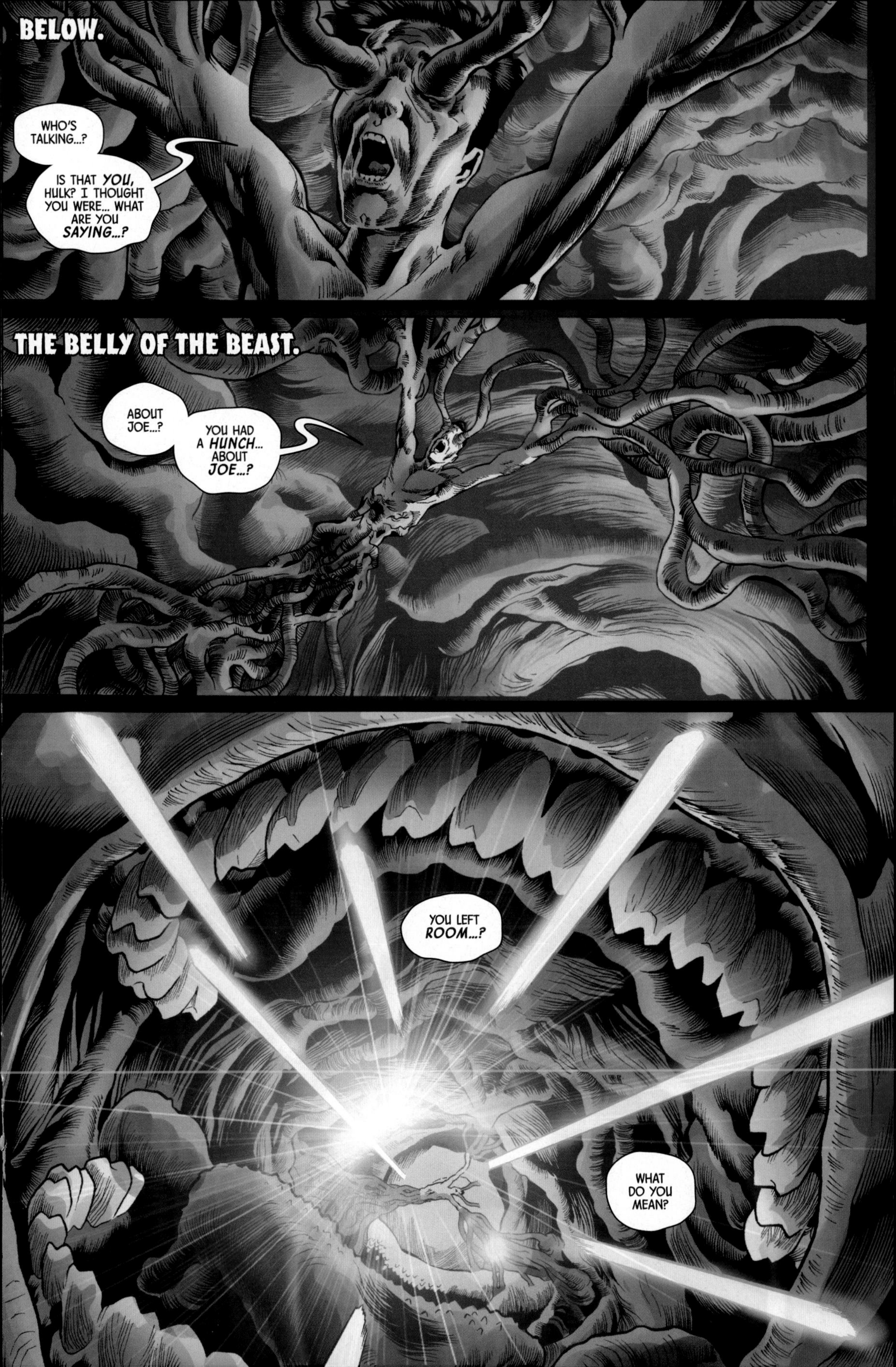
BELOW.
WHO'S TALKING...?
IS THAT YOU, HULK? I THOUGHT YOU WERE... WHAT ARE YOU SAYING...?
THE BELLY OF THE BEAST.
ABOUT JOE...?
YOU HAD A HUNCH... ABOUT JOE...?
YOU LEFT ROOM...?
WHAT DO YOU MEAN?

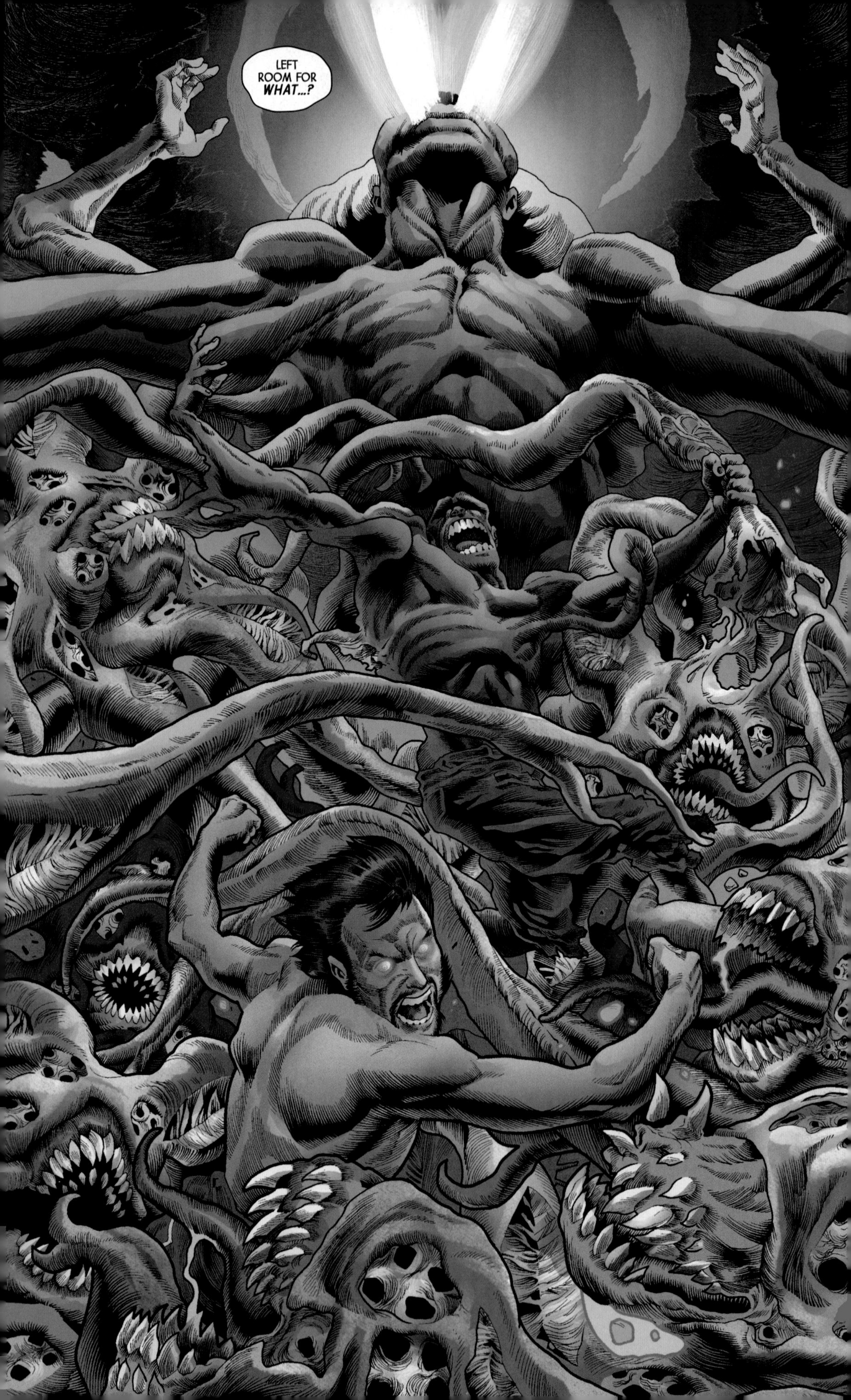
LEFT ROOM FOR WHAT...?

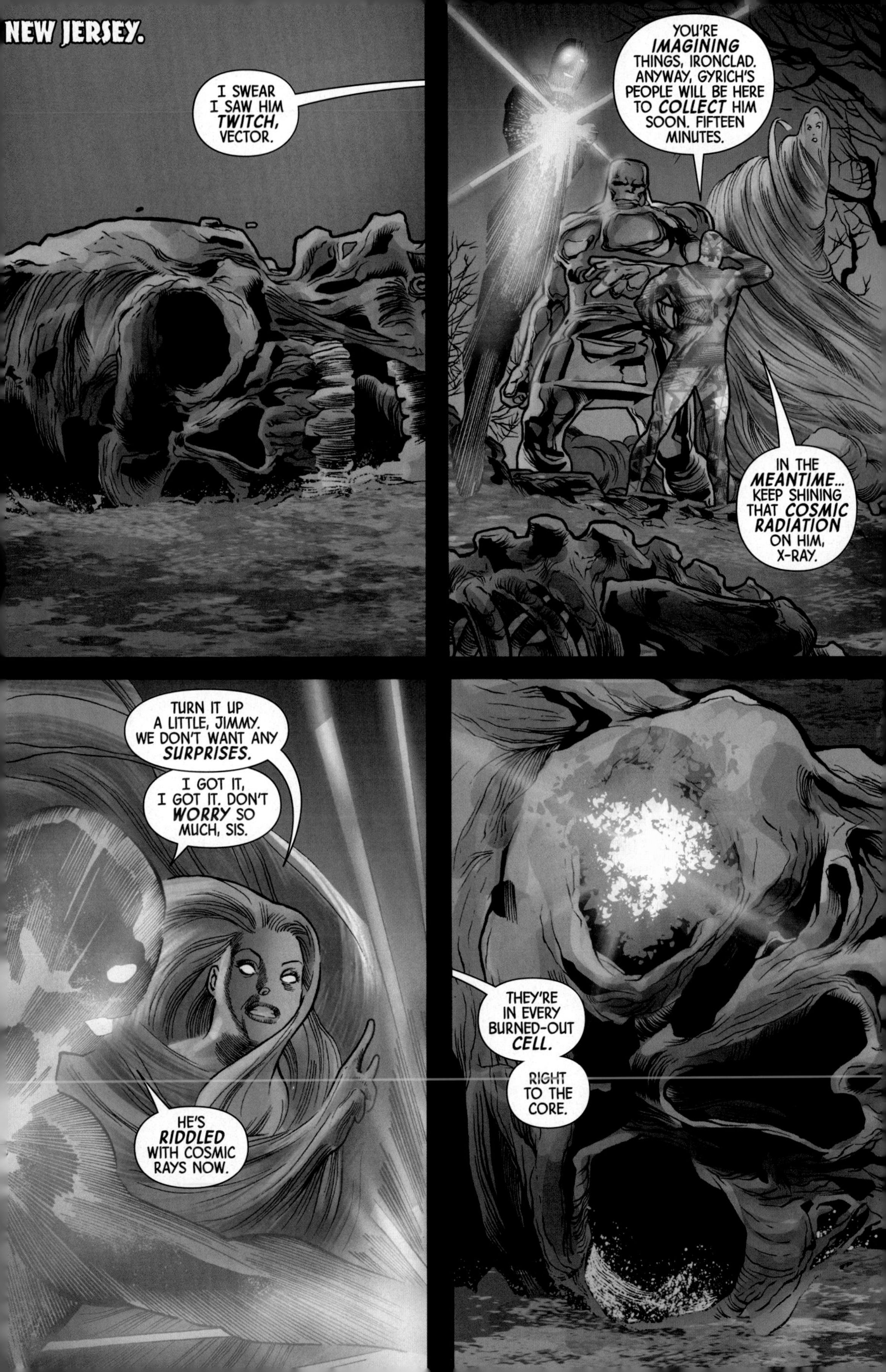
NEW JERSEY.
I SWEAR I SAW HIM TWITCH, VECTOR.
YOU'RE IMAGINING THINGS, IRONCLAD. ANYWAY, GYRICH'S PEOPLE WILL BE HERE TO COLLECT HIM SOON. FIFTEEN MINUTES.
IN THE MEANTIME... KEEP SHINING THAT COSMIC RADIATION ON HIM, X-RAY.
TURN IT UP A LITTLE, JIMMY. WE DON'T WANT ANY SURPRISES.
I GOT IT, I GOT IT. DON'T WORRY SO MUCH, SIS.
HE'S RIDDLED WITH COSMIC RAYS NOW.
THEY'RE IN EVERY BURNED-OUT CELL.
RIGHT TO THE CORE.

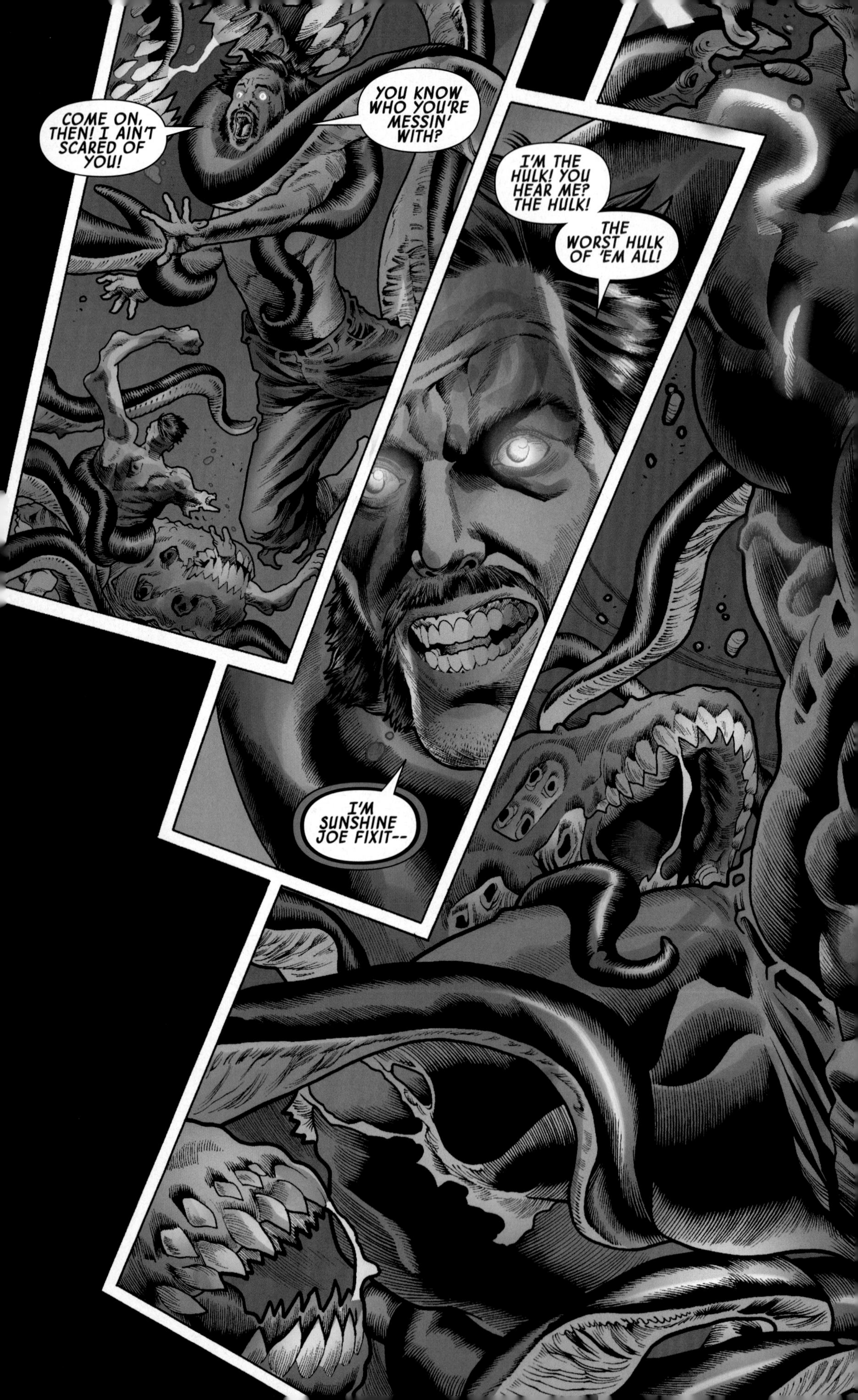
COME ON, THEN! I AIN'T SCARED OF YOU!
YOU KNOW WHO YOU'RE MESSIN' WITH?
I'M THE HULK! YOU HEAR ME? THE HULK!
THE WORST HULK OF 'EM ALL!
I'M SUNSHINE JOE FIXIT--

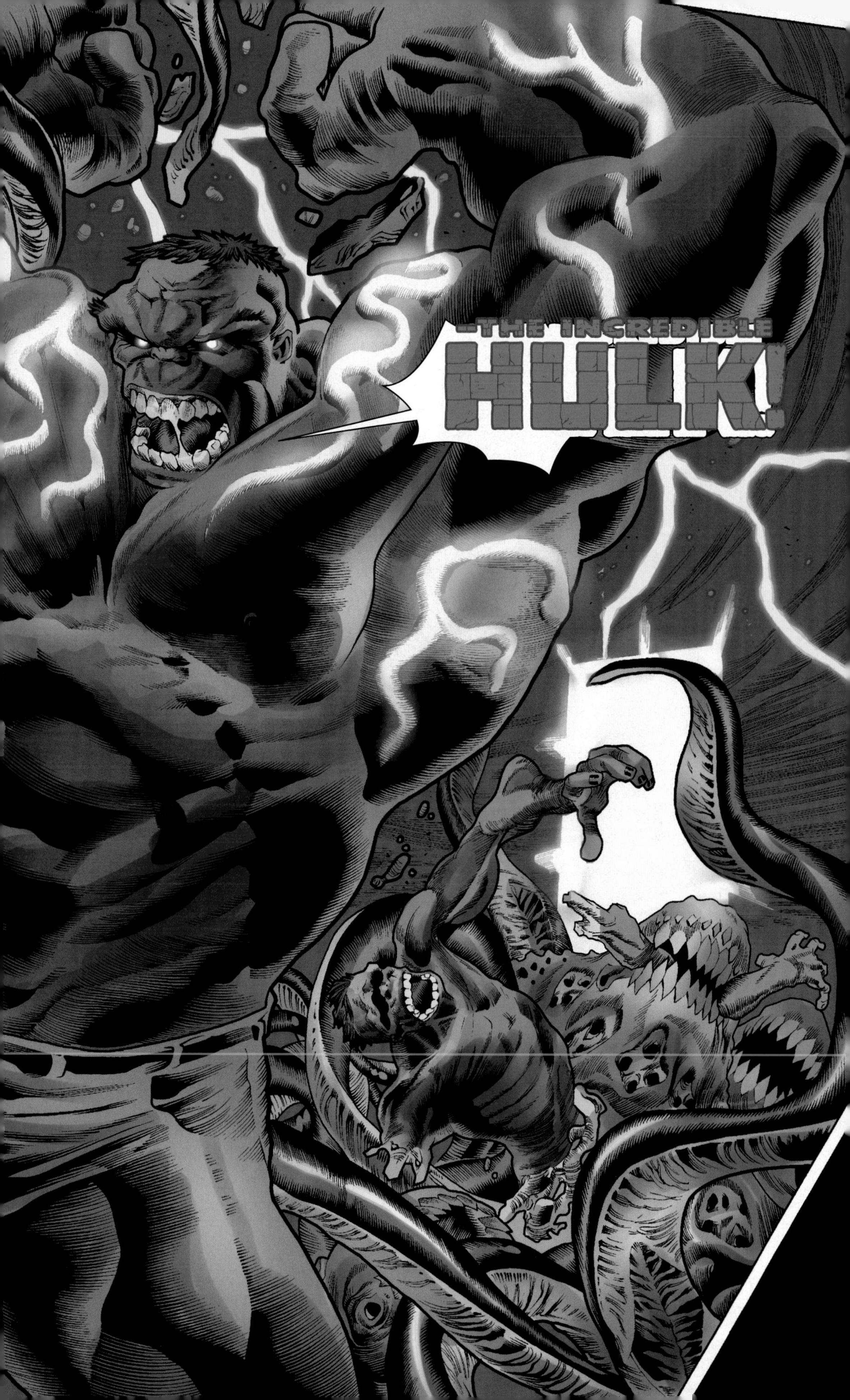

--THE INCREDIBLE
HULK!

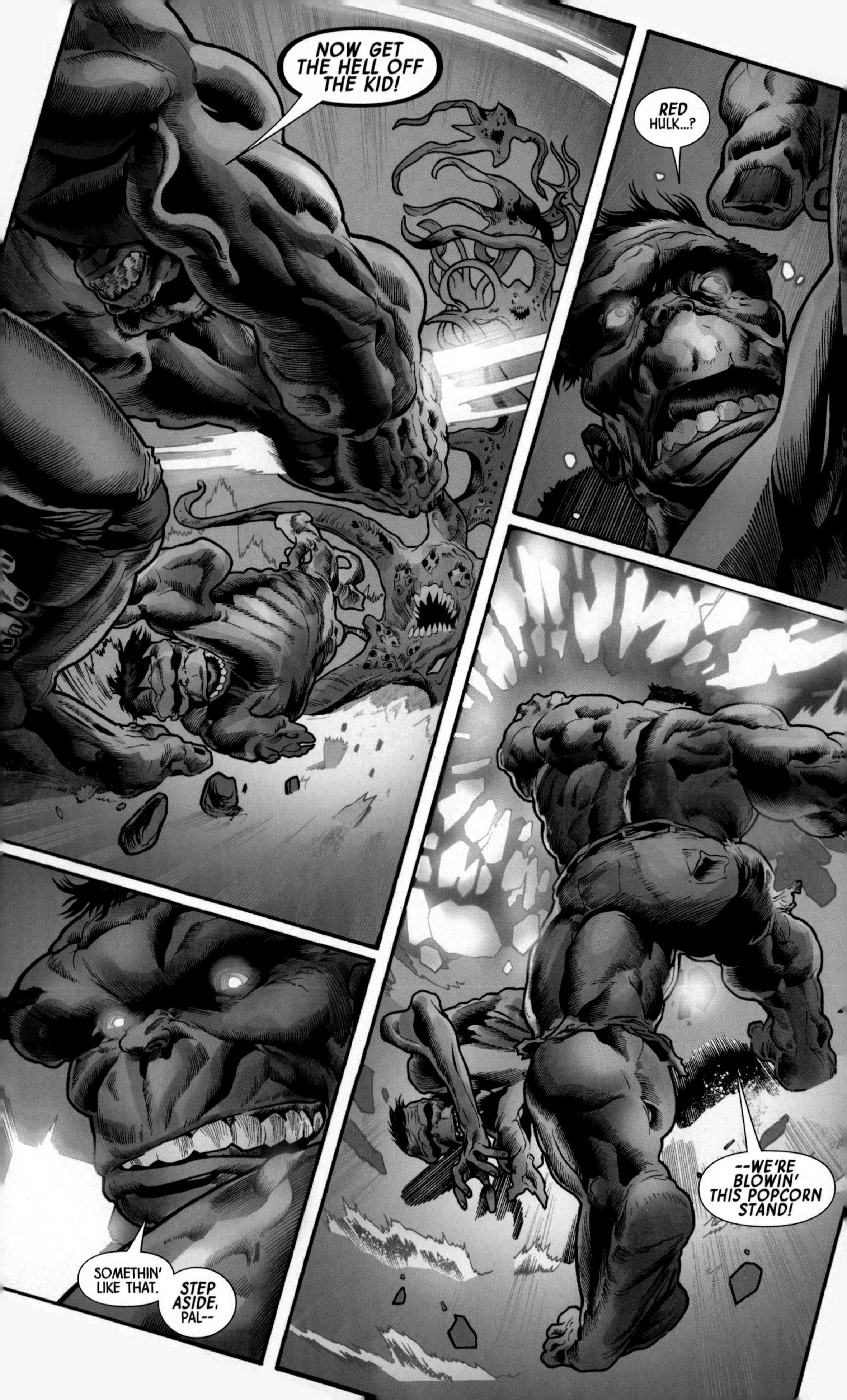
NOW GET THE HELL OFF THE KID!
RED HULK...?
SOMETHIN' LIKE THAT.
STEP ASIDE, PAL--
--WE'RE BLOWIN' THIS POPCORN STAND!

OH GOD-- LOOK AT HIM--
WHAT'S HAPPENING?
WHAT'S HAPPENING TO HIM?
...HEH.
SOMEBODY'S SCARED.
THAT'S GOOD. YOU OUGHTA BE SCARED. YOU ALL OUGHTA BE SCARED.
YOU HAD A REAL GOOD RUN...

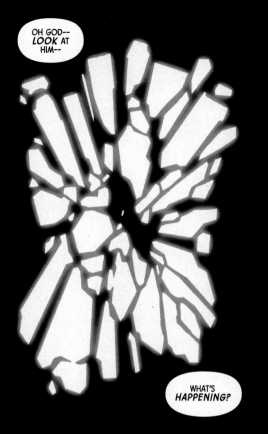

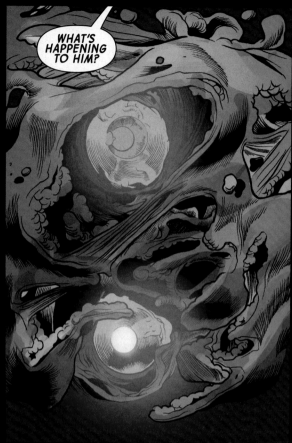

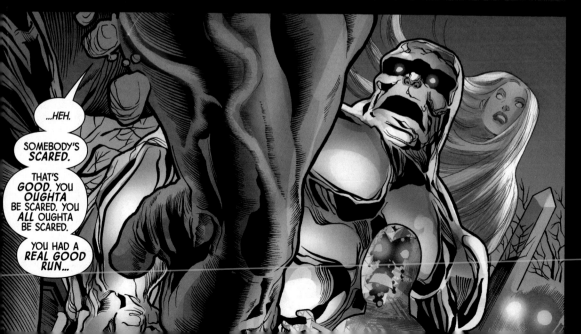

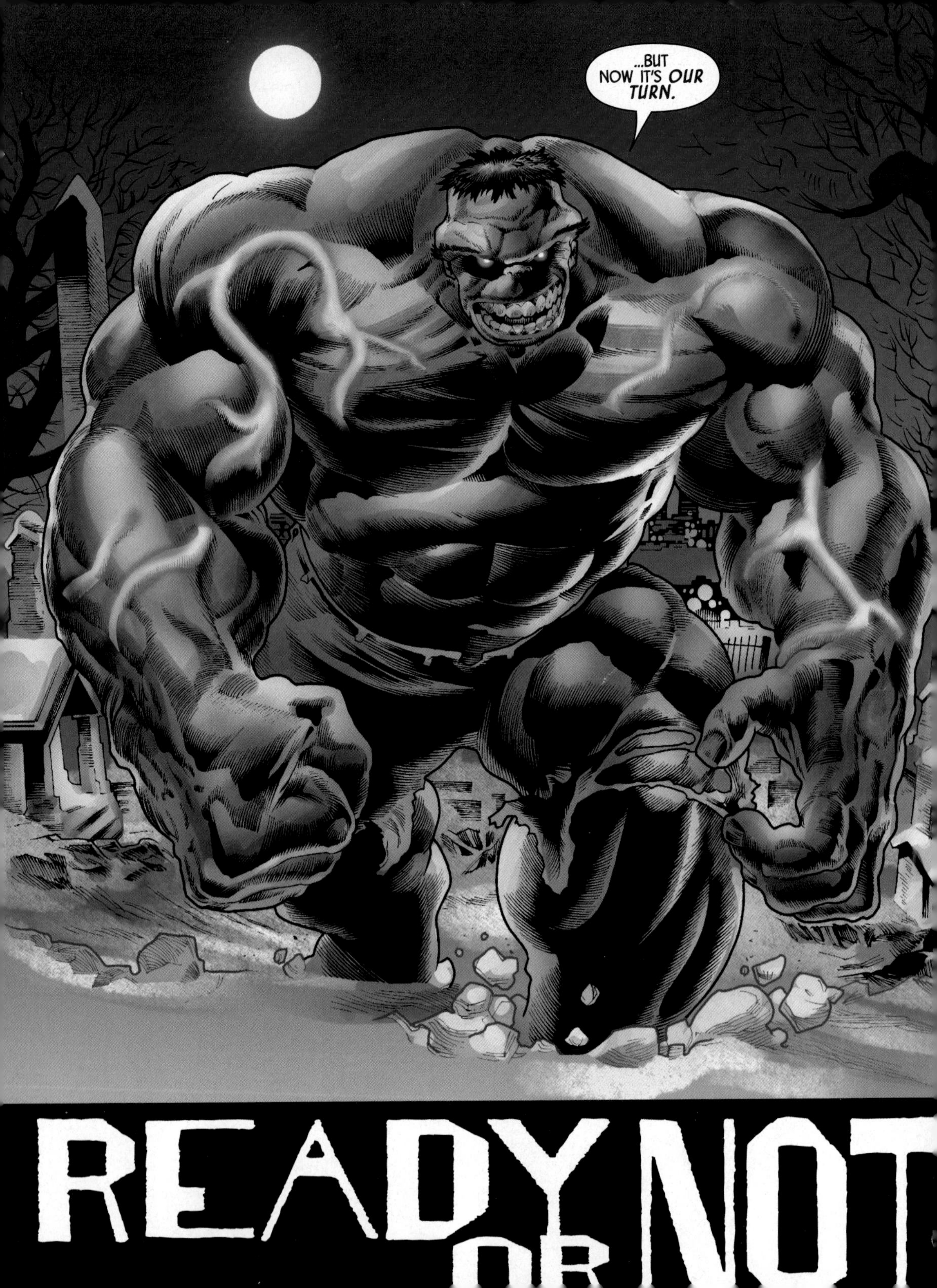
...BUT NOW IT'S *OUR* *TURN.*
READY OR NOT